IDEAL MARRIAGE

ITS PHYSIOLOGY AND TECHNIQUE

"Marriage is a science." H. DE BALZAC

THE RANDOM HOUSE
Lifetime Library

Ideal Marriage

ITS PHYSIOLOGY AND TECHNIQUE

by TH. H. VAN DE VELDE, M.D.

FORMERLY DIRECTOR OF THE GYNAECOLOGICAL CLINIC AT HAARLEM

Translated by STELLA BROWNE

Introduction by J. JOHNSTON ABRAHAM
c.b.e., d.s.o., m.a., m.d.

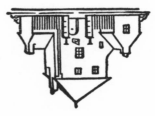

RANDOM HOUSE · NEW YORK · PUBLISHERS

INTRODUCTION

THIS is the book on the physical problems of marriage we have all been waiting for. It had to be written; and written exactly in this way—soberly, scientifically, completely, without a scintilla of eroticism, and yet with a sustained note of high idealism.

Of books of a kind on the subject there have been more than enough. Most of them have suffered from the same defect, namely, that they have been written by people with incomplete medical knowledge.

Dr. Van de Velde, who for many years was in charge of the Gynæcological Clinic of Haarlem, has all the scientific qualifications necessary to write on the subject with authority. In addition, he is happy in possessing the gift, rather rare in a scientist, of a clear literary style. He can write to interest as well as inform. That is why his book can be recommended so confidently to every physician who has the welfare of his patients at heart. In these days doctors must be able to advise on the subject. The consulting room is the modern confessional, and it is the duty of the members of the medical profession to give definite and accurate advice on any problem in sexology propounded with honest intent to them. How many of us can truthfully say that we are competent to do so? Not many, unfortunately, for the subject has never before, to my knowledge, been presented so simply and concisely. Such information has hitherto been hidden away in scattered articles in many languages. Here it has been collected together by the industry, and molded into homogeneity by the wisdom of this distinguished Dutch gynæcologist.

In this book, then, will be found all the data bearing upon the physiology and technique of sexual congress, clearly stated, without pruriency or mock modesty—in other words, scientifically.

In writing it, Dr. Van de Velde has placed the medical profession in his debt. None of us, probably, will accept all that he says. But all of us will be wiser for having read him.

It is a book that should be in the library of every doctor who looks upon his patients not as "cases," but as human, very human beings entrusted to his care.

J. JOHNSTON ABRAHAM

38, HARLEY STREET, W. 1.

LIST OF CONTENTS

CHAPTER III

GLIMPSES INTO GENERAL HUMAN SEXUAL PHYSI-

PART II

SPECIFIC ANATOMY AND PHYSIOLOGY OF SEX

CHAPTER IV

NOTES ON THE SEXUAL PHYSIOLOGY OF THE ADULT

CHAPTER V

CHAPTER VI

SEXUAL PHYSIOLOGY OF THE ADULT WOMAN . . 86

CHAPTER VII

PART III

SEXUAL INTERCOURSE
ITS PHYSIOLOGY AND TECHNIQUE

CHAPTER VIII

CHAPTER XII

FURTHER MANIFESTATIONS DURING COITUS: EPI-
   LOGUE OR AFTER-GLOW 244

PART IV
HYGIENE OF IDEAL MARRIAGE

INTRODUCTION,
DEFINITION, LIMITATION AND
ARRANGEMENT OF MATERIAL

CHAPTER XIII

CHAPTER XV

PREFACE

IN order, so far as possible, to avoid misunderstanding of this monograph on the part of superficial readers, the author is anxious to emphasize the following aspects of its contents in advance.

The book is the first part of a *trilogy*. It treats of the sexual basis of married life, and aims at *increasing the forces of mutual attraction* in marriage, through the evolution and improvement of physiological relationships. The second volume, "The Prevention of Conjugal Aversion," with which the author is now busy, deals with the problem of preserving happiness in marriage, from the purely psychological point of view, and attempts to *combat the forces of mutual repulsion*. The third volume is destined to treat the problem of *Fertility and Sterility in Marriage*—a problem of immense significance for marital happiness.

This first volume deals with the physiology of conjugal life, because knowledge here is the indispensable basis, both theoretical and practical, for success in marriage. It attempts to fill a *lacuna* which still exists in scientific literature for the medical man or woman, and at the same time to give doctors an opportunity to refer those patients who need instruction in this particular matter—and all doctors know how many such patients there are!—to the relevant passages, which will spare them the embarrassments and inadequacies of a possibly painful personal consultation. Finally, it attempts to help such married couples as have not recourse to doctors, without their intermediary advice by revealing manifold possibilities of achieving or enhancing happiness, of which they have often never heard or dreamed. Thus it is obvious that the book has to be written in terms which the laity can understand without difficulty.

The title of the volume is correctly translated by the term "The More Perfect Marriage": more perfect, that is to say, than marriage as hitherto known. But this exact translation would be somewhat clumsy, and the whole tenor of my observations and recommendations is proof that the title is not to be interpreted as confining married happiness to the sexual-physiological factor alone. Rather is it to be taken as a shorter form for "Complete and Ideal Marriage in Its Physiological and Technical Aspects."

PERSONAL INTRODUCTORY STATEMENT

THIS book will state many things which would otherwise remain unsaid. Therefore it will have many unpleasant results for me. I know this, for I have gradually attained to some knowledge of my fellow human beings and of their habit of condemning what is unusual and unconventional.

And, for that reason, this book could not be written earlier. So long as a doctor has to meet the requirements of his practice, he cannot permit himself to transgress the bounds of custom.

But he who is set free from those requirements—free at last to say what he believes to be both righteous and necessary—has the *duty* to speak out before the world.

So I must write down what I have learnt to be true and right; I could not face the evening of my life with a quiet conscience if I omitted to do so. There is need of this knowledge; there is too much suffering endured which might well be avoided, too much joy untasted which could enhance life's worth.

And I have now attained a suitable age and experience for this task. The scientist who has studied theory and practice for more than a quarter of a century; the man of letters who has expressed many thoughts in diverse forms; the experienced gynæcologist; the *confidant* of many men and women; the man to whom naught human, and naught masculine, has remained alien in the domain of feeling; the husband who has experienced all the joys and griefs of married life; and, finally, the man of fifty, who has learnt to contemplate life with a certain serene detachment, who is too old for "youthful follies," but still too young to have lost all desire—all these various entities have been called to contribute to a work written by one pen alone.

I could have escaped the unpleasantness referred to above by the use of a pseudonym. But I cannot have recourse to such protection. As a scientist, it is my duty to sign my own name to a serious medical and scientific work. Also, my advice and suggestions here are offered in a wholly responsible, *i.e.,* ethical, spirit, and would lose half their moral purpose if proffered anonymously or under an assumed name.

So I will meet all blame and annoyance arising therefrom with untroubled mind, and in the hope—nay, the *certainty*— that many men and women, even if they dare not say so, will breathe their thanks in the privacy of their nuptial chamber.

TH. H. VAN DE VELDE, M.D.

Val Fontile,
  Minusio-Locarno,
    Switzerland.

IDEAL MARRIAGE

ITS PHYSIOLOGY AND TECHNIQUE

PART I

INTRODUCTION AND GENERAL PHYSIOLOGY OF SEX

CHAPTER I

PRELIMINARY.   MARRIAGE, ACTUAL AND IDEAL

I SHOW you here the way to Ideal Marriage.

You know the honeymoon of rapture.   It is all too short, and soon you decline into that morass of disillusion and depression, which is all you know of marriage.

But the bridal honeymoon should blossom into the perfect flower of ideal marriage.

May this book help you to attain such happiness.

———————

Marriage—in Christian civilization at least—is often a failure.   On that point there can be no manner of doubt. It *can* be the gate of an earthly Eden, but it *is,* in actual fact, often a hell of torment.

It should be, in the true sense of the word, a Purgatory, that is, a state of purification; but how rarely is that attained!

Then, should we abolish marriage?

Many voices have clamored for its destruction, but they have not shown a more excellent way.

And a far greater number have defended this immemorial institution—the most distinguished thinkers among them.

Marriage is sacred to the believing Christian.

Indispensable to the Social Order.

Absolutely necessary in the interests of the children.

It offers the only—even though relative—security to the woman's love of love, and of *giving* in love.

And men too, on the whole, find in the permanent recognition and responsibility of marriage, the best background for useful and efficient work.

For all these reasons, and also because I believe the permanence of monogamous love-unions to be in the line of sexual evolution and to offer the strongest altruistic leaven to the primitive egotism of Nature's mighty urge—I, too, believe in marriage.

Much is suffered *in and through* marriage.

But *without* marriage, humanity would have to suffer much more.

But, accepting marriage as an institution, we have to decide whether we shall also accept the negation of happiness and the acute positive misery which we must often attribute to this cause, as inevitable; or whether we shall try to heal and help.

No one who, like a doctor—particularly a gynæcologist or sex specialist—is constantly in a position to know what goes on "behind the scenes" of married life, can hesitate for a moment with his reply. He must risk *all* in order to improve human prospects and potentialities of enduring happiness in marriage.

The four corner-stones of the temple of love and happiness in marriage are:—

(1) A right choice of marriage partner.

(2) A good psychological attitude of the partners, both to the world in general and to each other.

(3) A solution of the problem of parentage which meets the wishes of both partners.

(4) A vigorous and harmonious sex life.

Every serious writer on these topics has given wise advice on the choice of wife or husband; doctors, theologians, philosophers have uttered their warnings, centuries ago, as urgently as in the past month!

So I need not recapitulate what has already been said. It lies outside the limits of this specialized study. But I will once more express regret that all the wisdom of the ages is still so much disregarded and that the majority, far from exercising *discrimination and selection,* blunder blindfold into marriage; and also add my testimony to the "cloud of witness" to the paramount importance of *sound health* as a preliminary requisite. For nothing—or almost nothing!—handicaps the chance of happiness in marriage from the very first, so severely as ill-health on either side.

The psychology of marriage is also not directly relevant to our theme.

I would advise all whom it may concern—that is, all married people—to read the two excellent books by Löwenfeld,[1] "On Married Happiness," and Th. von Scheffer,[2] "Philosophy of Marriage" respectively, or, rather, to study them closely. And men may find much good food for thought in the fifth chapter of Gina Lombroso's "Soul of Woman." [3]

Scheffer says, "Marriage is at once a concession and a demand. But if it is to thrive, there must be constant thought for the other partner!" It is also "perhaps the strongest educative factor in the whole school of Life, and, like all schools, Life is no idle game." [4]

Its greatest peril is weariness, satiety, *ennui,* and the resultant alienation through which the woman generally suffers more acutely than her partner, who can take refuge in his main interest and preoccupation—his work; whereas her nature, more profoundly and exclusively emotional, is dependent on personal relationships.

Gina Lombroso, daughter and secretary of the famous anthropologist, Cesare Lombroso, wife of the historian,

---

[1] Löwenfeld, "Ueber das Eheliche Glück." Siebener Publishing Co., Berlin.
[2] Th. von Scheffer "Philosophie der Ehe." Rös & Co., Munich.
[3] Gina Lombroso, "The Soul of Woman."
[4] Havelock Ellis, "Little Essays of Love and Virtue." A. C. Black, London.

Guglielmo Ferrero, mother of two children, and herself a doctor (both of philology and medicine) writes: "The loneliness of mind and heart to which a man can condemn his wife, is much more painful and injurious than tyranny and violent brutality, which public opinion so decisively reprobates. For these ills are visible, grossly corporeal, and often only temporary, for the reaction of public opinion which they immediately provoke offers in itself some protection and remedy. But the loneliness of desertion is an invisible, unimaginable anguish, which in itself makes resistance vain, and poisons every hour of the day, and all the days of an unhappy life, for it is a *negation* of life and hope, and the discouragement, the disintegration of purpose it produces becomes more complete and incurable with the years, and more unendurable than any swift and violent pang.

"A man should make it his business to let his wife participate in his work, should take an interest in her difficulties, should guide her activities, reassure her timidities and doubts." He can do all these things, for "there is no 'man's job' in which a woman cannot help him, to some extent, materially or mentally; there is no terrifying anxiety and perplexity (of hers) which he could not dispel with a word. Let him give her a share in his work, let him take the trouble to understand and guide her, and she will believe that she is loved and appreciated, and she will be happy, whatever sacrifices may be demanded of her in return." I cannot refrain from quoting the thoughts which Signora Ferrero has so deeply felt.

And in the same manner—or on the same lines—many other specialists in human nature have expressed themselves. Albert Moll,[1] in the first (1912) edition of his "Manual of Sexual Science,"[2] said: "The link between husband and wife is re-enforced especially, when it is possible for her to stand shoulder to shoulder with him in his life-work, to be an adroit and efficient help-mate, even in details and indirectly. Perhaps this is the reason why we find such comparatively happy marriages among small tradespeople,

---

[1] Famous German specialist in sex questions, author of "The Sexual Life of the Child," etc.
[2] "Handbuch der Sexualwissenschaften." Berlin.

where the woman often helps by serving in the shop, or among artisans, where she also often 'lends a hand with the job.' "

I entirely endorse these opinions, and would only add that the wife can do much to avert that fatal marital *ennui* by independent interests which she persuades him to share. For instance, an interesting book, or journey, or lecture or concert, experienced, enjoyed and described by her, with sympathy and humor, may often be a talisman to divert his mind from work and worry, and all the irritations arising therefrom. But, of course, he, on his side, must be able to appreciate her appreciation and her conversation.

In these comparative trifles, which are actually so tremendously important, in the exhilaration or depression they produce, intuitive and affectionate *tact* must be the guide of both partners. Only with such *tact* as guide can they ascend the happy mountain on which Paradise is built.

The constant peril of mental and psychic alienation in marriage may be combated in the ways I have just mentioned.

But the most effective means of defense—outside the sexual sphere—is always and undoubtedly *a strong mutual interest in some subject that appeals to both with approximately equal force.* This subject may vary, from the cultivation of flowers to the collection of postage stamps, from music to sport, from the game of chess to the science of motor cars! A common hobby keeps mutual sympathy fresh and active.

But what mutual interest could unite a married pair more closely than the love and care for the children they have themselves produced? Children are the strongest mental link in normal married life, and those who ignore this ancient truth will often have occasion to repent.

Nevertheless, who should know better than the gynæcological specialist that the problem of offspring is not so simple and easy of solution, for many modern people as for those enviable parents who see no problem, but leave the matter to the operation of higher forces—Nature or God? The gynæcologist has occasion every day to meet unhappy frustrated mothers, for whom one disappointment follows another, for whom barrenness means the shattered happiness of their marriage.   Every day, too, he is compelled to see the tragedies of a marriage-bed which the husband deserts, out of fear of the consequences of fulfilled desire; or of so many—ah, far too many—where the wife awaits the husband whom she truly loves, in fear and trembling, for the same reason.   He knows—and he alone—*how many* marriages are shipwrecked, entirely and only because of the fear of unwanted pregnancies.   The discussion of these immense contributory factors in married weal or woe is part of the task I have undertaken.   But to discuss them helpfully we must have knowledge of the normal functions of sex.   So, in this treatise, we will first consider the physiology of marriage.

And this is the argument I have here set forth: vigorous and harmonious sexual activity constitutes the fourth cornerstone of our temple.   It must be solidly and skillfully built, for it has to bear a main portion of the weight of the whole structure.   But in most cases it is badly balanced and of poor material; so can we wonder that the whole edifice collapses, soon?

Sex is the foundation of marriage.   Yet most married people do not know the A B C of sex.   My task here is to dispel this ignorance, and show ways and means of attaining both vigor and harmony in monogamous sexual relations.

I address myself to the medical profession, and to married men.

To the doctors—because they should be the guides of the laity in these matters, too.

They *should* be!   How little they really *are* such guides, and why they so fail, is shown in this citation from Ludwig Fraenkel's "Normal and Pathological Sexual Physiology of Woman." [1]   "I have let the Sexologist speak in such detail, firstly because he is perhaps the relevant specialist on these questions, and also because the majority of gynæcologists,

---

[1] From Vol. III. of Liepmann's "Brief Manual of General Gynæcology." Publisher, F. C. W. Vogel, Leipzig (1914), p. 41.   ("Kurzgefasstes Handbuch der gesamten Frauenheilkunde.")

owing to a refined *but certainly misguided* [1] reticence or prudishness, know really very little about them." [2]

And I also address myself to married men, for they are naturally educators and initiators of their wives in sexual matters; and yet they often lack, not only the qualifications of a leader and initiator, but also those necessary for equal mutual partnership!

They have no realization of their deficiencies. For the average man, of average "normal" genital potency, who performs his "conjugal duties" regularly and with physiological satisfaction to himself, still imagines that he has thereby met all the requirements his wife can make. And if she is not satisfied, and remains in a permanent condition of "suspended gratification," then, with regret or indignation according to his own type of temperament, he simply puts her down as one of those "sexually frigid" women (from 20 to 80 per cent. of all women are supposed to be sexually frigid—a conveniently and conspicuously wide margin of error!), laments his bad luck, and drifts further and further apart from her.

If he has been fortunate enough to wed a woman of warmer and more spontaneous temperament, who is obviously not indifferent to the rites of marriage—if those rites take place in the same invariably scheduled manner, with no varieties of local stimulation or sensory adornment—sexual satiety will in a few short years intrude itself into the consciousness of both, and equally imperil their marriage. For monotony can only be relieved by variation, and, to the uninstructed man, the only possible variation seems to be in the *object* of his efforts; and the rift in the lute is there, and widens.

The thought that the defect and the failure might be on

---

[1] My italics.

[2] In the most recent years, this reticence has fortunately been gradually discarded by the most eminent gynæcologists, as may be seen, for example in E. Kehrer's monograph, "Causes and Treatment of Sterility from the Modern Point of View, together with a Contribution on Disturbances of the Sexual Function, especially Dyspareunia." (1922. Publisher, Steinkopff, Dresden.) But for the greater number of medical practitioners and even gynæcologists, Fraenkel's comments are still deplorably true.

his side, that he himself might have prevented the alienation which he truly deplores—this enlightening and humbling truth never dawns upon him!

For he does not know that there are numberless delicate differentiations and modifications of sexual pleasure, all lying strictly within the bounds of *normality,* which can banish the mechanical monotony of the too well-known from the marriage-bed, and give new attractions to conjugal intercourse. Or, if he guesses this truth, he thinks it implies degeneracy and debauchery, for he fails to understand that what is physiologically sound may also be considered ethically sound.[1] He thinks his wife is "far above that sort of thing," leaves her more and more to herself, seeks the diversity of stimulation he needs outside his home, and often ends in *real* debauchery in consequence!

This average husband does not even know that his wife's sexual sensations develop and culminate to a slower rhythm than his own. He does not know *at all* that he must *awaken* her with delicate consideration and adaptation. He cannot understand why the Hindoo women, used to the sexual assiduity and skill of their own men, mock the clumsy Europeans as "village cocks"[2]; nor does he appreciate the point of view of those Javanese who boast, not of the joy they received, but of the delight they gave.[3] He does not guess that:

> "The sweet fruit of divinity consumes
> And fades to nothingness in women's wombs
> Because men know it not, and will not know!
> Because men are too small and weak of heart
> To use their flaming power; but give their art
> To haloes on veiled brows! Not flesh aglow
> With raptures that they dream are theirs alone.
> Yea, they would seize life's central sacred fire
> And bear it hence like jewels of a throne,
> But the assuagement of her deep desire
> It is that crowns the Godhead in his own."[4]

---

[1] And is even considered so by the Church. I shall refer to this later. See Chapter XVII.

[2] Havelock Ellis: German version by Kurella of "The Sexual Impulse." Publisher, Kabitzsch, Leipzig.

[3] Communicated by Breitenstein in "Twenty-one Years in India: Borneo." Cited in Ploss Bartel's "Woman." Publisher, Neufeld & Hennis, Berlin.

[4] Translated from Werner von der Schulenburg: 'Don Juan's Last Love."

The essence and significance of Don Juan is a mystery to most men, or is grossly misinterpreted. They should read Marcel Barrière's "Essai sur le Don-Juanisme Contemporain," and learn that the soul of this arch-lover was not seeking the base triumph of snatching and throwing away, but ever and only the ecstasy of giving the joy of love.

And in this sense the husband should act the part of Don Juan to his wife over again. Then, in giving delight, he will himself experience it anew and permanently, and his marriage will become *ideal*.

And if *erotic genius* does not characterize him, the man needs *explicit knowledge* if he is to be capable of inspiring such desire and imparting such joy.

He must *know how to make love*.

The ensuing chapters may be of help to him here. They can, in certain portions, be read by educated laymen without any difficulty. Other portions, however, need close and careful study. For I aim at giving my instructions and deductions an entirely scientific tone and basis, though at keeping free from superfluous pedantry. This manner of treatment, as well as the nature of the theme, make it impossible to avoid the use of many foreign words and technical terms. Readers who do not exactly comprehend any of these words can ask a doctor to explain their precise meaning.

For, to achieve our purpose, is well worth study.

CHAPTER II

1. *The Evolution of the Sexual Impulse*
Sexual Sensations and Internal Stimuli

LIFE is dominated by the urge of self-preservation and by the sexual urge. The former preserves the individual, the latter the race. For biological purposes racial preservation is more urgent than individual survival, therefore the urge of sex is stronger than hunger, stronger than fear. Among animals, the most apt and vigorous males are the first to risk their lives in nuptial combats for their mates; the same is true of primitive man. And in civilization we may daily observe that human beings expose themselves to all possible dangers and difficulties in order to satisfy this imperious longing, and frequently sacrifice life itself on the Altar of Love.

I cannot doubt that the sexual impulse is fundamentally an impulse to reproduce. But it is equally certain that the two impulses have become increasingly separate, distinct, and independent. This is even admitted by theologians. Thus a clergyman, Pastor Ernest Baars, in the periodical *Sexual Problems* (1909, p. 753), admits "That the desire for parentage has receded into the background, compared to the desire for sexual relations." This urge to reproduce (the parental impulse) has modified its initial force in civilization. It is more active in women than in men, and not expressed in an indiscriminating "urge to reproduce," but rather in the longing for maternity, the "cry for the child." In this form, it can be observed in the majority of women.

The development in men is different. Here, the only

vestiges of a direct and definite *reproductive urge* may be traced in the fervent—and not infrequent—longing to have a child by some *special dearly-loved woman,* to perpetuate in human form the communion of souls and bodies, which is the equivalent of the desire for the child of the particular beloved man in the normal deeply-enamored woman.[1] But this longing, which in congenial temperaments is enhanced by a pseudo-mystical wish for immortality, in the continuance of germ plasm and the inheritance of special qualities and faculties, has little or nothing of the elemental force of primitive urges and impulses.[2]   It can be at the utmost only an intellectualized yearning.   Still less primitive and "instinctive" are the other motives which may make a man want children.   They are all intellectualized, all thoroughly "rational," whether the determining factor be "family" and descent, monetary considerations, sociability, convenience or sheer vanity; but, of course, all or any such secondary motives may assume a dominant and compulsive character.

Thus, among civilized races, the urge to reproduce has ceased to "play lead" among the components of the sexual impulse, which appears as a further stage of evolution; an advance in psychic power and complexity.

Many eminent authorities (for instance, *Hegar* and *Eulenburg*) consider the sexual impulse as an *urge to copulate,* apart from reproduction.   I cannot agree on this.   Copulation, *i.e.,* functional sexual intercourse, is certainly the core and summit of sexual desire, but we must reflect that sexual activity is not necessarily identical with complete intercourse; that the urge to such activity generally, if not always, exists in children, long before they have any idea of the possibility of copulation (or coitus, or intercourse).   We

---

[1] *Cf.* the final words of Adalbert von Chamisso's poem, "Sweet friend, thou gazest on me with amaze," from the Cycle, "Woman's love and life," which have been immortally rendered in Schumann's accompaniment, especially in the repetition "Thy likeness looks at me—thy likeness!"

[2] As will be observed I use the terms urge or impulse in the narrower specialized sense employed by *Krafft Ebbing,* not in the more general sense employed by Wundt, which only implies inclination or wish.

may also consider that other forms of sexual activity are often preferred to normal intercourse.

I also consider it superfluous to seek more precise formulation of the term "sexual impulse," especially when we eliminate the direct "reproductive urge," as I have done in this study.

It is an urge or impulse to sexual activity (or manifestation or expression) which has its seat, i.e., its initial origin, and its irradiations not only in the genitals, but in the whole body and the whole psychic personality. Hence its power is almost supreme, almost divine, and extends far beyond its specific province. Let us only consider one example of that power: the incalculable influence of the sexual impulse on Art in all its forms. (Erotica.)

The sexual impulse, in all its manifestations, is largely dependent on the *activity of the sex glands,* and not only on their external secretions (sperm and egg cells), but especially on their internal secretions or *hormones.*

It has now been proved that the genital glands (as well as *many* other glands—if not all!—and other non-glandular tissues) produce certain chemical substances, which are not externally employed but regularly absorbed into the blood as it circulates through the body. These substances, however tiny the amount secreted may be, can have the most potent effects on the whole physical organism or on its component parts. Those secreted by the genital glands, even before maturity, have crucial importance in determining the growth of the whole genital apparatus, and of the specifically sexual characteristics, qualities and functions. If the genital glands are defective or poorly developed, or even totally lacking—as, for instance, after certain surgical operations in early youth—the normal action of their internal secretions cannot have due effect on the growing boy or girl, and thus there evolves, not normal youth or maiden, but the eunuchoid, the castrate, who deviates sharply from both sexual norms in muscular development, in chemical metabolism, in psychic constitution—and the more so, the earlier and more complete the cancellation of the sexual hormones.

The internal secretions or endocrine secretions of the female genital gland (ovary) give the specifically *feminine* trend, both to body and mind of the adolescent and the adult woman. The male genital gland (testis) operates in a precisely opposite direction, but, by a similar process, it makes the boy into the typical man. This is proved when the genital glands are excised in animals, especially young animals, and the corresponding glands of the opposite sex grafted, in their stead, with certain precautionary measures. The mental qualities of the animal, its sexual inclinations and attempts at contact or coitus are then determined entirely by the ingrafted glands, and the structure and functions of its body are transformed, so far as the stage of anatomical development it had reached when the operation took place, still permits.

Nevertheless, sexual characteristics, inclinations and emotions, even, to some extent, sexual functions, are not *exclusively* dependent on the activity of the genital glands; and this is specially the case in fully mature adults. If they were so dependent they could not survive the cessation of such activity. But sexual feelings and manifestations persist in many individuals whose genital glands are no longer functional, whether this atrophy is due to accident, surgical operation or malignant disease, or—as in the case of all women at a certain period of life, which generally falls between the forty-third and fiftieth year—due to the natural process of dissolution. The "internal secretions" of the other endocrine (or ductless) glands probably have great influence, both on the degeneration of the genital glands and on their full activity. And we must also reckon here with another important factor: the adaptation and habitual reaction to sexual intercourse resulting from experience. And the *inherited* sexual inclination is even more potent than the acquired psychic faculty. Both, however, are primarily based—both in human and anthropoid evolution—on the effective functioning of the genital glands.

Thus we may say that the sexual impulse originates exclusively in ovary and testis respectively, but, in the modern adult human being, has become interwoven and interdependent on hereditary and acquired psychic concepts, on the one side, and on individual glandular activity, internal and external, on the other side.

Albert Moll, in his "Investigations into the *Libido Sexualis,*" has distinguished two instinctive components: the urges to *contrectation,* and to *detumescence.*[1]

I agree, on the whole, in principle, but prefer to colloquialize these rather repellent terms and to extend their meaning. I would observe that lines of demarcation cannot be drawn too rigidly here, for both trends merge into one another, and can never be kept wholly distinct.

Contrectare is Latin for "to touch." Moll uses it in the sense of physical contact with a person of the opposite sex. I apprehend this impulse as an irresistible urge to *approach* the opposite sex as closely as possible, and will therefore use the term *impulse of sexual approach.*

Instead of the urge of detumescence, I prefer to write impulse of *sexual relaxation* or *relief of tension.* Here I envisage not only the specific local relief, but also the general bodily, and specially psychic, satisfaction which should accompany it. The *impulse of sexual consummation* (or satisfaction) is a more adequate expression, as it renders both the *local and generally bodily well-being and gratification in immediate and intimate association with the summit of sexual tension, in unison, and its relief.*[2] But as *relaxation* corresponds with Moll's *"detumescence,"* I shall use that term as well as *consummation,* according to whichever of these phrases, coined by me, appears most suitable.

The view of *Hermann Rohleder,* as expressed in "The General Sexual Life of Genus Homo," and supported by other experts, is that there is a third component trend, an *impulse to tumescence.* This I must reject; I can find no distinctive element here. For the increase of tension up till

---

[1] From *tumescere,* Latin, to swell; detumescence—subsidence of a swelling. Detumescere and detumescentia are artificial Neo-Latinisms.

[2] I may add, that whoever wishes to read a lucid, perfectly decent and artistically exquisite description of the typical manifestations of the impulse of approach and of general relaxation, in an innocent normal girl, should turn to Claude Anet's "Petite Ville," and the first story, "Mademoiselle Bourrat."

the beginning of actual *coitus,* is accompaniment and effect
of the *impulse to approach.* From the beginning of coitus
till the complete orgasm (which is both the summit of
approach and the first stage in the relief of tension, and
therefore doubly satisfying), the increase of tension, although it continues and reaches its attainable maximum, is
no independent phenomenon but the means to an end, *i.e.,* to
attain the desired satisfaction and relaxation. Therefore,
from the moment coitus begins, this tension is part of the
urge to sexual consummation.

Although the impulse of sexual relaxation is strongly
affected both by purely external stimuli and by psychic
concepts, it is also under the influence of specific local
conditions of the genital glands. This is especially the case
in the male, for whom the relief of tension can sometimes
be a mere *evacuation* or *discharge of accumulated seminal
matter.*

Among animals, the females also show extensive interdependence of the excretion of ova and the relief of sexual
tension. This is most pronounced among certain species of
fishes. Among higher animals, this interaction between the
sexual impulse and the process of ovulation is clearly evident
in the so-called "rut" or "heat." In the process of human
evolution, ovulation and sexual desire in women have
become more and more dissociated from one another. But
this severance is not so complete as is generally assumed,
even in the average woman of today. In Chapter V we
shall refer to certain indications that there is still reflex
action and interdependence here.

To briefly and systematically recapitulate: the sexual
impulse or impulse towards sexual activity is fundamentally
dependent on the secretions of the genital glands; the
internal secretions or *hormones* of these glands determine its
first component trend, the impulse of sexual approach, while
the external secretions govern its second component trend,
the impulse of sexual relaxation, consummation or satisfaction. (Of course, this definition cannot be taken absolutely literally, but with a grain of salt!)

All manner of emotions and mental processes have

crystallized round the *impulse of sexual approach:* they form the complex, the abstract conception of *love,* without personal differentiation and fixation.

But this is but a brief stage in the sexual evolution of the individual. In a—shorter or longer—period of time, the emotions of love focus and concentrate themselves. Psychically, the complex becomes more massive and intricate, and interlocks with ever-fresh groups of ideas, so that finally its empire extends over too large a portion of the whole field of consciousness. The association of ideas becomes more definite and continuous and takes a direction towards a certain individual type. The object of love, glimpsed at first only in dreams or day-dreams, is revealed in clearer, more human form. The ideal figure of the beloved (man or woman) is modeled by the Pygmalion of Imagination. And then—the meeting with the ideal in human form, breathing, visible, tangible, flesh and blood! And whatever defects the human object suffers in comparison with the ideal beloved, are of no importance, for the love impulse attributes all that is desirable, all that is admirable, to the beloved being.

A first shy, stolen meeting—a word—a look, given and returned; the immortal flame shoots upwards, love is born in a sense of indescribable exaltation and joy.

And the impulse of approach, sublimated into love, now unfolds itself more and more frankly and fully. It thrives and puts forth leaves and buds, and gradually the lovers attain full union and communion. In that moment, when youth and girl are fulfilled in and by one another, the impulse to approach and the desire for consummation find each other, and merge into a new integral emotion. Love is come of age, and is in flower. Now, and now only, can it bloom aright.

I must admit that psychic complexes, to which we dare not deny the proud name of love, because of their depth, their permanence, their variety and delicacy of emotion, may be, in exceptional cases, directed towards more than one object at the same time; nevertheless, I consider the

essentially monogamous stamp of a highly evolved love—
such as I refer to—as established beyond all doubt. So long
as any one loves ardently with both soul and senses, the
mind is so pervaded by the image of the beloved, that the
lover remains monogamous in essentials, even in circumstances where racial or religious customs, force or need,
compel occasional sexual intercourse with others than the
beloved.

It is otherwise if the impulse has not attained the dignity
and power of love, or has deteriorated from that high
evolutionary grade.   In such conditions the primitive
proclivity to polygamy emerges unmistakably in both sexes,
more especially in the male.

Marriage is the permanent form of monogamous[1] erotic
relationships.

As such, marriage represents a distinct advance ethically;
it is also evolutionary in so far as it gives the fullest opportunity for the primitive urges, which are initially purely self-
regarding and self-centered, to extend themselves in action
and consciousness towards *altruistic* objects, *i.e.,* the preservation and welfare of other persons.

From this point of view, lovers who celebrate their
marriage ceremony are participating in a sacred covenant,
and not by any means only in the ecclesiastical sense of

---

[1] *Note on Monogamy and Polygamy.*—Clarity is necessary here in de-
fining terms. *Monogamous* is the adjective applied by anthropologists
to persons, male or female, who contract only *one* marriage in their lifetime: *i.e.,* they do not marry again after losing wife or husband, as the
case may be. *Polygamous,* in its correct sense, is applicable both to persons who contract two or more marriages in succession, after their first
one has come to an end—through death or divorce—and to the man who
has more than one wife at a time. *Polygamous* is also correctly applicable
to the women who live in marriage with more than one man, simultaneously, but they are generally termed *polyandrous* (the masculine equivalent,
polygynous is rarely used).

The lack of clarity here is increased by the *colloquial usage* of the
terms monogamous and polygamous, as *referring to sexual relationships
in general* in contrast to its anthropological significance, which refers to
recognized responsible marriages only.

I want readers of this treatise to definitely understand and accept my
usage of "Monogamy" and "Polygamy."

I employ both terms as applying to both men and women, and to sig-
nify one or more than one sexual relationship during the same, fairly
long period of time, *i.e.,* actually conterminously or simultaneously.

sacredness.[1]   For they are promising one another the highest, the loveliest, and the hardest task that man or woman can undertake.   Namely, to control the current of their erotic emotions and direct it always towards each other!   And throughout long years, not once, but "unto seventy times seven," to give each other that supreme joy which is the best gift that human beings can share!

Love which has unfolded both its highest potentialities of joy and of dignity and moral value, through marriage, can permanently bless both partners.   It *can* do so; but, how often do the fairest feelings fade, the most solemn intentions subside!   "The spirit is willing, but the flesh is weak"; and sometimes even the spirit does not remain "willing" for long!

Incompatibility of temperament and outlook, differing grades of evolution, reaction to atavistic manifestations: we may add up a long list of dangers, difficulties and disasters, but their results can only be appreciated by those who themselves experience their grief and horror and humiliation.

For the fundamental difficulty is this: that as soon as sexual attraction is extinguished, *sexual repulsion and enmity* manifests itself.   For there is such a thing as *enmity and repulsion between the sexes:* at least, among human beings.   There is no doubt of its existence, and it emerges into prominence whenever the power of mutual attraction ceases to operate; and with a vehemence proportionate to the power of the former attraction.   It can become systematic hostility, intense hatred: many dramas of literature and real life are the proof (*e.g.,* Strindberg's).   And in marriage it is a perpetual menace, especially because—in its earlier stages at least—it so seldom reaches the full consciousness, and reveals its true nature.

And in this perpetual combat between instinctive sexual attraction and equally instinctive sexual repulsion, there are only two ways of preserving the happiness and permanence

---

[1] To *consummate* a marriage and to *contract* a marriage are quite distinct actions.   This is so fully recognized, that in countries where laws and religion refuse to admit *divorce,* they leave a loophole for *annulment* of marriage, where it can be proved that the marriage has been *contracted,* by the civil and religious ceremony, but not *consummated,* by the first act of coitus (sexual intercourse).

of the union: the finest and strongest altruistic emotion first and foremost, and then the prompt and constant enhancement of the attractive factors, so that antipathy remains dormant and has no opportunity to develop.

But *specific sexual incongruence or incompatibility* must first be guarded against, and the impulse must be developed to at least approximate activity and intensity in both partners; *relapses* must specially be avoided. And all this is possible! But certainly not easy. It is possible if the process of *courtship* is ever renewed afresh. If both partners "meet each other half-way"; are attentive, and adaptable to one another's needs; display initiative and ingenuity in stimulating and satisfying one another's needs; and by *a culture of erotic technique* beyond all present marital usage. That is: happiness is attained and preserved in the ideal marriage.

CHAPTER III

GLIMPSES INTO GENERAL HUMAN SEXUAL PHYSIOLOGY

11. *Sexual Sensations and External Stimuli*

IN the preceding chapter we observed the evolution of the impulse of sex, from the simple urge to reproduce, through various stages of development, culminating in *ideal marriage*. And we have obtained a definite idea of the manner in which the various elements composing the impulse to sexual activity, may be and are, influenced from within the organism by physiological processes, and psychological trends and experiences.

We must now endeavor to represent the impressions and sensations arising from *external* causes, which may either stimulate or inhibit sexual activity.

The *internal* stimuli may be divided into "somatic" (effect of internal secretions and of circulation and congestion in certain cavities and ducts of the body), and psychic (mental images, associations, phantasies). Similarly, we may distinguish between such external stimuli as are pre-eminently physical, and such as belong rather to the psychic and mental sphere.

But there is such constant interaction and interdependence between all these various types of stimuli, such mutual enhancement, inhibition and modification, that no sharp dividing line of classification can be drawn. This is true equally of the external and internal stimuli; and the most intensely psychic impressions and sensations can only be received through some one of the sensory channels.

Nevertheless, some division and classification here is appropriate and helpful.

We will first consider such *Psychic Impressions* as act powerfully on the sexual emotions; and here we find that all such natural phenomena as give rise to *terror and anxiety,* can cause strong sexual excitement.   This may partly be due to the wish for *protection or even simple companionship in danger,* which leads the woman to seek man's protection and the man to attempt to protect her; and this relationship of protection, given and received, stimulates and facilitates the *impulse to approach.*

But this is certainly not the only reason, for the sexual effect of fear and terror may be manifest when and where there is no possibility of protection or association, against natural phenomena, as has been observed unequivocally in cases of masturbators (sexual self-relief). We do not know whether in the case of such physical and climatic catastrophes as earthquakes and tempests, there are atmospheric disturbances which directly affect the higher nerve centers in the brain.

But it is suggestive that—as *Virgil* knew long ago—the atmosphere of an approaching storm has a particularly exciting and disturbing effect sexually; an *approaching* storm, *bien entendu,* before thunder and lightning have begun.

And not only *fear,* but *grief* may arouse sexual emotions. Here, again, there are obvious psychic factors, such as the longing to console, or to *be* consoled; that fellowship in sorrow, whose bond is peculiarly strong; the unconscious wish to escape from painful and depressing thoughts.   But, quite apart from such auxiliary influences, there is an *appreciable* instinctive association of *grief with love,* as can be confirmed by every one who studies his own or others' mental processes and characters.   Probably the cause of this association and interaction is connected with the removal of customary inhibitions and restraints by such disturbances of psychic balance as are caused by strong grief, and which also release primitive impulses in the sexual sphere and make them more consciously active and conspicuous than usual.

But here is a paradox.   Impressions which arouse a *maximum intensity of anxiety, dread and fear, have a repressive effect on sexual excitement when such sexual excitement is already present;* or can totally prevent its emergence, even under strong local stimulation.   Thus it often happens that a woman whose affections and sensations are otherwise strong and normal, is unable to attain satisfaction in coitus because of her fear of pregnancy; or that the male organ, having already attained erection, subsides again without functional relief.

Strong grief and fear have much in common with all other emotions and mental processes which are sufficiently vivid and absorbing to distract the conscious will from the activities of sex. For it is unquestionable that the whole range of mental and emotional complexes may either increase or diminish the sexual impulse indefinitely.

This may have such disadvantages as I have mentioned above. But reasonable and considerate persons may often utilize general psychic influences for their own or their partner's happiness, whether to control or enhance their own impulse to approach the beloved, or to accelerate or prolong sexual reactions.

I have treated these matters at some length in order to show the extreme intricacy and complexity of sexual influences and factors; how they are interwoven physically and psychically, how they shift and deflect or re-enforce one another, and can hardly be differentiated one from another. It would be needless circumlocution to re-emphasize this complexity on every occasion in future. I shall therefore, having drawn attention thereto, deal as simply as possible with my material. But my readers should never forget the labyrinthine intricacy of sexual matters, either in theory or in practice. This is probably the most difficult and mysterious region of the human soul, and those who ignore it expose themselves to endless delusions, and—most painful disillusions.

The impressions conveyed by the *psychic personality of individuals,* to the sexual impulse of other individuals, may be either repulsive or attractive. This is especially the case with certain qualities of particular *selective* significance. *Generosity and courage* in a man appeal to the feminine impulse to approach; cowardice in a man inhibits and repels women. *Modesty and dignity* in girls and women attract a man with peculiar power, whereas the opposite type of behavior generally excites his repugnance. But qualities or activities outside the sexual sphere may also be powerfully influential. The high regard and esteem for such qualities in a person of the opposite sex is not infrequently the foundation on which love is built. *Admiration* is even more prominent in this connection: the admirer is attracted, and the *admired* also!—from which circumstance we may infer the enormously important *rôle* of personal vanity and approbativeness in sexual life!

Alongside the various psychic qualities we meet the attractive forces of *sensory impressions* between the sexes. And the evolution from the simple impulse of sexual approach to Love, consists in apprehending and selecting the particular individual who combines in themselves the greatest number and highest degree of psychic and sensory attractions. This is termed "Sexual Selection" by many authorities.

And even after the evolution of Love, these charms and attractions do not lose their value. They are necessary to preserve love, for courtship can only be inspired and effected afresh under their spell.

"Love," says Stendhal, "means taking pleasure in seeing, touching, perceiving with every sense, and in the closest possible contact, some one whom we find lovely and who loves us." [1]

Let us therefore pass in review the erotic influence of the various physical senses.

It is considered uncertain whether or no the sense of *taste*—flavor—has any influence in this respect. In any case, I admit it is not great. And it is difficult here to disentangle the sensations of *taste* and *smell;* for mouth and nose are closely connected. *This intermingling of flavors and olfactory sensations* is specially close as regards sexual sensations. This also, I freely admit.

Nevertheless, I am inclined to attribute a certain sexual

[1] Stendhal. "De l'Amour," Book I., Chap. II.

significance to the *sense of taste*. I am, of course, not referring to the famous axiom that "the way to a man's heart is through his stomach," nor to the fact that a well-cooked and chosen dinner (even a "dry" dinner, *i.e.*, without the aid of alcohol), shared in each other's company, often helps the impulse to approach in both partners. For in neither instance is there *any direct sexual reaction to special flavors* or *consistencies in food*. Rather do I allude to experiences which would seem to prove that certain products of exudation or secretion in a being passionately loved—as, for example, the *saliva*—may stimulate desire by some subtle savor they impart. And this stimulation of desire may sometimes be considerable, but here much—or all—depends less on the qualities of the substance in question, than on the susceptibility of the percipient, which varies enormously as is the case with all sensory stimuli, both as between different individuals, and in the same individual at different ages and conditions.

I would emphasize, at this point, that I deal throughout this book only with such emotions and sensations as lie within the limits of *normal sexuality:* limits which are wide and various enough in all conscience! Morbid deflections, twisted and abnormal desires have no place in the physiology of marriage, in spite of their primitive ramifications, manifold diversity, and extraordinary frequency in the whole field of sexual life. And ideal marriage should be kept free from their taint, with all the knowledge and power at our command. "The pathology of love is a hell whose gate should not be opened at all," says Remy de Gourmont.[1] And we shall be ever careful to keep those sinister portals closed.

The *sense of hearing* has, I think, been underestimated unduly by many authorities with reference to its erotic effects. As Heine[2] says—or sighs!—

> "If I but hear the short sweet song
>   My dear sang long ago,
> My breast is rent and swept along
>   On a wild flood of woe."

---

[1] "Physique de l'Amour. Essai de l'Instinct Sexuel." Paris, Mercure de France.
[2] Buch der Lieder.

And who could surpass Heine in his knowledge of love?
And melodies associated in memory with love's happiness in
the past have a compulsive power, even when they are
"songs without words." For the memory attaches itself
to the melody, not—or hardly at all—to the accompanying
text. The melody was primarily associated with the erotic
experience, and thus the sense of hearing is the channel
which brings its enhancement to the sexual sphere.

Indeed, the realm of sounds, harmonic and melodic, has
erotic witchery of the utmost power for those who are both
æsthetically and sexually sensitive. No one thus doubly
endowed, can feel the tidal orchestral wave of the second
act of Wagner's "Tristan and Isolde" submerge his consciousness, without the deepest sexual response.[1] Nor
enjoy the much rarer delight of hearing Johann Strauss's
"Wiener Wald" interpreted by an adequate orchestra with
rhythm and élan, without the most delicate sexual vibrations.

Shakespeare called music[2] "the food of love." Nothing
could better express its erotic power.

Probably the chief factor in this influence is *rhythmic*.
Rhythm, in every manifestation, has a primæval sexual
significance, as the psycho-analysts specially emphasize.

Music is not the only form of auditory impression with a
powerful sexual appeal. The sexual impulse is far more
often powerfully stirred by the intensely personal medium
of the human voice; of a special voice.

The tone-color of a voice, and the intonation of a single
word—and it may be a word with no special meaning or
associations in itself—may excite incredible intensity of
desire. The unique and precious significance that a woman's
voice can give to "you" or "thou" [3] can suffice to over-

---

[1] No careful observer can for a moment be under the delusion that his
emotions are even in the smallest degree attributable to the *ocular impressions* (actors and stage *décor*) or the *words* of the libretto; they are
aroused by the music and by that alone. The rest is disturbing rather
than entrancing. A critical study of many performances of "Tristan" can
only confirm this knowledge.

[2] "Twelfth Night," Act I., Scene i.

[3] In all continental countries lovers have the specially significant intimacy
of "tutoyage," at their disposal.

whelm a man's powers of endurance and control, or to bring
about the climax of erotic expression in the orgasm.

Should any reader be disposed to comment that this
supreme result is not wholly due to auditory impressions,
but that the attitude and expression of the beloved's form
and face, especially her *gaze* contribute largely to this ecstasy, my answer would certainly be that this is possible and
often, indeed, generally, the case. But vision is not *necessary;* the sense of hearing *alone* can also convey the highest
bliss. As an instance of the magic of love's voice, I can tes-
tify that it has an undiminished power over the lover-lis-
tener, even when heard through a telephone receiver, and
memory is apt to cling with special tenderness and tenacity
to such auditory impressions—a proof of their importance.
I know of cases in which the tones of a dead woman's voice
heard in a telephone conversation were the most precious
memories of a former love.[1]

NATURAL AND PERSONAL ODORS

Personal qualities or idiosyncrasies are of great significance in the association of sexual emotion with the *sense of
smell*. This is the case both in perception of and reaction to
olfactory stimuli, and as regards the *special personal
odors*.[2] Here there are important *racial* variations, and
both olfactory susceptibility and the range and intensity of
personal odors are probably greater in women than in men.

Olfactory susceptibility is a very diverse and uncertain
factor. There are persons in whom it hardly exists. There
are certainly many who have no conception of the sexual
significance of odors and who are not conscious of any
specific reaction to odors. Inasmuch as they are here
anæsthetic and inappreciative, they lose a delectable relish
to love. I would advise such persons to give their attention
to the subject of odors, to become acutely conscious of the
enjoyment they derive from the subtle and various scents
exhaled by the body they love.

---

[1] *Cf.* Alice Meynell's beautiful lyric ending "Your words to me—your
words !"
[2] Dan M'Kenzie. "Aromatics and the Soul." Heinemann, 1923.

There are also individuals whose sense of smell is highly developed. Savants who love to classify and label mankind have grouped them into a special category; they belong to the "olfactory type," and resemble our remote ancestors and primitive races, among whom *smell* is a more important erotic stimulus than *sight*.

And human beings differ in their own individual odors as much as in their olfactory reactions. It must be of course understood that the term "personal odors" does *not* include such noxious by-products as the effluvia of unclean bodies or clothing, of the gases produced by waste matter in the bowels, or of breath saturated with garlic or other injudicious food! Or, indeed, of *all and any such sexually repulsive and disgusting results of lack of proper personal hygienic or æsthetic care,* which must be avoided as the negation of all wholesomeness and charm.

Even more imperative is it to avoid the peculiarly offensive stenches which accompany certain forms of degeneration and disease; especially perhaps those affecting respiration, as they cannot be concealed. A chronically disordered digestion, carious teeth, rhinitis, etc., can be the *coup-de-grâce* of love. Islâm recognizes and respects the intense sexual repulsion caused by such afflictions. One of the four grounds which entitle a Mohammedan woman to obtain a divorce is "when her husband is an Akbar, that is, when he suffers from bad breath, or purulent rhinitis, or ozœna." [1,2]

Any normal member of the canine species proves that human beings each and all have their own special smell, to the careful observer, though he may not perceive any difference. For the dog recognizes his master by smell alone, singles him out from among his fellows and follows his trail or "scent" without hesitation or error.

There are human beings who can perceive individual differences of this kind; but they are less numerous in the Western-Atlantic civilizations than among Orientals and in the tropics. Nevertheless, among us, too, the peculiarly

---

[1] A Greek word meaning "stink-nose" literally.
[2] Dr. Hussein Himmet, "Sexual Disease and Marriage in Islam." 1917. Müller & Steinicke, Munich.

personal emanation exhaled by the hair and the whole skin
of the beloved being can be a source of pleasure. Does not
the lover who has breathed the entrancing fragrance of the
beloved's breath seek to breathe it ever anew? "What is a
kiss?" said one who was an experienced adept in love. "Is
it not a fervent attempt to absorb, to *breathe-in,* a portion of
the being whom we love?" [1]

These emanations from breath and hair are very slight
and faint; therefore they can only exercise definite attraction
when proximity is very close, or in actual contact. But the
odor of perspiration can generally be perceived in the first
stages of approach, and its influence, whether in the direction
of attraction or repugnance—even disgust—may be decisive.

It is decidedly *idiosyncratic, i.e.,* differs widely in different
individuals. Moreover, it is chiefly exuded by the axillary
glands situated in the armpits; and in women, when dressed
in light evening attire and during the rapid movements
and close proximity of *the dance,* it is particularly noticeable.
And in these circumstances an impression may easily be
produced which is anything but inviting, but arouses in-
superable antipathy. For in many women and girls the
odor of the armpits is distinctly and unpleasantly "animal."
And they often are totally unaware of it, which is doubly
unfortunate both for them and for others! The advertise-
ment of a deodorant in the London *Strand Magazine* absolutely hits the mark on this point!

Cases in which the odor of perspiration is attractive from
the first are relatively rare, but they exist. As a rule, however, this particular personal odor is at first indifferent or
slightly repellent to the lover, but it may be intensely stimulating when he has reached a certain degree of erotic excitement.

But in all these intimate matters the personal tastes of
the "consumer" are as important as the idiosyncrasy of the
"producer" of the odors in question. This was strikingly
proved to me during a visit from two young men of my
acquaintance, who were also mutual friends. The conver-

---

[1] Giacomo Casanova, "Filosofia dell' Amore."

sation touched on a certain young lady. One of the youths
—he was only twenty-two—said carelessly, and certainly
without in the least realizing the true significance of his
words: "Oh, no, I don't like her as a dancing partner. She
is a nice girl, but—she has such a disagreeable smell!" The
friend, of the same age and equally *naïve,* replied: "Do you
really think so? I don't understand that at all; it is just
the smell that emanates from her that I like!"

And by mere chance, about a week later, I was witness of
an almost identical conversation between two young girls
of eighteen, equally innocent and outspoken, about a man
with whom they had both danced.

As an example both of the delicacy of perception of odors
in some persons and of the variations in the human exhalations of one and the same person, let the following facts be
recorded.

I had a young girl patient of about seventeen years of age.
She often "ran a temperature." As soon as this happened
her mother knew she was "feverish" merely from the odor
which she could perceive even at some paces away, and
though no one else noticed any such change the maternal
"diagnosis" was always confirmed by the thermometer.

A further instance is so remarkable that I will not deprive
my readers of its details. I know of a case in which a young
married lady can perceive and differentiate the momentary
mood and psychic condition of her husband—whose breath
has been affected by constant smoking—by the varying
odors emanating from his skin! She describes these odors
as follows: Slightly sweet when he is in a good humor;
slightly sour in fatigue; and extremely *acrid* in anger and
strong excitement, becoming the more pungent and penetrating the more he loses emotional balance and control.

Another most important odor, unlike those above mentioned, is entirely confined to women, and to them only at
certain seasons. I mean, of course, the odor or odors of
menstruation. These emanate chiefly from the monthly discharge of the genital organs, and have certain characteristics
common to all women, but varying so widely in *timbre,*
intensity, and personal peculiarities that they can have an
individuality or idiosyncrasy of their own. But they must

be carefully liberated from *adventitious odors, the result of lack of personal cleanliness and coagulated decomposing blood-corpuscles,* which too often accompany them, and are extremely unwholesome and repulsive.

The whole menstrual odor may be masked by clothing and, above all, by frequent and fastidious change of under-linen. Nevertheless, it is generally perceptible, especially to persons of olfactory type, and this is the case not only as regards the special region affected—the genitals—but the odor extends in most women to the exhalations of the skin —sweat glands—and breath, and varies here most widely and *personally.*

The menstrual odor, like the odor of perspiration, may have a threefold effect on the impulse of sexual approach. It may be wholly repellent; distinctly pleasant, and condi-tionally pleasant, *i.e.,* slightly repellent at first, but attrac-tive, even delightful, when a certain *pronounced* stage of tension and desire has been reached. The group of persons who from the first attract or are attracted by the menstrual odor is certainly a very small minority; the third group, the *conditionally* attractive or attracted, is larger than might be supposed; but the first group, that of those who feel or inspire disgust in this respect, *is an overwhelming majority.* A warning to women! "A man forewarned can deal with two," says the old proverb, and we may add, "A woman forewarned—with three!"

In both women and men there is a specific characteristi-cally sexual odor of the genital organs. It, too, is idiosyn-cratic, and varies in degree and type. When it is not exces-sively pronounced—which as a rule it is not—we may say that the normal genital odors exercise an attraction over normal persons of the opposite sex. But this form of attrac-tion can only come into play when the couple have attained a considerable sexual intimacy (at least within the conven-tions of our civilized code).

And as soon as the normal natural odor is tainted by the results of uncleanliness (stale sweat) or any morbid dis-charge its character changes and it rouses a strong sexual repugnance and antipathy.

The genital odor is stronger in women than in men.

When the whole organism is stimulated and ready for coitus this odor is increased by the lubricating secretions of the accessory glands of the vulva; and in many women there is apparently an increase of the odorous exhalations of skin and breath as well.   This phenomenon may then serve as a special means of excitement and allurement for the male lover.

Another important specific genital odor is that of the seminal secretions in the man.

This also has variations.   There is, first of all, a good deal of difference between *races*.   The seminal odor of Orientals is stronger and more acrid than that of the "Caucasian" West.   The semen of the healthy youths of Western European races has a fresh, exhilarating smell; in the mature man it is more penetrating.   In type and degree this very characteristic seminal odor is remarkably like that of the flowers of the Spanish chestnut (Marrons), which also vary according to the condition of the trees and the atmosphere, and are sometimes quite freshly floral, and then, again, extremely pungent and quite disagreeable.

Again, the same individual man may vary greatly in his seminal odor, as has been corroborated by trustworthy and independent testimony.   After mental and emotional excitement the smell of the semen is more acrid, after muscular exertion more aromatic, and after several repeated acts of coitus in rapid succession it becomes fainter, but "stale" and unpleasant.   I have heard its variations described as parallel and concomitant with those of perspiration of the whole epidermis, and the descriptions of its various phases showed remarkable unanimity, though given independently by several women, and referring to different individual men.

It is therefore obvious that the seminal odor must cause distinctly different olfactory sensations in sexual intercourse.   But the medical man who has often occasion to investigate spermatic secretions in the laboratory finds, curiously enough, that the various specimens only differ very slightly, and then almost entirely in degree of intensity. Of course this may be because he endeavors so far as possible to ignore or inhibit the sense of smell, in the course of this kind of research, as it is apt to cause disgust and even nausea. On the other hand, the specific seminal odor is affected by exposure to the air and by being discharged from the male organ (for so long as it is contained within the glands semen has no smell, or hardly any), and this atmospheric action increases the intensity of its smell and obliterates all individual shades of difference.

But women who are adepts do not hesitate for a moment in confirming the existence and significance of these individual shades of difference. I know of one highly talented and delicately sensitive woman who abruptly terminated a *liaison* on finding, at the first act of sexual intercourse, that the special seminal odor of the man was intolerably unpleasant to her.

It may be said *in general* that the odor of semen is exciting and stimulating to women, and unpleasant, even nauseating, to men. But the *mental associations* are here so powerful that they may completely displace or negate the primary sensory impression, so that most men feel *no* repulsion at the odor of their own semen, but pronounced nausea at that of other men's.

For a woman (in coitus) the odor of the beloved man's semen is delightful and excites her anew; but that of an unloved mate fills her with loathing.

The larger portion of semen once deposited in the vagina soon ebbs or drips away again. What remains inside soon loses its distinctive smell. But the resultant blend of male and female secretions inside the vagina, after coitus, exhales a fainter but quite distinctive odor, which can easily be recognized by experts, and is perceptible to persons of the "olfactory type" on underlinen and clothing.

It excites both sexes when perceived, but here, too, the mental associations to which it gives rise—especially the subconscious speculation as to its origin—are no doubt influential in enhancing the primary impression.

The final specifically sexual odor which I must mention, can perhaps rarely be consciously observed but appears to me of such significance, from several points of view, that I will not omit to record it, especially as, so far as I know, it has not yet been described. I base these observations on three cases, women, who quite independently of one another told me that from fifteen minutes to an hour after completed coitus their breath began to show a slight seminal odor, which lasted from one to two hours. They themselves were not aware of it, but their husbands noticed it at once. In the case of two of these married couples this circumstance often led to a repetition of the act of sexual intercourse. The husband of one woman declared to me that the merging and saturation of the beloved person of his wife with the product of his sexual activity, as shown by the faint tang of semen in her breath, and the reminder of the delight felt in the act, had both appealed to his imagination so strongly that he experienced a renewed transport.

This explanation of the stimulation as due to mental images and associations which were only set in motion by the specific olfactory impression seems to me entirely convincing, and much more probable than the hypothesis that the man's sexual emotions were directly aroused by the homologous seminal odor.

There is no doubt that the facts were correctly observed and recorded by the women. I tested the breath of two of these ladies and detected the specific odor;[1] and the third case was confirmed by a colleague. Further confirmation on these lines has not been carried out by me, with the exception of one doubtful instance. There is not often an opportunity for observation here, because the odor, where

---

[1] This circumstance proves: (*a*) the reabsorption of chemical components of the semen into the genital organs of the woman; (*b*) the penetration and saturation of her bodily secretions and blood with spermatic substances; and (*c*) their elimination and diffusion through the action of her lungs, in respiration.

This process of reabsorption has a physiological value to which we shall later return. The mucous membrane of the uterus is very sensitive and absorbent, that of the vagina less so, though it is also capable of saturation. This capacity has been *exactly* demonstrated in recent research, namely, by means of microscopic investigation, of serum-treatment and of other conclusive tests. Nevertheless, the simple fact of the effect of semen received in coitus on the breath of the woman is sufficiently impressive, as proving its elimination and excretion through the lungs. This phenomenon reminds me of the oft-repeated test in which women whose uterus was treated with tincture of iodine showed a decided iodine smell in their breath shortly after the substance had been introduced.

perceptible at all, is so faint that it can only be recognized in the closest proximity to the mouth of the object, and the question is delicate and intimate.[1]

If we recapitulate our observations on natural genital odors, we must conclude that even among civilized peoples the sense of smell has important influences on the sexual impulse. In general, sexual odors and all strong physical odors have a negative or repulsive effect on persons of culture at the first stages of approach: they arouse or increase sexual antipathy. But after the first stages of approach are completed and a certain degree of propinquity or intimacy attained, sexual odors may increase desire and facilitate closer contact. But, on the other hand, a sexual approach which has almost attained its goal can be checked or *completely frustrated by local odors, especially such as suggest dirt or disease.*

Under these circumstances it is easily understood that human beings, from the earliest times, have had recourse to natural substances or artificial products whose scent masks or enhances personal odors.

PERFUMES AND THE SEXUAL IMPULSE

This theme is important and complete enough to form the subject of a separate monograph. It would please me much to write such a monograph, but our knowledge is not sufficiently advanced; on many topics under this heading we can, as yet, only generalize. And, therefore, one could only write another of the many books now being written about sexual love in all its aspects, and written in a spirit in which I prefer *not* to treat the subject.

Although I am even now in a position to make certain observations and record certain facts of fundamental im-

---

[1] In the few further cases in which I was able to attempt observation, the specific odor was absent. This may be attributable to a temporary loss of sense of smell on my part, but this explanation could not dispose of all the cases which were examined at wide intervals of time. Or the lack of odor might be due to defective elimination by respiration; or to imperfect or negative action of the absorbent *mucosa* of the uterus; perhaps because the semen had not entered the uterus, as is known to occur often and by deliberate design.

These observations confirm the experience of certain women who have recourse to deodorizing mouth washes, such as *odol.*

The typical specifically *masculine* scent is provided by Nature, in *musk*. This substance is secreted only by the adult male musk-deer, in special glands in the neighborhood of the genitals; its quantity and quality improve in the spring when the animal is in rut.

Musk is used much more extensively by perfumers than is generally supposed. But it is one of the most strongly odorous substances known to us, and should only be used in strong dilution and combination with other scents. For many men have an innate repugnance to the scent of musk when it is pronounced and characteristic—an antipathy which is, of course, quite normal and physiologically justified. There could be no objection to the frequent use of musk as a component in the most luxurious soaps, powders, lotions and essences, if it were always properly diluted and blended with discretion—which is far from being always the case.

Another staple substance may be mentioned here: the *negative feminine lavender*. The Arabians of the sixteenth century were already aware of the fragrant blossom as an antidote to "an evil smell from the vulva." And the lavish use which our ancestresses (at a time when bathrooms and *bidets* were infrequent luxuries) made of these delicate dried flowers between mauve and blue, sprinkling them loosely or tied in little bags in their linen cupboards, among their undergarments, certainly suggests a similar purpose. For lavender is an excellent deodorizer, if the unpleasant genital odor is not excessive and/or is not the result of uncleanliness or morbid discharges. In other words, lavender neutralizes a too pronounced specific odor of the female genital organs, and is probably also efficacious in counteracting excess of other feminine exhalations, which should explain the widespread popularity of lavender-water and bath-salts scented with lavender. But if these toilette articles are really to succeed in this purpose, they must be compounded by experts and used according to knowledge. Take lavender as an illustration, for other perfumes: a *Vinaigre de toilette* prepared with lavender can increase the deodorant effect by a special acid reaction, especially in the genital region; whereas, in an alkaline preparation such as soap, the same result would not be attained, for alkalis emphasize the specific genital odors.

Moreover, a "Lavender Water" will hardly be an effective deodorant, if the perfumer has *fixed* the lavender odor by combining it with tincture of musk! as I have found directed in the recipe for a certain English preparation. Not because of the specific "masculinity" of musk, but because musk has the power of stabilizing and accentuating other odors, especially personal odors.[1]

This brief illustrative example will show how complex are the factors to be reckoned with in an intelligent sexual use of perfumes, and how various their mutual interaction.

But I must not allow myself to be led into treating this fascinating subject at too great length, so will conclude by deducing certain definite rules from the observations I have made, which may be taken as fundamental and indicate appropriate lines of further research.

All genital odors are heightened by alkalis, diminished by acids.[2] Camphor,[3] Amygdaline[4] (Bitter Almond),

---

[1] A good essence of lavender may be compounded as follows: 1 liter of lavender-water, one-eighth of a liter of rose-water (without any musk or other animal substances), and 75 grammes of salammoniac. It can then be tinted a pale blue with phenicine (indigo).

The "Vinaigre des Quatre Voleurs," a well-known essence, contains an alcoholic extract from the leaves of lavender, mint, rue, rosemary, cloves, and certain other less important ingredients, together with camphor, in an acid solution. So far as I know, it was not originally intended as a genital deodorant, and has never before been recommended as such. Nevertheless, it is admirably adapted for this purpose and is a reliable, though not highly luxurious, toilette article, being compounded of suitable neutralizing ingredients without any, such as musk, which have the opposite effect.

It is obvious that such preparations should only be used well diluted, in sitz-baths and *bidets,* and if as vaginal douches, then only under medical advice.

[2] Note in this connection that normal urine is more or less acid; when drinking water with lime as a constituent is taken (the so-called "hard" water) the reaction is somewhat alkaline. The evaporation or decomposition of urine, whether inside or outside the body, also tends to be alkaline. But certain medicaments can preserve the acidity of urine, within the body.

The vaginal secretions are normally slightly acid. The amount of acidity varies with the physiological condition. Under certain circumstances, especially when mixed with other normal or pathological secretions, or when affected by certain bacteria, the vaginal products become alkaline.

The slimy "libidinous" secretions of the urethral glands and Bartholin's glands have an alkaline reaction. Blood, serum, and sperm have an alkaline reaction; sweat an acid reaction.

For Notes[3] and [4] see next page.

Lavender neutralize the genital odors, and probably other personal odors. Musk (and probably also other odorous substances of animal origin)[1] fixates all personal odors, whether genital or other, and enhances them, when it is used in the smallest possible amount. In a more concentrated form it dominates and obliterates all other odors, and displays its specifically *male* and sexual character. Among other less specific but strongly dominant odorous substances I will cite only one: Peppermint.

Whenever extraneous[2] perfumes are employed, great care is necessary to insure that they shall harmonize, not only in their own ingredients, but with the personal odors of the individual who employs them. Further, that they do not contain substances which have the effect of emphasizing the qualities which the user wishes to modify or disguise.

VISION

The sense of *sight* does not require such full treatment of its sexual influence as the sense of smell. I have had observations to make regarding the latter, which are new, or, at least, which have not been previously systematized or emphasized. But I can only repeat what has been known to all, and from time immemorial, of the charms and allurements of sex through the medium of vision. For I need hardly emphasize its enormous importance in initiating sexual attraction and approach. With very few exceptions, it is the sense of sight that gives the *first impressions* between the sexes. And these *may* be decisive and conclusive. But, fortunately, *everything* does not depend on visual impressions, for otherwise there would often be only a very slight prospect of the awakening of love or of its preservation!

---

[3] As in the preparation of cold creams.

[4] For instance, in "Eau de Violette" or violet water, which contains 2 per cent. of oil of almonds, and in the "Pâtes d'Amande" for the complexion. But not in "Amandine," which is a saponaceous substance, as superfluous alkaloids can neutralize the deodorant properties of Amygdaline.

N.B.—Almond preparations are more widely used on the Continent than in Great Britain.

[1] *E.g.*, Ambergris.

[2] *Extraneous* is here used in contrast to *personal odors.*

For, in contrast to the senses of touch and smell, which grow in importance with the approach to actual *contact,* the sense of sight loses its paramount place more and more. Certainly if the impressions it conveys remain favorable, it may still exercise a potent spell. But if there is not much beauty to perceive, this same sense of sight may be dominated, and, as it were, *canceled* in an astounding fashion, by habit, conscious purpose, mental images, and by impressions through other sensory channels, and especially through psychic factors.

As the Dutch poet *Cats* wrote:

> "Listen, my friend, and know the reason why:
> All beauty lies in the beholder's eye."

The primary sexual characters, *i.e.,* the genital organs, have, as a rule, little visual charm for adult civilized persons. They only increase desire when it has already reached a certain pitch.

But the *secondary* sexual characters are extremely important as stimuli to the impulse of approach; especially those which indicate aptitude for sexual intercourse and for its natural results.

Thus a man is peculiarly attracted by a woman's full and finely-formed breasts; and a woman by a man's tall stature and powerful build.[1]

---

[1] Therefore a man is instinctively repelled by those signs of defective womanhood which can only bring catastrophe in married life. And his natural instinct here guides him wisely: how wisely, is proved by the following passage from an article by *M. Hirsch,* in the *Zentralblatt für Gynäkologie,* 1923, No. 39: "I term those women *intersexual,* whose external organs or proportions show one or more marked masculine or undeveloped feminine characteristics: hair-growth, larynx, pitch of voice. shape of face, genitals, mammary glands, extremities, angle and amplitude of hips and thighs. Even in the absence of such deviations, the woman whose instinctive emotions are under normal in degree or masculine in direction, must be deemed of intersexual type. This is especially the case with regard to the sexual impulse, which, in such cases, is either not definitely differentiated, and often shows an infantile fixation on the mother, or otherwise develops late and runs the gamut of abnormality, even as far as homosexual inclinations. The impulse of sex in these women is either slight, uncertain or capricious. Their whole sexual life, *so far as it runs on normal lines* from the beginning of menstrual activity to first intercourse, or defloration, through coitus, conception and parturition, is a succession of conflicts and catastrophes, whether bodily (dysmenorrhea, vaginism, dyspareunia, sterility, or toxæmias of pregnancy, and all possible complications at childbirth), or psychic. On this point I entirely agree with *Mathes.*"

The æsthetic sense[1] certainly blends with the primitive impulse in this mutual admiration of secondary sexual characteristics, but the decisive factor is this mighty instinctive urge, the very voice of life itself, with its needs and demands, whether they are *consciously* formulated, or, as is usual, submerged in the unconscious.

Bodily movements may appeal to the eye quite as much as bodily *proportions*. This is the case, whether such movements have a definite erotic purpose—as is partially the case in *dancing*—or whether they enhance the wholly unconscious and unpremeditated grace of line revealed in the rhythmic, slightly swaying walk of some women—their fascination is unquestioned.

And if we would know how a woman feels—often unconsciously—about the ease and power of movement in a beloved man, let us remember Goethe's Gretchen: "His kingly gait, his stature so tall. . . ." We may observe finally that the special influence of *movement* as a sexual attraction, seems—*like sound—to lie in its rhythmic character*.

It is only in colder climes that clothing has been worn mainly to protect circulation and keep up bodily temperature. In all warmer regions, tropical and subtropical, it originated wholly from the wish to adorn the body, to make it more remarkable and attractive, and to draw attention to certain special organs. The detailed research of various anthropologists arrives at this conclusion.

As a rule, however, among races *at a certain grade of civilization,* the male costume has generally served the purpose of protection from climatic influences. Only rarely do we find in the history of civilization a fashion which deliberately emphasizes the specific male characteristics. Perhaps the most conspicuous example were the "codpieces" [2] (French "braguettes")—little bags outside the close-fitting hose,

---

[1] At the Conference of the German Gynæcological Society at Heidelberg, in 1923, *Aschner* quoted and agreed with the statement by *Stratz* that only five women in every thousand can claim to be really beautiful.

Stratz is a famous specialist on anatomy and physical culture.

[2] Codpieces were first worn in the middle years of the fifteenth century, as may be seen in the Nancy Tapestries of the time of Charles the Bold, Duke of Burgundy. At the beginning of the sixteenth century they were exaggerated to an absurd degree. Dürer and his contemporaries depicted them as worn by the Landsknechts, or mercenary soldiery of his day.

worn in the mid-Renaissance. These bags or pockets contained the genitals and emphasized their size and shape at first sight.

The male costume of modern times is not as a rule specially sexually accentuated.[1]

The exact contrary is the case with female dress, which of late has followed primitive and tropical patterns, and aims not at concealing, but at enhancing physical charms. From the earliest times, and even when it had to serve as covering from intense cold, it has tended to accentuate and follow the lines of the secondary sexual characteristics. Examples are numerous: for instance, the low-cut bodice—"décolleté" of the seventeenth and eighteenth centuries; the corset, which in its original form *literally* lifted and pressed forward the bosom, in a dangerously painful fashion; and the wasp waist, which was constricted in order to emphasize the curves of bust and hips. Or again, the "Tournure," or "bustle," of the 'eighties, which was at first only meant to discreetly indicate the roundness of the feminine posterior—in itself an important sexual attraction,[2] but which became so exaggerated and unwieldy that it ended by giving the ladies of the most fashionable society a deplorable resemblance to Hottentots.[3]

Fashions such as those of the Directoire and contemporary periods, which instead of uncovering the largest possible amount of epidermis, drape the covered portion in light and clinging fabrics, which suggest rather than conceal outlines and give additional suppleness to movements, have a particularly alluring effect—much more so than that of nudity. Women have always recognized and utilized this form of charm, in their veils, shawls, shawl-dances, etc.[4]

---

[1] Since the "codpiece" fashion, there have been a few faint attempts at something similar. *Cf.* Viollet-le-Duc "Dictionnaire du Mobilier," Tome 3, p. 80.

[2] *Cf.* the antique statue of "Venus Kallipygos"—Venus with the beautiful buttocks—in the National Museum at Naples.

[3] The Hottentot women have a peculiar and enormous development of the adipose tissue of the hips and buttocks, "steatopygy," which is considered most beautiful by the men of their race.

[4] In this respect, too, there is nothing new under the sun. *Cf.* the frescoes at Knossos, in Crete, as described by *Ahrem:* "Woman in Antique Art." (Publisher: Diederich's, Jena.) These Knossian women wear corsets and flounced skirts.

But the strongest sexual impressions received by the human eye are those which other eyes transmit.[1]

Victor Hugo (quoted by Krauss "Woman," publ.: Hoffmann, Stuttgart) has said that "Love stories have so overworked the power of love's gaze, that finally people agreed to discount it. We hardly dare, nowadays, to admit that two human beings loved one another because they looked at one another. Yet—love dawns thus, and only thus. The rest—comes afterwards. Nothing is more true, more real, than the primeval magnetic disturbances that two souls may communicate to one another, through the tiny spark of a moment's glance." How—*i.e.,* through what microscopic muscular contractions and co-ordinations—the mechanism of mutual glances operates, how people "ogle" one another or "make eyes" in colloquial language, is as hard to analyze as it is to estimate the psychic significance and purpose of this process.

The old rhyme, "The heart is in the eyes, thou must look there," is truest in matters of love. And this mutual interchange of emotion from eye to eye is continuous, from the first shy homage of irresistible attraction to the rapturous gratitude of fulfillment.

The impressions received visually from the impersonal world are far less important for the sexual impulse than personal images. Of course writings, letters, printed matter, drawings, portraits, statues, etc., depicting human persons have a different effect from other extraneous objects: they are media of personality and have a certain individual significance.

But utterly impersonal things may also arouse sexual emotion. An appreciable number of perfectly normal people experience sexual stimulation in contemplating a lovely landscape. For a smaller number of normal persons, there is a definite sexual appeal in the abstract beauty of line and color. They are in a small minority, but they exist, and all serious students of sex know of such æsthetically-emotional men and women.

---

[1] As Gretchen says: "The magic of his smile and glance . . ."

The most important of all the senses, in sexual matters, is *touch*.

The sensory organ of touch extends over the entire surface of the epidermis or skin, and the adjacent portions of mucous membrane; but all parts of the epidermis are not equal in their tactile sensibility.

Our treatment of this subject may best be served by separating the stimulation of the nervous structure of the genital organs from the general tactile sense. We will treat the tactile stimulation of the genital organs in a later chapter, and deal here and now with the sense of touch in general. And here we must primarily distinguish an *active* and a *passive* sense of touch.

The *active* tactile sensations are those experienced in contact with anything, by that part of the body which *touches* the object. The chief active tactile agent is the hand, more especially the fingers and their tips; the tip of the tongue is also highly sensitive, but the toes and soles of the feet are of little importance in this respect, even in people who habitually go barefoot.

The lips of the mouth are midway between *active and passive tactile agents*. They have a share of both kinds of sensation, as is exercised in their chief sexual office—the kiss, simultaneously and with equal effect. But we shall consider this in detail in a further chapter.

Passive tactile sensations, those which are received by the object touched, are diffused throughout the surface of the body and the exterior mucous membranes. Moreover, the tissue and organs situated below the epidermis can receive sensations from a specially vigorous or continuous touch, more or less resembling those of the outer surface proper.

In general, we may say that *under favorable psychic conditions,* the stimuli received by the passive tactile sense, are of a sexually exciting kind. This effect is increased the more appropriate the exact part touched, the more adroit the manner and variation of the touch; and both psychic and sensory appreciation may be increased by experience and practice. We shall discuss these stimuli in detail when we treat of (preliminary) love-play (Chapter VIII). Here it must suffice to state that while the whole epidermis may be sexually receptive to touch, there are certain parts of it which are pre-eminently so.   Their technical name is *erogenous zones.*

The erogenous zones are mainly grouped around the openings of the body (orifices), or in their neighborhood. I cannot wholly agree with Havelock Ellis and the other authorities who consider erogenous zones dependent on the connection between epidermis and mucous membranes. Only the surface of the lips has this peculiarity. But it is noticeable that not only the area around the *genitals,* but also round the *anus* and the mouth—as apart from the lips— and nose, have the *erogenous* peculiarity. That is also the case, though in a lesser degree, as regards the *lateral portion of the eye-sockets* and the surroundings of the *aural orifices.* Indeed, the *lobe and helix* of *the ear* are a definitely erogenous zone in many persons; and the same is true of the *lobule.* But this zone requires vigorous stimulation, such as *suction,* before the sexually-stimulating effect is produced, though it can then be very effective.

There are, however, passive erogenous zones which are not immediately connected with any orifice.

It might be maintained that the deep fold or crease which on either side separates the buttocks from the upper part of the thighs—and which is extremely responsive to *light* touches—and the inner curves of the upper portion of the thighs, are more or less adjacent to the genital and anal zones.

But that can certainly not be said of the specially sensitive areas on either side of the end of the "false rib"; behind the angle of the lower jaw and round to the nape of the neck, along the edge of the hair! There are further erogenous areas, besides those just mentioned, but they differ in different persons, and widely.

The sexual sensibility of the mammary glands, especially the nipples, is of peculiar intensity and importance.

Gentle kneading, rubbing and squeezing of these glands with the palm of the hand is sufficient in most women to arouse sexual excitement. If the nipple is further stimu-

lated, either by manipulation with the fingers, or even more
so, suction with the lips and tongue, it causes the whole
breast to swell (as there is an increased blood supply, tension, and in some cases secretion of milk), and the nipple itself, and even part of the areola, to become rigid and protrude: there is also a regular reflex action on the genitals,
which is perceptible in uterine contractions. And the local
stimulation of the nipple has a protracted as well as vehement sexual appeal for women.[1] Even the suckling of an
infant seems fairly often to excite unmistakably sexual trans-
ports. At least, many writers have so testified. *Does their
evidence refer to normal women—or not?* I dare not venture on a decisive opinion here. *Physiologically* such an
effect is probable; *psychologically* it is not. Only experience
can decide, and that is not easily verified or compared. I
can only say that the comparatively small number of women
to whom I have felt justified in addressing this question have
replied *without exception* that they have never felt definite
sexual pleasure when suckling their children—even although
they were well acquainted with the erotic effect of the stimulation of the nipple in sexual relations.

For we shall have occasion to deal with this erotic effect
in the love-play between the partners.

Active tactile sensibility can lead to extreme sexual excitement when a human body of the opposite sex is touched with
erotic intentions or in a favorable psychic mood of the
"unconscious." And if the psyche is already "attune to
love," the slightest, lightest, chance contact can arouse the
deepest thrills.

But if the person who touches is indifferent to the person
touched, or if sexual associations are resolutely inhibited,
either by conscious purpose or other mental preoccupations,
an exhaustive examination of the genitals can take place

---

[1] Contrariwise, a sufficiently strong local stimulation of the genitals
causes the nipples to become turgid and erect. On the basis of this phenomenon, which has been apparent from the earliest times, the anatomists
of the Middle Ages assumed that there was direct muscular connection
between breasts and genitals, without the intermediation of the spinal
centers. The first to record this was *Leonardo da Vinci,* and tradition
says that he considered it of the highest importance. His famous drawing
of a human couple in the act of coitus illustrates this regular interaction
in the woman, very clearly.

without the sexual feelings being roused by the active sense of touch.

But in the case of a neutral—not resolutely inhibitory—frame of mind, it is extremely probable that the active tactile sense will produce sexual stimulation of a degree of intensity proportionate to the sexual character of the parts touched.

Thus we conclude that the sense of touch is the most important of all the senses in sexual matters; but that just this sense of touch is peculiarly dependent on psychic conditions, in order to exercise attraction and not repulsion, and can therefore only operate when a certain degree of propinquity has been attained.

FIRST INTERMEZZO OF APHORISMS

1.

Without marriage there is no happiness in love.

Madame de Staël.

2.

What is marriage? Community of purpose, of activity, of experience, between man and wife.

The worst that can happen in a marriage is not that the wife should suffer, but she should waste away in unsatisfied yearnings, that she should be bored, that she should be lonely and a widow before the time.

Then is it to be wondered at, that she is alienated from her husband? Oh! had he from their first days together, and from the first difficulties they encountered together, really made her his own, had he shared his intentions, his desires and his disquietudes with her—if they had watched and kept vigil side by side, tormented by the same thoughts—then, indeed, her heart would have been proved and preserved as his. For common pain and grief is a strong bond between those who love one another. To suffer together means—the renewal of love.

Jules Michelet.

3.

Marriage must continually vanquish a monster that devours everything: the monster of habit.

Honoré de Balzac.

4.

Good fortune doth befall a girl
    Through a good husband: he's a pearl,

And I will die as sacrifice
If such a marriage is not Paradise.

Quotation from *Jacob Cats.*[1]

5.

All cattle, great and small,
  All fishes in the sea,
    The feathered songsters all,
      Would gladly wedded be!
Would gladly woo and win their loves. Why lonely
  Do I remain, and languish, only?

Jacob Cats.

6.

Dear friend, dost know why that sweet urgent pain
Drives us to port, through love's wild sea?
He who was cleft by love, doth seek again
Union with that lost part that now is *she*.[2]

Jacob Cats.
From "Pictures of Love's Meaning,"
Amsterdam, 1658.

7.

If God had meant woman to rule over man, He would have taken her out of Adam's head. Had He destined her to be his slave—from his feet. But God took the woman out of the Man's side, for He made her to be an helpmate and an equal to him.

St. Augustine.

8.

The greater the man's soul, the deeper he loves.

Leonardo da Vinci.

9.

Woman is weak, and in marriage, she should submit her will to man's. As a return, man owes her the sacrifice of his selfishness and *self* will.

Balzac.

---

[1] Jacob Cats lived from 1577 to 1660, and is known to this day as "Father Cats," in Holland. He was not only an eminent politician and accomplished linguist, but, above all, he was famous for putting the proverbial wisdom of the people into poetic form.

His method was generally to take some well-known saying in classical or modern tongue, or some idiom, and frame it in a brief or elaborate rhyming paraphrase, with some sexual lesson as its moral. He then illustrated the proverb with an appropriate woodcut, which he prepared himself with skilled craftsmanship, and appended relevant proverbs, idioms and verses in many different languages, and in amazing profusion.

[2] This verse and others in many different languages refer to a woodcut of the creation of Eve from Adam's rib. It has the title, "Quod perdidit optat" ("What he has lost he longs for").

10.

The husband draws and absorbs his wife's life into his own circle
of experience, with irresistible power.

Goethe.
("The Natural Daughter.")

11.

A wife is for her husband, that which he has made her.

Balzac.

12.

A woman's torment is not the man's tyranny—but his indifference.
Michelet.

13.

There is no tepidity, no half-and-half love. He who cannot embrace a woman with dominant virility will be neither respected by
her nor loved. He bores her—and with her, boredom and hatred are
near neighbors.

Michelet.

14.

A "cold," passionless woman is a woman who has not yet met the
man she is bound to love.

Stendhal.

15.

List thou that doth lament thee
  That Woman's chilly "No" torment thee!
That thou didst court a wilful fair,
  And suffer anguish and despair.
Take courage and resolve that she
And she alone can comfort thee:
  And bear thy pain, for this I tell
Thee surely, all can soon be well.
  With honeyed flattery and by dint
Of wooing, sparks are struck from hardest flint! [1]

16.

Let this be your honor! Always to love more than ye are loved,
and never to stand second in his heart!

Nietzsche.
(From "Thus Spake Zarathustra.")

---

[1] This verselet is illustrated by a picture of a gentleman and lady seated
before an open fire; he is paying court to her. In the background a boy
is striking sparks from a flint. The motto is "With effort one can extract
fire from flint."

17.

When two people love each other, nothing is more imperative and delightful to them than *giving:* to give always and everything, one's thoughts, one's life, one's body, and all that one has; and to feel the gift and to risk everything in order to be able to give more, still more.

Guy de Maupassant.

18.

Perfumes are as much a human necessity as prayer, as leechcraft, as water and as bodily exercises.

Omar Haleby.
"El Ktab." [1]

19.

The fragrant atmosphere of a *boudoir* is an allurement less easily avoided than is commonly supposed. Indeed, I know not whether the wise man who trembles at the scent of the flowers his beloved wears at her breast—is more to be envied or pitied!

Jean Jacques Rousseau.

20.

The sight of any conspicuous beauty of nature or of art immediately recalls the image of the beloved!

Stendhal.
"De l'Amour."

---

[1] An encyclopædic Arabic treatise on the Art of Love, written in a serious and helpful spirit.

PART II

SPECIFIC ANATOMY AND PHYSIOLOGY OF SEX

CHAPTER IV

NOTES ON THE SEXUAL PHYSIOLOGY OF THE ADULT WOMAN

1. *Introduction and Definition. The External Genital Organs*

THE reader who carefully studies the above headings will at once clearly understand that we do not propose to give a detailed treatise on female genital physiology, but, on the contrary, strictly define and limit the subject-matter of our observations.

We deal here with the adult woman in the married state. Thus we ignore the earliest stages of development and the period of puberty and adolescence. Pregnancy and childbirth are also outside the special sphere of our inquiry. We shall only have to refer to them occasionally.

There is also no good purpose served by an exhaustive treatise on all aspects of adult female sexuality. It would be too unwieldy and also both unintelligible for the layman and superfluous for the medical practitioner, who is able to refer to various monographs and manuals, especially to the recent monograph by *Ludwig Fraenkel* of Breslau. Here the student can find all he needs, including a complete bibliography of the most recent relevant publications. I propose to make use of Fraenkel's work in the following pages.[1]

I shall confine myself to discussing and elucidating those special departments of the normal, specifically sexual functions of the adult woman as are directly necessary to enable my readers to understand the physiology and technique of marriage. On that particular subject I have contributions to offer which are not found in the professional manuals of physiology and gynæcology.

It may be stated, once and for all, that there are here many disputed points and many problems that still await solution. It would only confuse my readers to engage in controversy on these questions. I shall endeavor to frame my descriptions and deductions according to the present level of scientific knowledge, and to base them on my own investigations and experiences. There is no doubt that many of our opinions will have to be more or less modified within the immediate future. But I do no think that there will have to be much modification of my conclusions and suggestions on the *practical side.*

Students of the *physiological functions* of any special organs must first have a clear conception of their *anatomical structure.*

I shall endeavor to make the anatomy of the genital organs clear to my lay readers by means of diagrams. I shall then forthwith enumerate the special functions of the various organs, with special reference to their importance in practice, as advocated throughout this book.

In the diagrams there are appended both the English and the Latin terms. When latinized expressions are most commonly used and intelligible, these are employed.

In the text we shall use both sets of terms, but more often the Latin, as these are more "medical" in tone and less likely to be offensive or suggestive by their associations on certain topics.

---

[1] In Halban-Seitz Encyclopædia: "Biology and Pathology of Woman." (Publisher: Urban and Schwarzenburg, Vienna.)

The female genital organs are divided into internal and external. The external female genitalia are visible if the woman lies on her back and her legs and outer lips (*labia majora*) are separated. These organs are depicted in Plate I. This diagram is drawn to scale, not only because of lucidity, but, above all, because the genitalia vary very much individually in size and shape; especially, for instance, in the diameter and lengths of the *labia minora* and in the shape of the hymen. If the thick and fleshy outer lips (*labia majora*)—which are surrounded with hairs and generally touch each other in women who have not borne children (*Nulliparæ*)—are separated by the fingers and the vulva or *pubic cleft* revealed, the various other portions of the outer genitalia can generally be clearly distinguished.

The first exterior genitalia to be observed are the inner lips or *labia minora,* which are often quite small. In the diagram they are colored brown (No. 10) in order to distinguish them from the inner surface of the *labia majora* (No. 7), which are tinted gray. The *labia minora,* on the average, are from 25 to 35 mm. long, from 8 to 15 mm. high, and 3 to 5 mm. thick.[1] They gradually decrease and disappear towards the perineum, or are merged into a narrow *rim,* the *frenulum labiorum* (No. 17), which joins them just behind the entrance to the vagina. This rim or frenulum disappears, as a rule, after frequent intercourse. In front the *labia minora* grow narrow, and are joined at the base of the clitoris, in the clitoridal *frenulum* or rim (No. 6).

The clitoris (No. 5 in the diagram, and tinted green) is the foremost organ contained in the pubic cleft, and is furnished with a gland or tip (clitoridal gland, *Glans Clitoridis*) which protrudes slightly and is situated between the upper edges of the outer lips. The shaft of the clitoris, tinted pale green in the diagram, slopes slightly from front to back, and is covered with a delicate fold of tissue, the *preputium clitoridis* or foreskin of the clitoris (No. 4, indicated by five curved black lines). So it is not clearly visible and appears as a slight swelling; but it is easily discernible to the touch

---

[1] Estimate of *Waldeyer,* "Topographical and Surgical Anatomy." (Publisher: Cohen, Bonn.)

and can be felt against the pubic bone. In many cases, especially those of arrested development, the prepuce covers the gland or tip of the clitoris, but it can be pushed back so that the tip of the clitoris becomes visible. The foreskin covering the shaft can be *moved,* but not *drawn back.* In the second diagram the clitoris is also depicted (No. 27, also green), and appears as a structure protruding with a downward curve from the *symphysis.* The clitoris is an organ of voluptuous sensation[1] exclusively. Accordingly it is provided with an abundant network of *nerves,* whose numerous fibers are chiefly clustered immediately beneath the surface of the *glans,* and are peculiarly apt to receive and transmit stimuli. The most sensitive portion is the junction of *glans* and *frenulum.* Even the lightest contact—and more especially a *light* and *gentle* contact—here arouses acute sensations of pleasure.

The further structure of the clitoris serves the same purpose as its nerve-supply. Like the specific male organ—or penis—with which it corresponds (or is *homologous*)—it is a network of blood-vessels, and when these are charged with blood it swells and becomes hard and stiff (turgid). This phenomenon is called (in both cases) *Erection,* and is the result of sexual stimulation, physical or psychic: the clitoris, when erect, appears one and a half times larger than when it is in repose.

Moreover, the prepuce draws back, and this tip protrudes so as to receive further stimuli by contact. At the same time the angle of the organ to the vulva becomes more obtuse, and there is a minute but perceptible elevation and forward movement of the whole structure, which further facilitates friction and stimulation. But the clitoris is not capable of such a marked change of angle and position as the erect penis; and the male organ attains both positively and relatively a much greater expansion, though the clitoris is more highly endowed with nerves and therefore more easily stimulated.

It is significant that the clitoris, in common with the rest of the female genital apparatus, only attains its full develop-

---

[1] Technical term for sensation of sexual pleasure (Voluptas).

ment and dimensions with regular and constant sexual intercourse.

But even in virgins the clitoris can become enlarged and active, if they themselves are in the habit of applying local friction—in other words, of practicing *masturbation* (or sexual self-relief).

Between the gland and the prepuce of the clitoris on the sides of the *frenulum* is the *preputial sack* (in the lower part of the white space in Plate I.).   In this sack, in the tiny folds of the prepuce, is found a greasy secretion, the white fluid *smegma clitoridis,* which, if not carefully removed, solidifies and becomes almost *flaky.*   This substance has a certain importance (which is not nearly enough emphasized) as the result of its chemical composition.   It contains ingredients belonging to the same *acid* type as valerian: for instance, capric acid, and especially the capryllic group ($C_8H_{16}O_2$).

The significance of these components will immediately be clear to the lay reader if he realizes that such acids may, on the one hand, have pronouncedly pleasant specific odors— for instance, like that of fresh pineapple pulp; but, on the other hand, are also responsible for the stench of rotten cheeses and the peculiar unpleasantness of profusely perspiring feet!   And the "pineapple" scent can quickly change to something very different in the processes following exposure to the air.[1]   The *smegma clitoridis* is mainly responsible for the specific feminine genital odor, with all its personal *nuances* and semitones.[2]   There is a certain, though limited, attractive and selective function in this humble product, for if secreted in a moderate amount, and exhaling a very faint yet fresh odor, it can have a distinct appeal to the opposite sex.

[1] In my garden is a flowering shrub of the Viburnum species, whose fresh blossoms have an unmistakable—though faint—fragrance like that of the wholesome female genitalia.   When the flowers fade, there is a change in their pristine scent—a scent which is distinctly attractive to men, even to inexperienced youths, while most women dislike it.   This changes its character and becomes generally repulsive, with a rancid, penetrating *acridity,* which is all too familiar to gynæcologists in their consulting rooms!

[2] The personal odors of sweat, grease and other exudations are also largely determined by acids of the capryl type.

But if the *smegma* collects in excessive quantities—and it *is present to excess if it is at all visible to the unaided eye!*— the normal odor becomes obtrusive, or, far worse, it changes, through the process of fermentation, and very rapidly, to a putrid repulsive smell, which is extremely offensive, and must inevitably have a fatal effect, even on a desire which has been already aroused.

The most unfortunate and extremely disgusting results occur when, owing to neglect of personal cleanliness where it is most needed, the natural local secretion becomes mixed with the products of urination, menstruation, and even with excrement! A regular process of putrefaction sets in and affords a forcing-house for bacteria! And there are other consequences, less obviously nauseating, but dangerous. The by-products generated by the chemical forces in putrefaction are at once rancid and acrid, and cause irritation of the neighboring membrane and tissues, whose symptoms are redness, swelling and watery discharges. The local inflammation increases the unpleasantness of the putrid odor and causes acute itching and burning sensations, which make sexual intercourse difficult and very painful.

Thus the *smegma clitoridis* must be promptly and regularly removed. The sins of omission in this respect are without number, and not at all only on the part of generally uncleanly or slovenly women, but in those who are careful to wash all other portions of their bodies. No lay person would credit the facts which are constantly revealed to the gynæcologist in the course of his professional duties. There is this excuse, that neglect to properly cleanse the genitalia arises often from *ignorance of their structure* and/or from a certain modesty and aversion to handling them. Also there are in this little organ—the clitoris—so many tiny folds and interstices that even a specialist may have difficulty in completely removing secretions which are in themselves somewhat oily and adhesive. But such removal is absolutely necessary, not only for the reasons given above, but because the smegma and the bacteria which may infect it are a danger in the case of operations and of deliveries in the matter of asepsis.

The smegma is mostly exuded on the inner surface of the

prepuce. But it can also be found on the outer surfaces, in the deep grooves between the outer labia and the prepuce, and the recesses running between the inner and outer labia. It is not there so specifically odorous as on the clitoris, but otherwise its importance is the same. Fortunately, it is also more accessible and easily removed, so that its presence in profuse quantities between the labia is a sign of gross personal uncleanliness. Nevertheless, a doctor ceases to be surprised at anything!

If we continue our study of the external female genitals or vulva, we turn to that portion which is bounded in front by the *frenulum labiorum* (No. 17) and lies between the inner lips or *labia minora:* it is called the *vestibulum vaginæ,* or simply the *vestibule.* In the diagram it is No. 11, and is colored pink. Within this space is the sexual orifice, or *introitus vaginæ* (mouth of the vagina), in the diagram No. 13, colored blue: in maidens this is closed by the *hymen* (tinted blue, streaked black, No. 15) or virginal membrane, popularly called "maidenhead." Further forward is the much *smaller opening of the urinary passage (ostium urethræ),* which in the diagram is colored blue and numbered 8, together with the double orifices of the larger and smaller vestibulary glands.

The significance of these glands and their mucus secretions is understood only by very few people at the present day.

On either side of the mouth of the urinary passage, and slightly behind it, is an orifice about the size of a pin-head, giving access to the duct of a gland called after its discoverer, Skene: these are the *glandulæ vestibulis minores,* and their ducts are between 1 and 2 cm. in length. (No. 9 in diagram.)

The orifices of the ducts leading to the larger vestibulary glands (*glandulæ vestibulis majores,* or, more generally, *Bartholin's glands,* also after the discoverer) are also hardly visible. They are two tiny openings on either side of the entrance to the vagina (*introitus vaginæ*), just inside the fold formed by the outer surface of the hymen and the inner surfaces of the *labia minora.* In cases where the *labia minora* are shorter than in the diagram, and do not extend

so far backwards, the *glandulæ Bartholini* open into the
narrow rim between the hymen and the base of the *labia
majora,* or outer lips.   When the hymen is ruptured, those
orifices are sometimes found in its remains (*carunculæ
myrtiformes*).   Or it can be almost impossible to ascertain
their exact position.   The glands themselves are at the most
between 1 and 1½ cm. in length, and situated at a depth of
about 1 to 1½ cm. from the surface of the vestibule.   (No.
14 in diagram.)

Both Skene's and Bartholin's glands manufacture a perfectly transparent, thin and very slippery mucus secretion,
which, as a rule, is only exuded under the influence of sexual
stimuli, particularly as a result of *initial psychic excitement.*   In normal cases, the amount of mucus is just sufficient *for purposes of lubrication of the introitus vaginæ,*
and, together with similar urethral secretions of the man,
enables *coitus* to be carried out.

It is obvious that when the amount secreted by these
glands is inadequate, difficulties may arise, which must be
met by artificial means.   More uncommon are the cases of
excessive lubricating secretion, which prevents normal
stimulus by friction in *coitus.*   But specialists recognize the
existence of many such cases.

There is not much to be said about the mouth of the
urinary passage, or *ostium urethræ.*   It is generally on a
slight projection of the vestibular surface, and varies a good
deal, individually, in size and shape.   The *introitus vaginæ*
demands much more detailed attention.

We must first consider the membrane which partly closes
it in the normal unmarried woman.   For though the *hymen*
disappears as a rule in married life, it plays an important
part in the first act of intercourse, which may be of lasting
effect.

It varies enormously in different individuals, both as to
size and shape.   As a rule, it may be described as a crescent-
shaped, and very thin continuation of the posterior (back)
vaginal wall, which stretches forward and nearly closes
the *introitus* from behind.   But there are other not infrequent variations of form: ring-shaped hymens, or

hymens with two congenital perforations or even more than two.

During the first act of sexual intercourse, under normal circumstances, the hymen is torn, or at least perforated, generally in two places, on right and left, at its posterior junction with the vulva; this penetration is usually accompanied by a slight loss of blood, which may, however, be quite considerable. It is much more easily effected in some cases than in others, but is almost always *painful* to a greater or less degree. This pain depends on the size, thickness and tension (inelasticity) of the membrane itself, quite apart from such preventable mistakes as nervous terror on the woman's part and roughness on the man's. As regards tension (tightness or inelasticity), it must be emphasized that in mature women, whose virginity has remained intact till over thirty years or age, the hymeneal membrane shares the increasing toughness or hardness of all the bodily tissues, and offers frequently considerable difficulties in coitus. The *thickness* of the membrane also varies individually: I will merely record that at its base—or its junction with the posterior vaginal rim—it is generally a couple of millimeters, and slightly less on the outer edge; it *never* is of the gossamer-like tenuity which popular superstition attributes to it.

Yes, indeed! Who shall recount the errors of popular belief or superstition about the hymen? The nonsense talked and credited here, not only by primitive savages, but among modern educated people, is beyond belief. And not only absurd, but often dangerous. For these erroneous ideas can lead to quite false and unjust conclusions as to the chastity of women or the reverse. So we must stress the fact that one of the variations of form in this membrane (*hymen fimbriatus*) has deep scallops on the inner edge, which only experienced gynæcologists can distinguish from the perforations of complete or incomplete intercourse.

The contrasting type of structure may lead to errors in a precisely opposite direction. In these cases there is either abnormally slight development of the hymen, or else it is fairly normal in shape, but so loose and dilatable that it is not perforated during intercourse, and even survives the passage of the child at birth! But the latter cases are, of course, very exceptional. In the other extreme—the hymens with so tiny an orifice or such a thick and fleshy *introitus* that (as in the case of the exceptionally tough membrane) perforation is impossible in the normal manner, recourse must be had to medical help.

Even when the remains of the membrane are recognizable after perforation (or *defloration*) has been accomplished, they generally disappear after the first delivery. Or can only be detected in small, flat—or pimple-like—protuberances on either side of the introitus.

In Plate I. we have depicted the *introitus* as a hole: but this has been done for the sake of clarity in explanation. Actually, it is never visible as a hole, unless the woman assumes the knee-elbow (quadrupedal) position (in which the intestines sink forwards, and a vacuum is formed in the abdominal cavity), and at the same time the posterior vaginal wall is pressed back. Then there is a rush of air into the vagina, it becomes dilated, and it is possible to see into the interior of the passage through the *introitus,* which assumes the shape of a round hole.

But otherwise the *introitus* only opens to an object which presses the two vaginal walls apart. This object may enter from without: *e.g.,* the male organ, or a finger, or a scientific instrument in coition or medical examination: or it may pass from within—*i.e.,* from the *uterus*—outwards, as a child's head and body during birth or the menstrual secretions at the monthly courses.

Normally, the *introitus* is closed, both because of the elasticity of its rim and the support of the local muscular structures and because of the pressure of the lower portion of the vaginal walls.

As a rule, these two first-mentioned factors suffice to completely close the vaginal orifice in virgins or in women who have not long been adapted to sexual intercourse. This is specially the case when there are still perceptible remains of the perforated membrane. In such cases only a tiny portion of the anterior (front) vaginal wall is visible from outside (represented in the diagram as No. 12, tinted black). In women who have been married for any length of time, a larger portion of this vaginal wall can generally be distinguished; after the first child is born this is accentuated, and after several births the lower *posterior* vaginal wall also protrudes slightly. This is partly due to the diminished elasticity of the vaginal rim (black border of the blue area in diagram) and its associated muscles, and partly to the gradual sinking and drooping of the walls themselves. The causes of these changes are the numerous *lacerations,* of a more or less serious character, which occur even in normal births. Invisible lacerations in the *vaginal walls* and surrounding tissues, and others which are visible— though, as a rule, only visible in the few days immediately following a birth—in all directions, but mostly backwards through the vulvo-vaginal ring, which closes the *introitus.*

The woman in labor knows only too well that one of these lacerations, if it is directed backwards and about in the center of the vulva, often severs not only the *frenulum* or rim of the inner lips (No. 17), but affects the perineum (No. 18) *too.* But she knows not at all that a lacerated perineum *always means that the vagina is also lacerated.* Women quite fail to realize what this means for their future. They and their husbands know that the treatment of a lacerated perineum means the trouble and pain of a *suture.* So they often try to persuade the doctor in attendance to "get it over and done with" as quickly and superficially as possible, or, indeed, to *omit* all treatment! "because you know, doctor, you yourself say it is only torn a *little,* and so I expect it will heal of itself, without sutures!" And the doctor, alas, all too often agrees, or, at least, he performs the suture with the patient in the lateral position, without special care, and without suturing the vagina, because it means less immediate trouble for the woman, her family, and, to be frank, also for himself.

I must admit that, for a long time, I myself took no other measures. I followed obediently in the footsteps of my teachers, and copied the procedures I observed in most great hospitals and clinics of different countries,[1] unconscious of the need, in a perineal suture, to achieve anything more than an *apparent* restoration of the perineal surface, which generally can be produced, even by such simple means.

But, with time and practice, I have perceived that the results of superficial perineal sutures are wholly inadequate, both hygienically and æsthetically. There are nearly always little interstices which disfigure the surface of the vestibule, especially the hinder portion. The *introitus* gapes and loses elasticity, for the tissues around it have not healed and the muscles lose tone and control, because they have been torn too, and not properly reunited. Above all, I have learned how great the significance of these little changes may be for future sexual life, and for the happiness of a marriage: they mean that coitus has lost much of its charm for both partners. Thus it becomes obvious that every perineo-vaginal laceration should be most carefully stitched; and this I have, since I recognized the need, endeavored to do. This entails reuniting the deeper lying tissues, and especially muscles, as carefully as possible, and using as much dexterity and ingenuity over these genital sutures as are habitually used in operations on the face and throat. A perineal and vaginal suture *is in no respect a minor operation, but a major: it demands, as indispensable conditions, technical proficiency, adequate instruments, experienced assistance, good lighting and sufficient local anæsthesia.* We may justly demand that doctors shall supply these conditions, and that women (and husbands) shall expect them, instead of making difficulties because of the "time and trouble" necessary for success, and accusing the medical attendant of pettifogging triviality.[2]

---

[1] Latterly things have much improved in this respect. In the clinical departments attached to University Schools of Medicine, perineal sutures are completely and correctly carried out; the budding medical man is instructed in their technique, and they are carefully described in textbooks. But "practical" obstacles often make mincemeat of all this theoretical knowledge and these good intentions!

[2] When the attempt to restore a normal *introitus* has either been neglected or failed, previously, I can only urge that it should be made after another birth has taken place. It means then, no extra confinement to bed for the woman, and the chances for complete recovery are excellent, if she has proper care after her delivery, in spite of the possible invasion of

Before proceeding to treat of the *internal* genitalia, we must mention another double (bilateral) structure, which is situated between 1 and 1½ cm. below the surface on either side of vulva and introitus, and near the vaginal walls. These so-called *bulbi vestibuli* consist of a network of broad, thin-walled, sponge-like blood-vessels, which become congested and swollen (like the clitoris, described above) in response to sexual stimuli, whether psychic or local.   The front or anterior portion of these bulbs is smaller than the other: they converge towards the apex of the triangle in which the clitoris lies.   Behind, they become larger.   In its normal, undilated state, each bulb is between ½ and 1 cm. thick and 1 to 1½ cm. broad.   The length is from 3 to 5 cm. The posterior extremity is rounded off and just covers the gland of Bartholin on either side, reaching about to the posterior vaginal wall.   Its outer edge lies at the base of the *labia majora,* its inner edge bounds the inner lips, and at the rear it touches the vaginal wall.   Thus the two bulbs form together a *horseshoe-shaped cushion* opening towards the rear, and surrounding the vestibule and introitus of the vagina.   When they become congested and expand, the outer lips share in this congestion and expansion; they curve over and outwards, and their inner surface becomes visible, while the vulva also seems to pout and slightly open itself.   The whole genitalia seem to swell and protrude, and the readiness for intercourse is thus strikingly apparent, locally.   These horseshoe-shaped *bulbs* form a cushion-like protection to the vaginal orifice, which is less distinctly *seen* than *felt.*   They add greatly to the friction in coitus and increase pleasurable sensations in both partners.

---

the lacerations by uterine secretions.   This is because the reversion of organs to their previous position, which occurs normally after births, is very helpful to the healing process of the sutures.

CHAPTER V

THE SEXUAL PHYSIOLOGY OF THE ADULT WOMAN

11. *The Internal Genital Organs*

In discussing our subject, as stated above, we will take
Plate II. as our text. It is drawn to scale, and represents
the lower part of a *vertical section* through the exact middle
of the body; that is, a section straight from front to back,
which would bisect nose and navel and spine exactly. This
vertical section also exactly bisects the *pubic cleft* between
the *labia majora* (34, yellow) and *minora* (33, light
brown), and the groove which separates the buttocks, or
nates (28, dark gray) behind. It passes through the clitoris
(27, green), *ostium urethræ* (or opening of urinary passage, 30, blue), *introitus vaginæ* (31, blue), and hymen
(32, white and black diagonal lines), cutting or bisecting
them into two halves, and also through the bony pelvis,
which is represented in front in the symphysis pubis (22),
and behind in the sacrum (12) and coccyx (24) longitudi-
nally divided. Above we see the spine (7). Bony and even
massive portions—such as vertebræ and pelvis—are colored
yellow. In the spinal column and sacrum the vertical section
of a canal is indicated (6, pale blue). This is the neural—
lower down, the sacral—canal, which does not further
concern us.

Another important feature of the pelvis is the so-called
rump or *promontory* (8) at the junction of the lumbar
vertebræ and the sacrum. If we draw a line between this
point and the center of the upper and inner rim of the pubic
bone (22), this will exactly bisect an *imaginary* flat surface
or plane, occupying the middle of the body and inclined
slightly forwards. The surrounding wall (or circumference) of this plane is easily recognized by the pelvic bones,

and has enormous significance in childbirth and the practice of obstetrics. Within the circumference of the pelvic bones, and below the symphysis pubis lies a cavity called the *pelvic cavity*. Within this bony casket, hidden and protected from accidents, lie the internal genitals, or sex organs. They, too, are bisected in our diagram: so are the bladder and urethra (20, 21, 23, 30), as well as the lower part of the rectum (25).

Thus the vagina (26) and womb (14, 16, 18, 19) are artificially divided in two halves, which are symmetrical (match exactly).

But the innermost organs of all, the tubes (11) and ovaries (10) are in pairs, and lie on either side of the womb. In order to make the diagram comprehensive and clear, and as it shows in vertical section the right side of the body and the dexter portion of the various cavities and glands, we have depicted the right ovary with its *duct* or tube. But these would *really not be in a vertical section, but behind the surface, here depicted, and in the right half of the pelvic cavity.*

In this diagram we have not reproduced the various layers of muscles and connective tissue; they lie in the white areas of the diagram, and we do not at present consider them. The positions and proportions of the *actual genitalia* are much more easily understood if we keep Plate II. as simple as possible.

Four cavities are represented in vertical section in Plate II. The abdominal cavity (5, pink), the vagina (26, blue), with its continuations; the uterus (blue), and the oviduct or tube (11, blue); the bladder (21, blue), with its passage or urethra (30, blue); and the rectum (25, blue) or lowest portion of the intestines, with the anus (29).

We first consider the neighboring organs, whose relations with the genitalia are of importance.

The rectum (or lower gut, or strait-gut) is the lower extremity of the large intestine, or bowel; it descends from the left side, reaches the middle line of the body, and curves slightly forwards, with an enlargement at the lowest portion of this curve, the *ampulla recti*. Externally it opens at the *anus,* closed by a strong muscle, the *sphincter ani:* the anal passage is much narrower than the actual rectum.

The rectum is a fairly broad duct, with highly elastic walls, capable of containing large quantities of solid excrement (*fæces*) ; these tend to collect in the *ampulla,* or bowel. If they are not promptly and regularly expelled or *excreted,* they become thicker and harder, and the overloaded and distended *bowel* presses against the vagina from behind, and can cause pain and difficulty in coitus.

Another disadvantage of the close neighborhood of rectum and anus to the sex organs is the constant and recurrent risk of soiling or infection through the *fæces,* which are extraordinarily fertile soil for bacteria. Therefore it will be understood that the *most fastidious and scrupulous cleanliness is necessary.*

In the diagram both *bowel* and *bladder* are represented as *half full.* The bladder empties itself by a contraction of its muscular walls, which decreases the size of the organ. At the same time the *upper and hinder* portion of its wall *approaches the lower and front portion.* When the bladder becomes filled with urine, it assumes the shape of a sphere, and its cupola rises behind the *symphysis* towards the lower abdominal wall, and presses backwards against the genital organs. And if this pressure occurs more frequently than is normal, and even—as in some cases—*habitually,* the results are serious. It can cause or accentuate uterine displacements, and thus bring about morbid conditions. And the bladder itself is gravely injured by such abnormal distensions, even on one occasion, and especially by frequent overloading, even to a lesser amount, for an unduly distended bladder cannot be duly contracted again, and it becomes more and more difficult to perform the act of *urination* or *micturition* effectively. The urine is passed more slowly than should be the case, and a small amount is not evacuated but remains behind in the bladder, and offers a perfect forcing-house for *bacteria,* which easily gain access to it. The urine decomposes within the bladder, and acute or chronic inflammatory lesions result, with all the appreciable dangers—not to speak of discomfort and pain—peculiar to such conditions.

It is apparent, therefore, that this humble act of evacuating, or "passing water," is decidedly important, and not by any means the trivial matter many people suppose. It is therefore necessary to speak of it in some detail, and to point out that imperfect evacuation and *retention of urine in the bladder* occur often among women and girls because of the bad habit of *not giving sufficient time to the performance* of this function. First of all, they wait to the last minute before they can bring themselves to use the closet, and then their one idea is to get it over quickly! Thus the unwholesome *retention* is favored in two ways.

This is especially the case when (in peculiar circumstances) urination must take place in a *recumbent position:* for many women simply do not know *how* to pass water lying down. Not only is there some retention in such cases, but the function itself is sometimes quite suspended. And when another position is out of the question—*e.g.,* occasionally after childbirth or certain operations—artificial aid becomes necessary which, however skilled, may always involve disadvantages.

So I must not omit to advise all women and girls to *avoid retention of urine:* empty the bladder completely, *take time enough,* and *go soon enough.* Also, to learn betimes how to pass water when lying down.

Finally, we may mention that the bladder does not open directly into the vulva, but has a passage, or duct, called the *urethra;* it is between 4 and 5 cm. in length, and curved slightly forwards. It is closed at the upper end by the muscle at the neck of the bladder. The external orifice (*ostium urethræ*), which we have already considered, has no closing apparatus.

The proximity of the sexual and urethral orifices in the *vestibule* can have very serious results for both sets of organs, *e.g.,* if either structure is *infected* it is most difficult to prevent the spread of disease to its neighbor. An additional reason for the most meticulous cleanliness.

We will now consider the central duct, or cavity, in Plate II.: the *vagina* (blue). The vagina is the *special copulatory organ* of woman, *i.e.,* the organ which serves the specific act of *coitus.* It is also the *efferent duct* for the passage of the uterine contents out of the body, especially during menstruation, parturition and confinement.

The vagina is a duct or tube of about 7½ to 10 cm., and its direction follows the axis of the pelvis, *i.e.,* is slightly curved forwards. In the intact organ there is a very slight curve backwards, at the extreme lower end, immediately above the introitus. This inclination is caused by a layer of elastic muscular tissue and sinews which encircle the introitus and form a sort of muscular hinge—though a relatively weak one—which presses the front wall backwards.[1] The vagina is also provided with a second, much more powerful muscle, which is attached to the inner surface of the symphysis, and encircles the vaginal wall in its upper portion, lifting it upwards and forwards. As these muscles perform an important function in coitus, and also otherwise, therefore they are shown in a special Plate III.: this supplements Plate II., and includes the muscles of genital organs as well as the muscle closing the *anus,* to scale.

In order to correctly understand the position and function of these muscles, we must observe that the most superficial, (*A*) the *sphincter vaginæ* (closing muscle of the vagina), or *constrictor cunni,*[2] forms part of a group of muscles composing the outer surface of the *pelvic floor* and somewhat difficult to delimit anatomically. But the inner and stronger group which grips the vagina from the direction of the symphysis is formed out of the inner portion of a very powerful muscle, whose outer extremities (not drawn in Fig. 3, for greater simplicity) encircle and reinforce the *rectum* behind, as the other parts do the *vagina.* This internal group of muscles, which somewhat resembles a hollow *cone* in shape, forms the deeper layer of the pelvic floor. When it contracts the most obvious effect is to raise the lower part of the rectum. Hence the name *musculus levator ani.* But the operation of the anterior portion (which grips the vagina and is reproduced in Plate III. as *C.*), can also be distinctly felt, for instance, in the course of a gynæcological

---

[1] Because it is attached to the *anus* behind.
[2] From *cunnus:* Latin for female genitals.

examination, if two fingers are introduced into the vagina and the woman is told to "press hard." The exact place where these muscles encircle the vagina sideways and from behind and join it to the symphysis is then quite perceptible, and the local contraction of the vagina is sometimes considerable. But a doctor who has taken particular heed of the efficient action (tonicity) of the muscles composing the pelvic floor, in the course of several rectal and vaginal examinations, must note with astonishment how much this *tonicity* varies individually. Most women and girls are only able to contract all the pelvic muscles at a time, and then only slightly. (Only the muscle which closes the rectum, the *sphincter ani*, can act independently and strongly.) But there are women who control the voluntary action of the pelvic muscles efficiently, and can not only contract them powerfully *"en bloc,"* but bring different constituent portions into play separately. This developed capacity for voluntary muscular action gives the vaginal portion a separate existence, so that I consider it appropriate to coin a special name for it: *musculus levator vaginæ.*

There is also sometimes voluntary control of the *constrictor cunni.* But this is rarer, and generally only amounts to a co-operation of these two muscles, apart from the rest of the pelvic floor. Nevertheless, a few women, specially adept and expert, do understand how to work the constrictor and levator, either independently or together, at will—a faculty of enormous value in the *technique* of intercourse. (Cf. Chapter XI.)

Voluntary control of the muscles of the pelvic floor is at least as important as that of the other bodily parts: for only through such control can we attempt to restore normality after the extreme distension and slackening of the parts following parturition, and thus to avoid permanent and progressive injuries. Yet the gymnastics of the pelvic floor is totally neglected by women, almost without exception. Nevertheless, such regular exercise is undoubtedly beneficial. Those women whom I was able to induce to exercise the *constrictor* and *levator* twice a day during pregnancy and confinement achieved a remarkable improvement. In order to achieve effective control we must remember that

general contraction of the pelvic floor (such as we have pro-
gressed sufficiently to prescribe to women after childbirth),
is quite insufficient.[1] Women must learn how to bring the
muscles into play *separately,* and use them either simultaneously or in succession. For this instruction is
necessary, and can only be imparted during gynæcological
examination. Gynæcologists should use such inevitable
professional occasions to be of help to their patients in this
way as well.[2]

In contrast to the above-mentioned muscles, which can be
controlled by conscious volition (and are therefore called
"voluntary"), and consist of *rigid* or *transverse* fibers, we
shall find in our further study of the specific feminine organs
only muscular tissues which consist of smooth fibers and
are termed "involuntary" because they are not operable
by the conscious will. Muscular tissue of this type contracts
in response to many diverse stimuli, mechanical and chemical, or direct and indirect, which are transmitted through
the *nerves.* Its contractions may be psychically influenced,
but only indirectly so. A regular normal control through
the higher (psychic) nerve centers is impossible. But this
by no means implies that *involuntary muscular* tissue has a
less important function to perform: the exact reverse rather
is the case, for its *rôle* is of the greatest significance in the
internal female genital organs. The walls of the entire
female genitalia are lined with smooth muscular tissue, including the vaginal walls, which also are richly furnished
with elastic connective tissue.

After this necessarily brief account of the different types
of muscles we turn again to our study of the vaginal organ.
This muscular duct or tube is covered internally throughout

---

[1] *E.g.,* the in themselves excellent movements "to strengthen the pelvic
muscles" by "separating and closing the knees," recommended to par-
turient women by *K. Reifferscheid* in Stöckels "Lehrbuch der Geburtshülfe." (Publisher, Jena, Gustav Fischer.) Even when his advice is
followed by simultaneously lifting the loins and contracting the *sphincter
ani* as strongly as possible, the only result is a *general* movement of the
pelvic floor.

[2] When gymnastics fail, a relaxed and weak pelvic floor can be benefited
by *vibro-massage.* In order to avoid erotic stimulation of the patient, I
recommend that this massage should be *rectal* not *vaginal.* It should
obviously be only carried out by an experienced specialist, and not during
pregnancy or the first weeks after childbirth.

with pink mucous membrane of a rather tough and firm consistency, but the walls are only about 4 mm. thick. This is really extremely tenuous: but there is enormous ductility and dilatability. This is quite specific and necessary in view of the demands placed on the organ at birth. Nevertheless, after such excessive expansion, the vaginal walls generally lose some of their elastic tension and the passage becomes wider and looser than before: this is unavoidable.

The lower two-thirds of the vaginal walls, both anterior and posterior, are each, as it were, furnished with an oval cushion of crossing folds. The front is the most developed, increases in size towards the introitus, and even protrudes into it (Plate I., No. 12, black; also black in Plate II.). This cushion-shaped protuberance lends the lowest portion of the vagina a slight backward curve. An excessive development here, such as occurs often in pregnancy, can be mistaken for a prolapse of the front vaginal wall. The whole structure of oval pads and crosspieces or ridges, together with the remnants of the hymen, accentuated by the working of the *elevator* and *constrictor* muscles, and the protrusion of the *bulbi vestibuli,* is an apparatus for gripping and rubbing the male sexual organ, during and after its insertion or immission into the vagina, and thus to produce the ejaculation of seed or sperm-cells, in the culmination of excitement, and at the same time, by pressure and friction, to insure this orgasm (or acme of pleasure and ecstasy) in the woman also.

In Plate II. the vagina is depicted as an open hollow space. This is done for the sake of clearness, but is not strictly accurate. It only opens when some object—or even the air —presses into it, as I have explained in detail when describing the introitus. Normally the two walls touch each other, or rather the front approaches and rests on the back surface, so that a diagonal section would give this)———(outline.

The upper portion of the vagina encircles and contains the drooping tip of the womb, the *portio vaginalis uteri,* closes the vagina, whose upper portion merges into it and is circular. It is known as the *vaginal vault* or *fornix vaginæ.* As the womb lies obliquely to the direction of the

vagina, and as the posterior or back wall of the passage is
appreciably longer than the front, there are two distinct
parts of the Vault or Fornix, the one flatter and lying in
front of the *portio (fornix anterior, laquear anterius,* or
anterior vaginal vault), and the other, much deeper, behind
the *portio:* this is the *Fornix posterior, Laquear posterius,*
or *posterior* vault, represented in Plate II. under No. 17.
When the woman lies on her back the posterior vault is the
lowest part of the vagina, the male seed is deposited or at
least *collects* there, and so it is also termed *"Receptaculum
seminis,"* i.e., the *seminal bag* or *purse.*

As shown in Plate II., this curve of the upper vagina
is bounded above and behind by a deep pocket-like recess
within the abdomen, called after the author who first
described it, *Cavum Douglasii,* or *Douglas' pouch.* (In
Plate II. the Abdominal (5) and Douglas cavities (15)
are both colored pink.)   Douglas' pouch droops more or
less far down between the vaginal vault and the fore part of
the rectum (there is much individual difference in the relative proportions here).   There is practical importance in the
fact that these parts are only separated by a very thin wall
of tissue, for the *peritoneum* is thin and sensitive and the
vaginal wall more tenuous just there than anywhere else.
In cases where the penis is disproportionately large and/or
the vagina disproportionately small, and the man disregards
this and uses reckless force in *coitus,* there may be a *laceration or rupture here,* which is excessively dangerous, owing
to the sensitiveness of the peritoneum to infections and the
bacterial contents of the normal vagina.

Regarding the vagina, we may further observe that,
though it contains no glands, its walls secrete a slight
amount of fluid which contains *lactic acid.*   The proportion
of lactic acid secreted *varies rhythmically,* and this rhythm
corresponds to the recurrent changes which we know as the
processes of *ovulation and menstruation,* to which we shall
refer presently in detail.   Approximately midway between
two menstrual courses (a time which coincides with *ovulation* or the expulsion of an egg-cell or *ovum* out of the
ovary), the proportion of lactic acid in the vaginal secretions

is at its minimum, *i.e.,* about 0.05 per cent.   And this is specially important in view of the fact that male spermatozoa retain their vitality and mobility longest in a weak lactic solution (from 0.05 to 0.1 per cent.) and perish with relative ease in a stronger solution.[1]

This lactic acid in the vagina has also a protective function as a medium for various harmless or even beneficial microorganisms or bacteria, and as an antidote and antiseptic against disease germs from outside.   According to *Zweifel,* this auto-antisepsis, as we may term it, is particularly efficacious against infections during confinements.

With this secretion there are normally mingled epithelial cells and some leucocytes (white blood corpuscles), so that in quite healthy genital conditions a slight amount of thin milk-white fluid is found in the vagina.   Apart from menstruation, anything exceeding this, in quantity or consistency, *e.g.,* any slime or pus, must be regarded as morbid.   A *thick yellowish secretion is an unmistakable sign* of disease.

The vaginal walls *absorb* as well as secrete.   Thus chemicals in contact with the vagina may be absorbed and incorporated into the other bodily secretions.   They circulate in the blood and in process of time, according to their specific nature, they pass out of the body, through the lungs, salivary glands or kidneys (as urine).

This absorbent quality of the vagina is not often fully appreciated.   In Chapter III. I have referred to it in connection with the sperm, or semen.   Here I will emphasize the fact that certain strong poisons, such as corrosive sublimate, which are sometimes used as douches to prevent conception, are not absorbed without grave danger.[2]

During pregnancy this absorbency is increased owing to

---

[1] Detailed investigations on this point by E. Gräfenberg, Berlin: "The Cyclical Variations of Acidity in the Vaginal Secretions," *Archiv für Gynäkologie,* Vol. 108, Nos. 2 and 3.

[2] As I write, I see an article in the *Zentralblatt für Gynäkologie,* 1924, No. 18.   It mentions a case—which ended fatally—of characteristic sublimate poisoning, in an unmarried lady of twenty-five, who had introduced a pastille containing 0.5 gr. sublimate for contraceptive purposes.   And refers to a similar case, after douching with the same chemical.   (*Ibid.,* 1923, No. 6.)

the greater blood supply of the genital organs. The walls are swollen, tender, and easily vulnerable, and bleed freely at the slightest scratch or bruise. Their color darkens from pink to deep purple. Similar changes take place in the external genitals; the *labia majora,* owing to the expansion of the tissues and blood vessels, are usually slightly separated and the vulva more or less open.

Finally, we must consider the changes in vulva and vagina with *the advance of years.* Generally they only become evident rather late in life (especially if the women continue sexual activity), although after several births a certain amount of "wear and tear" is very perceptible. The effects of frequent parturition are flattening of the pads in the vaginal walls and stretching and slackening of the passage itself. These can, however, be much diminished by the precautions advised above (careful and timely sutures of even the smallest lacerations, and gymnastics of the pelvic muscles).

The typical degenerative changes of old age involve loss of elasticity, flattening of the vaginal vault and shrinkage of its walls, which become perfectly smooth and very thin and even brittle: the passage contracts. There are corresponding changes in the vulva and *introitus;* the *bulbi vestibuli* and Skene's and Bartholin's glands decrease in size and the adipose tissue of the *labia majora* shrivels, so that the whole outer genitals assume a wrinkled and worn out appearance.

It is, of course, obvious that care must be taken to reckon with these changes, both in the *pregnant* and in the *post-climacteric states.*

The uterus or womb (also sometimes called the *matrix*) has a more complicated and fundamental office than the vulva or vagina. Nevertheless, we shall occupy less time and space in our description of the womb than of its accessory organs. For its main function is to receive the fertilized *ovum* out of the oviduct, to nest the ovum in the mucous membrane of its walls, to nourish and protect the product of conception till it sends the child forth into the light of day. Thus the womb is an organ of *incubation and birth* (reproduction), and a description of its functions belongs rather to a study of obstetrics than to the present work.

The womb consists of a hollow pear-shaped muscular structure (the muscles being smooth or "involuntary"), richly interwoven with elastic fiber and tissue lined internally with mucous membrane (*endometrium*) and externally by the peritoneum. Its upper broader portion is called the *corpus uteri,* or body of the womb (Plate II., No. 14) ; the narrower lower portion is the *cervix uteri* or *neck* of the womb (No. 16).

We have learned to know the lowest third portion of the cervix as the *portio vaginalis,* which is like a tap protruding into the vagina and closing it from above. This we must treat in greater detail, as it plays an important *rôle* in the sexual act. It can be better described by a picture than in any words. In Plate IV. we have the representation of the *portio* as it can be seen, at the furthest recess of the vagina, if the vaginal walls are separated by the fingers or a *speculum.* The organ depicted on the left is the *portio* of a *nullipara,* that is of a woman who has never borne children. On the right is that of a *multipara* or mother of several children, in natural size. The differences are conspicuous. In the first case the *portio* is narrow and the *ostium* or mouth of the womb almost round. The *portio* of the multipara is thicker and more massive, and the *ostium* more or less wide, slightly open, with a horizontal fissure, from which scars (of lacerations) generally ray out on either side. Only therefore in the multipara does the ostium at all resemble a mouth : it is really more like *lips* than a mouth. But this term is always used professionally, and the edges of the ostium are called respectively the anterior and posterior lips of the uterus or womb.

In the ostium *a round drop or plug of mucus,* which should be as clear as glass, is generally visible, slightly protruding. It consists of a thick substance with an alkaline reaction, secreted by the cervical membranes. It is known in medical terminology after the first medical writer who described it, as the plug of Kristeller, or Kristeller's mucus plug, which is habitually shortened to "the Kristeller." It forms a stopper to the mouth of the womb; but its function is double, for immediately after *coitus* it facilitates the entry of the spermatozoa into the womb. We shall later describe how this is effected. This mucus plug generally adheres so firmly to the neck of the womb and the ostium that it is difficult or impossible to remove it. Normally it is perfectly transparent or, at the most, clouded and milky-white. Any tinge of yellow in it is a danger-signal, and a drop of pus exuding from the womb instead of the Kristeller is a sign of morbid and inflammatory changes in the uterus, and should be medically attended to at once.

Finally we must observe the deeper recess of the *"laquear posterius,"* or posterior vaginal vault, which is visible on Plate IV. below the posterior *lip;* and the shallower front portion of the vault, or *"laquear anterius,"* which we have recognized from the brief preceding notes. But it is necessary to refer to Plate II. in order to realize the exact proportions and position of the uterus.

It must be clearly understood that the position of the womb, as depicted in Plate II., does not correspond to its usual position. In the diagram the uterus lies higher inside the abdomen than is actually the case, for its upper portion remains as a rule below the plane of the pelvis. This inaccuracy is partly intentional, in order to present a clear unimpeded view of the organs. But also, and principally, because both vagina and womb are depicted in approximately the position and dilation into which the fully erected and inserted male organ would bring them. The vagina stretched to its full length, with parted walls, and the *portio* and whole uterus pressed upwards.

Further, in actual fact, with a half-filled bladder, and empty closed vagina, the main body of the womb (*corpus uteri*) would be inclined more forwards, and upon the bladder the angle between *corpus* and *cervix* be more acute, and the *anteflexion* (forward curve or inclination) as the normal position of the womb is called, much more pronounced. And finally the *portio* would resume its slight backward trend, the moment it was no longer pressed upwards and lifted forwards by the anterior vaginal wall, *i.e.*, as soon as the phallos had withdrawn from the vagina; and therewith the *ostium uteri* would curve slightly backwards and towards the posterior vault or *receptaculum,* whilst the empty and relaxed vagina is again inclined slightly backwards, and its walls again close together.

These then are the distinctive differences between the *normal* (empty) and the *coital* positions of uterus and vagina. They have been represented in the coital position as appropriate to a work on the physiology of marriage, and also because elucidation becomes thereby easier and more complete.

Obviously the uterus, like other sex organs, possesses considerable *mobility.* And it can be displaced, more or less seriously, through various causes. We have already mentioned one agency that presses it upwards. There are other agencies of displacement: *e.g.,* the muscles of the abdomen can strain or force it downwards; an overloaded bowel can force the womb forwards, and a full bladder can press it backwards. Moreover, the womb is subject to various gravitational stresses and strains, in various attitudes of the woman. And this uterine mobility is not confined to the organ as a whole, and in regard to its neighboring organs, but extends to its degree of inclination and to the angle of *corpus* and *cervix.* In addition to this wide and quite normal range of mobility, there are numerous *lesions,* or injurious displacements which occur very often, so we may realize how delicately balanced, how *unstable* is the mutual relationship of the interior genitals, to each other and the adjacent parts.

And yet this equilibrium is preserved. How?

Through the suspensory muscles of the uterus, a complex structure of elastic *involuntary* ligaments, which *support* as well as *suspend.*

They comprise (1) The two rounded "motherbands" or *ligamenta rotunda,* which extend from either side of the upper part of the uterus, are covered by the peritoneum, and pass in wide curves to the groins and thence to the pubis and base of the *labia majora.*

(2) The second pair of muscles is the sacro uterine (or

ligamenta sacro uterina), which owing to their immensely powerful retractile sinews and fibers, are also known as *musculi retractores uteri.* They begin at the highest portion of the uterus, and behind (at the angle of *corpus* and *cervix*), stretch out on either side, under the peritoneum, encircle Douglas' cavity and the rectum, and are attached firmly on either side of the pelvis, behind.

As these retractor ligaments are important in coitus, as well as in pregnancy and birth, they have been included in Plate III. They draw the lower part of the uterus upward and backward, which specially promotes the return of the womb to its normal position of *anteflexion* as well as prevents prolapse in the enormous downward pressure of later pregnancy and labor.

The third pair of suspensory muscles passes from either side of the womb, downwards, to the inner sides of the pelvis. These so-called *ligamenta lata* or broad muscles, consist of an extension of the peritoneum, containing the nerves and blood vessels which supply the uterus, from both sides of the body.

But these three powerful sets of ligaments would not suffice to suspend the uterus securely. The most efficient agent here is the cushion-like elastic muscular tissue at the base of the *ligamenta lata,* around the *cervix,* which spreads out like a cushion, before, behind, above and below.

The investigations of *Ed. Martin* of Elberfeld, have demonstrated, that this protective structure makes it possible for the pelvic organs, especially uterus and vagina, to respond pliantly to every sudden or prolonged abdominal pressure—lifting, straining or "bearing down," coughing, etc.—without permanent dislocations. They spring back elastically into their pristine positions, *so long as the protective mechanism is still intact.*

But this elasticity can be permanently impaired, if it is subjected to too great a strain. Therefore it is necessary to employ remedial measures against such a strain. This can be done by re-enforcing the solidity of the *pelvic floor,* against which the pelvic contents are forced, by increased pressure from above. Thus there are two requisites for preserving the normal position of the pelvic organs: a *suspensory structure whose elasticity is still intact,* and a *whole and firm support, vigorous and adequate pelvic floor muscles.* Both these must contribute and co-operate, if the pelvic organs are not to suffer.[1]

The cavity of the womb, or *cavum uteri* (colored blue in Plate I.), is about 7 cm. in length in nulliparæ, and over 8 cm. in women who have already borne children. Vertically it occupies very little space. But diagonally it may be described as a triangle, whose base is the *fundus uteri.* The apex of the triangle is directed downward, and lies just at the angle between *corpus* and *cervix,* where it forms an extremely narrow orifice into the *cervix* itself. This orifice is *at the most* 3 mm. wide. The cervix at its other extremity, of course, opens into the vagina, by the *ostium uteri*— sometimes called *ostium externum,* to distinguish it from the contraction at the junction of *cervix* and *corpus,* which is termed the *ostium internum uteri.* At the corners of the triangular area, which are known as the Fallopian angles, the body of the womb again contracts into excessively narrow orifices, which give access on either side, to the Fallopian tubes, oviducts, or salpinges.

The cavity of the womb is lined with a mucous membrane rich in secretory glands, which has most important functions to perform in *nesting and nourishing the fertilized ovum.* These functions involve extensive changes in the uterus itself.

Every lunar month (of four weeks) the womb prepares itself to fulfill its office, and in this preparation it undergoes considerable change. If this preparatory process is in vain, as no ovum is fertilized—it is automatically obliterated and dissolved, as rapidly as possible, and the mucous secretions are expelled together with a considerable amount of blood and sanguineous fluid. This is the recurrent menstruation or monthly period. After the monthly period, only the lowest layer of mucous membrane or epithelium is left in the womb. It remains in repose, until it feels the impetus which prepares it to receive another ovum. If this

---

[1] The last sentences have been freely quoted from A. Hoehne (W. Stöckel's "Manual of Obstetrics," Fischer, Jena, 1920). They are a testimony in favor of the various precautions and remedial measures I have recommended above.

also is in vain, and fertilization (conception or impregnation) does not occur, the epithelial cells and secretions are once more expelled, in another period. Thus throughout the years of sexual maturity the phenomenon repeats itself in a recurrence which forms the menstrual or monthly cycle; unless it is interrupted and fulfilled by pregnancy.

We shall discuss menstruation in detail in the next chapter, in association with the simultaneous rhythmic changes in the vital processes of woman, and in its dependence on the function of the ovaries.

The muscular wall of the uterus is about 1 to 1½ cm. through; it is thickest in the body of the womb. The whole hollow muscle of the womb is enormously powerful; it has to expel the child in the convulsions of birth. For this supreme office it has been prepared during pregnancy to such a degree—by the increase of muscular tissue—that the organ has increased in weight from 50 to 70 gm. (50 in nulliparæ, 60 to 70 in multiparæ) to between 900 and 1,200 immediately following birth.

But even in the non-pregnant state the uterus can expel blood and epithelial cells with great force. Its muscular fibers extend in all directions, but mainly from the mouths of the tubes towards cervix and *portio*.

The uterus automatically rejects and tries to expel anything except the product of conception (embryo, or fœtus) before it is ripe for birth; and either a solid body or an accumulation of liquid is pressed down and out. Moreover, the muscle automatically contracts in response to stimuli conveyed through the blood or nerves.

The idiosyncrasy or special peculiarity of uterine spasms or contractions is that they begin slightly, increase in force, remain for a short time at maximum intensity, and then die away. Then, after an interval of repose, they begin again. This specific quality is most marked in childbirth (labor pains), but can also be verified outside and apart from pregnancy.

Moreover, strong uterine contractions are accompanied by a peculiar and unique kind of pain. The acute and terrifying nature of this pain, not only at births but on other occasions, is well known to women.

Only slighter contractions, especially those *which meet with no resistance,* are painless, or even imperceptible. Fortunately, this is the case with the uterine spasm or paroxysm at the supreme moment of sexual intercourse.

Externally, the womb is covered by the peritoneum or peritoneal membrane. Only the narrow strips on either side where the ligamenta lata are attached and the lower outer surface of the uterus are not covered by the peritoneum.

In Plate II. it is clearly shown that the peritoneum does not extend as far down in front as behind, and also that in front it does not reach the vaginal wall. It is closely wrapped and sheathed round the womb by the supporting muscles, but at the front, between uterus and bladder, it is loose, and forms a pouch or fold—the utero-vesical fold. On this particular area the peritoneum can be moved to one side.[1] To the forepart of the body, the peritoneum covers the greater part of the upper surface of the bladder, and continues over the front inner abdominal wall above the symphysis.

We have already mentioned the *posterior peritoneal fold* in the lowest part of *Douglas' pouch.* From there the peritoneum extends over the front of the spinal column and the sides of the abdominal wall.

In short, this very thin transparent membrane lines the abdominal cavity, and also covers the entrails. And the inner genitalia, with the exception of the vagina, lie within the peritoneal cavity, supported and covered by a duplicate of the peritoneum which extends throughout the pelvis. In Plate II. I have endeavored to represent them as clearly as possible, for the exact mutual positions are somewhat complicated. It should be understood that the area colored pink (the lower peritoneal cavity) is filled by the *intestines,* which surround the genitals on all sides.

The close vicinity of genitals and peritoneum is very important, for the accessibility of the genitals to the outside

---

[1] Thus in the diagram, the white strip between the brown uterus and the reddish peritoneum does *not* imply that there is an appreciable layer of connective tissue here, but is left for the sake of clarity.

world and their activity may transmit infections of various kinds into the deepest recesses of the body.

The oviducts or tubes (Plate II., No. 11), are joined to the uterus on either side. They consist of ducts, between 10 and 15 cm. long, and curving outwards towards the sides of the abdomen. At the junction with the uterus they are incredibly narrow, but become enlarged gradually towards the sides.[1] Nevertheless, throughout they are relatively slender, and very delicate and pliant.

The tubes are enclosed and supported by the upper free rims of the ligamenta lata. Their lateral, curved and cone-shaped portion lies independently in the abdominal cavity. In appearance the delicate longitudinal folds and numerous deep red fringes of the tubes recall a carnation in flower.

Thus we see that there is access, continuous though indirect, between the outer sexual orifice or *introitus* and the abdominal cavity. This is significant, although, of course, we must remember that there are obstacles in the close approach of the vaginal walls in the mucus plug of Kristeller, and the slight fluid secreted by the tubes. But if liquid is injected into the vagina or the uterus, it can penetrate into the tubes, and from thence reach the peritoneal cavity; and as the peritoneum is highly absorbent, poisoning (toxic effects) or inflammations, local or even general (peritonitis), may ensue.

The interior of the tubes has numberless longitudinal folds and creases, and the most delicate microscopic hairs or fringes, which are incessantly moving, waving and flickering in the direction of the uterus. These *epithelial* cells never cease to quiver throughout the life of the organism, and thus they act as miniature pumps for a capillary current which flows from the abdomen towards the womb. This capillary current helps to perform the special function of the tubes, namely, to bring together the male and female elements in generation (spermatozoa and ova), and to transport the fertilized ova into the womb. And the capillary current is of assistance to impregnation in two ways: *its action on ova and spermatozoa is complementary, but exactly opposite.*

The capillary current and waving fringes draw the ovum,

---

[1] Hence the name Salpinges (Greek for trumpets).

as it leaves the ovary, into the cone-shaped abdominal openings of the tubes, where it receives *fertilization,* and then waft it along to the uterus, where it is embedded and nourished.   And, on the other hand, the outward movement and suction in the tubes excites the sperm-cells, or spermatozoa, to vigorous counter-efforts: for it is a special peculiarity of these tiny cells, *which have a capacity for independent movement, that they swim by preference against the current,* and they must move upwards and inwards, in the direction of the ovary.

Thus the capillary current in the oviducts unites the two contrasting and complementary cells which seek one another. Meeting of two such cells, or fertilization or conception, generally occurs in the curved lateral portion of the oviduct; here the ovum develops for the first week, and is carried along the tube and deposited in the uterus.   The peristaltic muscles of the oviducts, which are in constant slight motion, mainly in the direction of the uterus, of course help the transport and suction of the fertilized ovum.   (See *Sobotta* and *Mikulicz* especially: the latter in *Zentralblatt für Gynäkologie.*   Nos. 30 and 42.)

The ovaries, like the tubes, are duplex or bilateral organs; they are oval in shape, and lie almost vertically, with the short ends uppermost.   They are between 3 and 5 cm. long, 1½ and 3 cm. broad, and ½ to 1¼ cm. thick.   Their consistency is elastic but very firm, and their upper surface subject to periodical irregularities, because of the formation and maturing of the *Graafian follicles* containing the ova.

The short, curved upper ends of the ovaries and both surfaces lie inside the abdominal cavity.   One flat, longitudinal surface is attached to the *ligamenta lata* at the back, on each side; moreover, the ovaries have their own muscle which attaches them to the uterine rim at the side, and another (the ligamentum suspensorium ovarii), which is marked in Plate II. as No. 9, and attaches them to the pelvic wall, so that, although their position shifts slightly, they are held in place.   The openings of the tubes lie in the immediate vicinity of the posterior rims of the ovaries, and the central portion of their surfaces.

In the ovaries the countless egg-cells, or ova, are formed and then extruded or expelled.

This process is continuous. Recurrently, tiny follicles or pouches are formed, full of a liquid substance, and containing the single ovum. In a period of four weeks the follicles ripen, alternately in the right ovary or the left—it is, however, not certain that this activity is in constant and regular rotation between the two sides. The follicles ripen till they are ready to burst, and they are called after the scientist who first discovered the whole process (Rejnier de Graaf, who died in Delft, 1673), the *Graafian follicles.* They grow till they reach the upper surface of the ovaries, which becomes curved and bulges forward till it bursts under the pressure of the distended follicle, which may reach the dimensions of a small cherry. The fluid, sprayed forth from the bursting follicle, carries the egg or ovum (which is only 1/5 mm. in diameter) into the abdominal cavity, in the neighborhood of the mouth of the tube; and the suction here carries it into the oviduct, as described above.

But the burst follicle has not ceased its functional activity. It develops a series of protuberances, and becomes a glandular body of a pronounced yellow color, called from this yellowness, the *corpus luteum.* This ovarian product excretes substances which are poured into the blood, and profoundly influence the whole organism, as well as the mucous membranes lining the uterus. If pregnancy follows the expulsion of the ovum, the corpus luteum extends and develops during some months. If no conception occurs, the corpus luteum is dissolved and dispersed, after a brief efflorescence, leaving only a minute scar on the upper surface of the ovary.

As each follicle takes four weeks to ripen, the majority of these very numerous structures do not attain full maturity. They pass into the stage of *involution* or *demolition,* and their component *cells assume glandular characteristics.* But these cells also secrete and excrete substances *which are absorbed into the blood, and affect all the vital processes: in this they are aided by the interstitial tissue of the ovaries* (endocrine secretions).

Thus the ovaries are organs with a *twofold secretion:* *external (ova) and internal.*

The external secretion is periodic and recurrent. The internal is partly recurrent, *but also, to some extent, continuous.*

We have alluded, in our second chapter, to the importance of these secretions and functions in determining sexual impulses. We must now consider how they influence menstruation, and the whole organism and activities of the adult woman.

CHAPTER VI

SEXUAL PHYSIOLOGY OF THE ADULT WOMAN

III. *Ovarian Activity, Rhythm of Vital Manifestations in the Female Organism, and Menstruation*

THE questions which we must now approach are extraordinarily complex, not only because of the intricate processes involved, but also because many of the factors are extremely difficult to understand, and some of the main elements are not yet understood at all.

Nevertheless, we must try to form a clear and correct idea of ovarian activity; for a woman's main physical manifestations, and, to some extent also, her mental and emotional life, are not only *affected but determined* by these organs.

"Propter solum ovarium, mulier est, quod est"; that is: Only by and through her ovaries, is a woman that which she is.

And we shall see how much truth there is in this old aphorism.

What is the exact double function of these organs? We shall, for the sake of clearness, refer in future to them as *"The ovary,"* although they are double in structure as in office.

It is twofold: to produce the ova, or female *gonad* (reproductive cell); and to protect and promote its development.

We already know a good deal about the first process (of secretion of ova and their expulsion), thanks largely to methods of microscopy.

Nevertheless, there are difficulties here still. When is an ovum expelled? Does this occur regularly, at constant intervals? And how is *ovulation* (expulsion of ovum) related to the discharge of blood every four weeks from the uterus?

Menstruation is obviously very important, because of its conspicuous regularity, and its association with the non-pregnant state.   Always and everywhere, in medical practice and everyday life, women and doctors have relied on menstruation as a signal, announcing by its appearance or cessation, the most important processes in the genital organs.   We shall take the menstrual period as our *time measure* in tracing the phases of the reproductive function as well as of many of the other organic activities.   We will divide the four-weekly, or lunar monthly cycle, into which the life of a normal adult woman in the non-pregnant state naturally and rhythmically falls, into phases beginning with the first day after the menses have ceased, and ending with the twenty-eighth after which they again appear.

On which day then, of the four weeks, does ovulation occur?   The answer to this question is important in practice as well as theory.   For, as the days immediately following ovulation are obviously the most favorable to impregnation, great stress has been laid on discovering them exactly, but without reaching any universal and reliable results. Of recent years, however, we have attained fuller knowledge here, especially following abdominal and pelvic *operations*. Such operations have been undertaken, not necessarily for the special purpose of ovarian research, but for removing injuries to other neighboring pelvic organs or growths, etc., in the generative organs, and have been spread over rather wide periods of time and not confined to special phases of the monthly cycle.   They have been supplemented by precise observations on women in whom the maturity of the Graafian follicle was in some way or another demonstrable.   As a result of this research, so much knowledge has been attained that I consider it justifiable, with certain reservations, to describe the process in the following terms:

About two days before menstruation begins, and an un-fertilized ovum has perished, a fresh Graafian follicle begins to mature in the ovary.   This ripening proceeds steadily, and according to my individual observations, confirmed by others, the process lasts till the eleventh, twelfth or thirteenth day between the monthly periods. Earlier or later ovulation is possible, and the earlier ovulation may especially occur under the stimulation of *coitus,* but on the whole it is probably true to assume *both as the normal and the average (or most frequent) day, for the bursting of the follicle and release of the ovum—the twelfth of the interval between menstrual periods.* The ovum is drawn into the oviduct, remains alive for about fifteen days, and, if not fertilized, perishes. Immediately a new follicle begins to develop, and another cycle begins.

The ovary is in constant fermenting tension, owing to the incessant ripening of little follicles. This tension is increased by the secretion of liquid in the tiny bladder of the Graafian follicle. The tension increases to a maximum just before this follicle bursts, and then abruptly falls. The amount of liquid is considerable, and its expulsion causes a decrease of tension in the whole organ, probably to something below the degree existing before the development of the Graafian follicle. This tension then slowly grows again, as another follicle matures, until this new cycle ceases, and another vital wave rolls in.

Thus tension follows and is followed by relaxation. In some women the organic tension of the ovaries is manifested in an intense desire for *coitus* (sexual intercourse) during the days just before the follicle bursts. I alluded to this in the second chapter.

In order to appreciate the complex mechanism by which Nature attains the reproduction and preservation of the species, we must bear in mind these *separate but interlocking factors:*—

(1) The possibility that sexual intercourse in the days preceding the bursting of the ripe follicle, can give an impetus to ovulation, both through congestion, increase of tension, and possibly by direct vibration.

(2) The fact that at this time the vaginal secretions have just the slight amount of acidity which favors the preservation of the spermatozoa.

(3) The further fact that immediately following ovulation, both the internal genital organs and the whole body are in the most suitable condition to offer the released ovum the best chances of survival.

Thus we realize in outline the processes by which the ovary fulfills its first function, in co-operation with the other genitals.

This rhythmic wave of activity, in the maturing of the follicle and tension of the ovary, is indicated by the lowest (black) line in Plate V.

What of the second ovarian function?

How does the ovary protect the expelled ova?

By producing, throughout the bodily organism, the best possible conditions for its preservation, conservation, and evolution.

Its agent is the glandular portion known as the *corpus luteum.* It is a gland whose secretions are internal, for it is *ductless,* and pours its *product directly into the blood,* which carries them to the appropriate and effective directions. Moreover, the corpus luteum is not a gland whose operation is *continuous.* Each corpus luteum is in active existence so long as the ovum, to which it belongs and for which it functions, also exists, and then for another eight days, during which it is demolished and dispersed. If the ovum is fertilized the corpus luteum persists, and becomes much larger than in cases where pregnancy does not supervene. But if the ovum dies unfertilized the corpus luteum diminishes at once, and its characteristic influence subsides. But meanwhile a fresh corpus luteum is developing, for the process of this development begins at once with the growth of a new Graafian follicle. And with the explosion of the follicle and its transformation into the corpus luteum, the action of its endocrine (or internal) secretion becomes evident. We cannot define with complete precision how far this activity progresses day by day, as can easily be understood in the case of internal and invisible organs like the ovaries. Nevertheless, the investigations of *L. Fraenkel, R. Schroder, R. Meyer,* and many others, have given enough data to enable us to say that the corpus luteum probably develops rapidly in the first four days, and more slowly during the next four, so that it is in full efflorescence after eight days. During the following six or more, generally seven days, the corpus luteum is in full activity, and even expands slightly, until, with the extinction of the ovum, it also becomes superfluous. Rapid dissolution sets in at once, and after another eight days it has so diminished as to be no longer functional. All this is represented by the *yellow line* in Plate V., which reproduces growth and decline of the corpus luteum, as well as the corresponding variations in its activity. If we compare the lower black line with the yellow, we see that these waves of development follow one another continuously; a new corpus luteum begins as soon as the follicle explodes, and a new follicular wave emerges as soon as the yellow subsides.

And the summits of these internal tides are the expulsion and extinction of the ovum. Regarding the interaction of the two processes, we only know that the corpus luteum checks and prevents the formation of a fresh follicle, because (in teleological terms) such a fresh follicle is unnecessary, so long as the preliminary changes for the reception and conservation of the ovum which has just been extruded are taking place. The extinction or expulsion of the ovum from the human body puts an end to the corpus luteum, which at once diminishes the amount of its specific secretion and grows smaller. Thus the check on the formation of a fresh follicle is removed, and such formation begins forthwith. Another ovum begins to grow.

But what exactly is the impetus given by the follicular explosion to the growth of the corpus luteum? And how does the extinction of the ovum initiate the decline of the corpus luteum?

Perhaps we may answer the first query by presupposing a special reaction of the serum in the blood to the liquid injected into the abdominal cavity when the follicle explodes.

An analogous answer to the second question has been propounded, but I fear this is too far an excursion into purely speculative territory, and prefer to place on record here, for the present, only a great note of interrogation.

An equally vigorous—if not more vigorous—exercise of activity by the corpus luteum causes the membranous lining of the womb to *proliferate and develop in order to afford a resting place and nourishment to the ovum*. Under the influence of the ovarian secretions, the membranes of the uterus, hitherto small in extent and comparatively passive, begin to increase and form the typical structures of pregnancy. This increase amounts to a positive proliferation of tissue. Its phases were first described and their significance revealed in 1907 by *Hitschmann & Adler* in Vienna: and fully elucidated through the exhaustive and exact microscopic observations of *F. Driessen* in Amsterdam. I have expressed numerically and geometrically, by means of curves, the results he recorded in the chief gynæcological journal of the Netherlands, in 1915[1] (*Nederlandsch Tydschrift voor Verloskunde en Gynacologie*). The curve of development for the uterine membranes is shown by the red line in Plate V. It emerges from a phase of latency or passivity, begins to rise on the second day after the emergence of the corpus luteum, and follows the steady increase of the corpus luteum's functional activity, a little behindhand, as the mucous membrane cells (epithelial cells) take time to grow. During this period of efflorescence the two curves correspond in a striking degree, and both reach their maximum on the same day. Immediately after the powerful stimulus exerted by the corpus luteum ceases, the curve of evolution in the uterine membranes also declines, and reverts, within a few days to its latent stage.

And shortly after this decline, after one, two, three or four days, but generally after *two* days, *menstruation begins*.

This is heralded locally by the dissolution and expulsion of the greater part of the freshly grown mucous membrane,

---

[1] Driessen designates the grades of evolution in the mucous membranes with the letters a, b, c, and d. I have used here the numerals 1 to 4, bearing in mind that these membranes never wholly disappear, but exist, though latent, in stage 1. I calculated the daily average from the many data brought forward by Driessen for each day. From these single daily averages, I then derived the *mean average,* by Bloxam's method. The figures for each day were added to those of the preceding and succeeding days and divided by 3. This method eliminates chance variations, so far as possible.

accompanied by the secretion of a thin blood-stained fluid, which may be full of blood, until the cessation of the menses. For the whole organism its significance is greater. It must be considered as one manifestation of a general bodily relaxation and reaction. We shall deal more fully with this aspect further on.

The red-dotted line also represents the results of Driessen's investigation of the mucous membranes, reduced to numerals and curves, by the present writer. It visualizes the secretion of glycogen in the uterine membranes. Glycogen, as the intermediate stage between sugar and carbohydrates, constitutes *an important reserve of nourishment;* its concentration and conservation in the cavity destined to receive and contain the impregnated ovum may therefore be regarded as part of the *preparation for pregnancy.* This curve, on the whole, runs parallel to the red line, rises two days after the formation of the corpus luteum, follows the functional activity of the corpus luteum, and drops abruptly as soon as the yellow body of the ovary begins to diminish and disperse.[1]

The sexual organs furthest from the central structures, namely the breasts, share unmistakably in the cyclic curve:[2] they too follow the three stages initiated by the corpus luteum; ascent, summit, and decline. Rosenburg has proved this by his microscopic-anatomical investigations of breasts at different stages in the menstrual cycle. He also demonstrated these changes in a curve, which is reproduced unchanged, as the *blue* line in Plate V. This blue line is inserted at the top of the diagram, as the breasts only subside and relax to a slight degree, but remain in evidence through-

---

[1] In delineating this curve, I have followed the same methods as with the preceding. But as the uterine mucous membranes never entirely disappear, but the glycogen does, the latter has an O instead of *Driessen's* letter a to show its non-existence. Thus *Driessen's* D corresponds here to the numeral 3, instead of as in the red line, to 4: and the whole curve designates a lower amount of substance. Finally, it may be pointed out that *Driessen's* investigations covered the interval from the first day to the twenty-eighth. But in order to make matters clear, I have prolonged the curve, in both directions. Thus the portions relating to days, 25 to 6, have been duplicated.

[2] A. Rosenburg, "Menstrual Changes of the Mammary Glands," *Zentralblatt für Gynäkologie,* 1923, No. 3.

out the cycle. Like the changes in the uterine membranes, initiated by the corpus luteum, the glandular enlargements and tensions within the breasts, described by Rosenburg, are to be regarded as preliminary to the transformations typical of pregnancy. Thus Nature, determining woman's organism expects fertilization of every ovum as it leaves the ovary. On each occasion she prepares for the changes which would follow such fertilization. And on each occasion, when fertilization does not occur, and the purposes of Nature are frustrated, the preparations are demolished and dispersed.

It is universally known that the breasts swell just before the menstrual flow begins; they become tense and hard, and even sometimes quite painful. But this phenomenon is *not* identical with the gradual changes in the breasts between periods, as described by Rosenburg. First of all, the two processes do not coincide, in *time*. And secondly, the perceptible enlargement just before the menses is much too rapid to be part of the twenty-eight days' cycle.

It cannot be said with certainty whether the cyclical changes described by Rosenburg can be *consciously felt:* perhaps by some women and not by others. But the normal brief enlargement before the menses, which is distinctly perceptible, is probably due to increased blood supply and dilation of the smaller blood-vessels. This may occur, not only in the course of endocrine (chemical) processes, but as reflex action, through the nerves.

A good example of such causation and an illuminating instance of the probable answer to the problems we are here discussing is found in the rapidly subsiding enlargement of the breasts which many women experience just midway between two monthly courses, *i.e.,* immediately before the rupture of a Graafian follicle.

In this case we may certainly rule out any actual increase of glandular tissue. Nevertheless, the breasts swell. They swell because of congestion of blood, due to the tension in the ovaries, which at that precise moment is acute (see the lower black curve in Plate V.). This congestion is often pronounced in the uterus as well. P. Strassmann gave an object-lesson on the effect of ovarian tension by injecting gelatine into the ovary. This could only act mechanically, by increased pressure, but it produced a similar congestion.

We have seen that the ovarian function has an extensive powerful influence in the genital sphere. Its influence on the entire feminine organism is equally important. We shall consider this in detail.

In 1875 it was observed and recorded by *Mary Putnam Jacobi,* followed by the Essay of Goodman,[1] and confirmed and extended since then by a large number of investigators, that the most important vital functions of the sexually adult woman show regular variations of intensity within a definite period.

An intense and active phase preceding the monthly flow is followed by a weaker phase of relaxation, corresponding to the menses. Then there is a gradual increase again, a culmination, and descent, and if impregnation is not achieved, the same process repeats itself throughout sexual maturity, generally with remarkable regularity and punctuality at intervals of four weeks.

This monthly cycle of increase, summit and decrease has been proved to affect bodily temperature, heart action, blood pressure, muscular power, the excretion of urine, the process of assimilation, and, as we have seen of late years, the significant organs of sex. And signs still appear and multiply that in many other vital manifestations of woman the same rule of periodic tension and relaxation may be demonstrated. It is, indeed, like the ebb and flow of the sea under the waxing and waning of the moon.

In a monograph published in 1904,[2] "On the Connection between Ovarian Activity, Cyclical Periodicity, and the Menstrual Flow," I pointed out that the periodicity referred to can be most easily verified in the changes of bodily temperature, which follow an obvious curve, parallel to that of other vital functions, and may be taken as representative of the rest. Further, I demonstrated that this is best shown by the early morning temperature, which if taken the first thing on awakening, and at the same time daily, is least

---

[1] *American Journal of Obstetrics,* 1878.
[2] By F. Bohn's successors in Haarlem.

likely to be influenced by such extraneous factors as muscular movement, digestive processes, and so on.   The results
should then be checked by *Bloxam's Method* (see above),
i.e., the mean temperature for each day should be added to
that of the previous and succeeding days and the total
divided by three; this will further eliminate the influences
of temporary conditions and events on the direction of the
curve.   I published such example curves in the monograph
referred to, and since then have received numerous other
data on the early morning temperature of women and
girls.

Any medical man can confirm these observations by per-
suading an accurate, conscientious, healthy and sexually
mature woman, who leads a regular life, to take her bodily
temperature with a reliable thermometer every morning
after waking, and note down the result.   But the adjectives
I have used here are no empty phrases.   The qualities they
denote are, on the contrary, absolutely indispensable in order
to reach dependable results.   I emphasized this in 1904, but
would again lay stress on these requisites, as since then investigators have neglected them and been unable in consequence to verify the cyclic curve.

I would even give additional emphasis to my previous
remarks and add that the woman who makes the test should
be a person of some education and comfort in the home; for
I seldom succeeded in getting particulars which could be of
use from women of the poorer classes in spite of very precise
instructions.   *These instructions must, of course, never indicate the results expected!* Moreover, the temperatures of patients in women's wards of hospitals are unreliable, both for
the reason mentioned above, and because the early morning
hour in a hospital ward is the most bustling and unrestful
of the whole twenty-four!   And such patients are indeed far
from normally healthy!

The views I expressed twenty years ago on the cyclic
curve of the feminine functions, menstruation and ovarian
activity, as revealed in the variations of bodily temperature,
need a certain amount of revision at the present date.   For
since then our knowledge has been enriched on two fundamental matters: concerning the significance of the corpus

luteum and its endocrine secretions—mainly thanks to the researches of *L. Fraenkel* and von Born; and concerning the recurrent proliferation of the uterine mucous membrane, which culminates in the menstrual discharge, and has been studied by *Hitschmann, Adler,* and more recently by *Driessen.* We have already discussed the interaction of these two functions, as shown in the curves of the red and yellow lines in Diagram V.

Let us accordingly compare these curves with the black line which shows the morning temperature (checked by Bloxam's method), as representing the *general* vital manifestations—in contradistinction to the genital or sexual.

I have chosen this particular curve because it refers to a woman in whom it was possible to ascertain the exact day of the follicular rupture.[1]

A glance at the curve suffices. The black line of the general vital functions is not only parallel with the red uterine line, but shows remarkable correspondence to the movement of the yellow line of ovarian activity (in the corpus luteum). It *follows* the yellow line in the most exact sense of the word, as would be even more conspicuously shown if I had used the original (crude) variations instead of checking them by Bloxam's method.[2]

It is extremely probable, in curves which show a marked

---

[1] This was possible because one of the ovaries was situated further down than usual, inside the Douglas cavity, and thus its expansion during the ripening of the ova was clearly and *uncomfortably* perceptible to its owner, as the enlarged ovary pressed on the narrow space in which it was suspended. The relaxation of pressure following the rupture of the Graafian follicle was felt as a pleasurable relief. Thus the woman herself could not only specify the *day,* but sometimes even the *hour,* at which ovulation took place! Gynæcological examinations always confirmed this self-diagnosis. The tense dilation of the ovary (which I was able to verify by frequent examinations during several years in its unusually accessible position) and its decrease in size and comparative flacidity after ovulation, did not permit of any doubts. Sometimes these objective phenomena were observed without their subjective accompaniments, which may have been due to such circumstances as a comparatively empty bowel, or the exact position of the follicle on the ovary.

I have had the opportunity to observe various analogous cases, and consider them very helpful in determining the exact time of ovulation, without operative interference and with considerable accuracy. In one such case, during a surgical operation, I was able to verify the statement that follicular rupture had just occurred, by the testimony of my own eyes.

[2] See Plate VI., the lowest line, in its deepest extremity, and the Bloxam line which accompanies it.

drop or *dip,* that this lowest portion denotes the day of ovulation, or follicular rupture.[1]   This was conspicuously the case in the woman whose temperature curve is shown in Plate V., and in similar cases.   Even if absolutely *complete data* are not to hand, it was possible to get temperatures for a few days before and after ovulation, and the rise of temperature on the succeeding days, together with its steady increase for some days, were unmistakable.

I am certain of the following theses: *that the sudden rise in bodily temperature does not only herald the functional activity of the corpus luteum (follicular rupture, ovulation) but is caused by this function.   Summit or maximum temperature and decline are similarly dominated by the efflorescence and the dispersion of the corpus luteum.*   My former theory of the menstrual phenomena does not correspond to the latest results, therefore I cannot maintain it unaltered, but just as little can I close my eyes to the interaction between the various functions demonstrated by these curves.

The corpus luteum by its specific secretions stimulates general vital processes, and causes increase or proliferation of the membranes lining the uterus.   Contrariwise, the diminution and cessation of its activity puts a brake on all the bodily processes, and disperses the extra uterine membranes which are expelled in the discharge, called menstruation.

It could be conclusively proved that the determinant here is *glandular secretion, and not nerve stimulus:* proved by the results of castration, organic transplantation, and so forth, recorded in gynæcological literature.   But to cite instances would claim too much time and space.

I will bring forward two further testimonies that the general vital processes, represented and expressed by the bodily temperature, are determined by the activity of the corpus luteum.

The first proof is this: if in the course of a surgical operation the corpus luteum is removed, menstruation results—as Fraenkel has already shown—and the temperature immediately falls abruptly, the recurrent vital wave breaks off

---

[1] But there is not *always* one lowest *point,* as may be seen in Plate VI., B.   There, this minimum point is not visible the first time, though distinctly so, the second.

before its time.   (There may be difficulties here, owing to
rise of temperature owing to operation itself.)

The second proof runs in the opposite direction: if the
corpus luteum persists instead of perishing as the ovum
becomes extinct, the temperature continues and does not
fall.   This is the case at the beginning of pregnancy.   We
have known, for some time, that the corpus luteum persists
and even increases during the early months of pregnancy.
We know, also, that menstruation stops.   We have learned
more and more of the progressive evolution of the uterine
membranes.   *Driessen* has made us acquainted with the
profuse glycogen secretion of the uterus in the early months.
We know the breasts steadily expand; and this is due to increased glandular tissue, as anatomical experiments teach us.

Thus, if conception or impregnation occurs, the premenstrual vital *crescendo* of ovaries, breasts and uterus
continues: in the terms of our curves, if pregnancy begins,
the yellow, the blue, and the two red lines, instead of sharply
dropping on the sixteenth day after ovulation, keep at their
maximum or even slowly ascend.

We have not hitherto known that the same was true of the
black line in our Plate V. (bodily temperature).   But I am
now in a position to reproduce the temperature curve of a
young and healthy married woman, who menstruated with
regularity at intervals of twenty-eight days, and who became
pregnant for the first time while she was taking her daily
temperature; at my special request, she continued to take
and record her temperature daily, till the labor pains
began.   Before pregnancy, and again after childbirth, the
rhythmic rise and fall of vital processes were marked.   After
impregnation the monthly discharge ceased, and with it the
sudden *vital ebb*.   Temperature, curiously enough, remained
till the end of the fourth month at the same medium degree;
it sank gradually during the fifth and sixth months, and
more rapidly in the seventh.   It should be noted that a
month in pregnancy means a menstrual month of four
weeks, or twenty-eight days.

At the beginning of the eighth month there is a new temperature level corresponding to the middle (mean?) temperature during menstruation, and persisting between twelve

and fourteen weeks, till labor pains began—with remarkable stability.   I regret that I cannot here reproduce my V curve chart of this case: it was almost 1½ meters long, but it is of such interest and significance that I have given it in abbreviated (or skeleton) form, together with a section of the original [1] in Plate VI.

This temperature curve of pregnancy corresponds to the state of the gravid corpus luteum (corpus luteum graviditatis), which remains in activity and expansion till the end of the fourth month, then slowly disappears.   The curve of pregnancy shows no four-weekly variations any more than the vital curve of the woman who has passed beyond sexual maturity, or of the girl who has not yet attained it, or of the man.   The cyclical ascent and descent of the vital functions in sexually mature women, together with menstruation, which is a part of this cyclic movement, are wholly dependent on the activity of the ovaries.

I have dealt with these processes in such detail because they are of the greatest importance in the daily life of women, and therefore in that of their husbands and those who are associated with them.

For these intricate processes do not occur without becoming perceptible to the consciousness.   Far from it: her physical comfort and mental efficiency, her powers of resistance to disease and difficulties in all ways, are strongly affected.   Days of activity and serenity, full of spirit and sweetness, are followed by others conspicuously different.

The equable and active days correspond to the ascent and summit of the vital wave[2]; the others to the decline and ebb,

[1] This lower curve can be viewed as a second illustration of the normal rhythm, and also offers the chance of comparison with the line, corrected according to Bloxam's method.   The skeleton curve was obtained by using Bloxam's Point for every fourth day.   The case has other points of interest.   The date of the sexual act which caused impregnation is known definitely, for it was the only occasion during that particular period of time; and the date of ovulation which preceded coitus by three days (on the twelfth day after the previous menstruation) is extremely probable. Birth pains began exactly 280 days after ovulation (ten lunar months) and not 280 days after the last recorded menstrual discharge as has hitherto been assumed in obstetrical practice.

[2] It is significant that most women feel especially vigorous and in good spirits at the beginning of pregnancy.   In the middle months, sooner or later, this mental and bodily health may be impaired, by disturbing influences of various kinds, incidental to pregnancy.

that is to say, in the two days before the menstrual discharge and throughout its duration. Also, often during the trough of the wave, especially when the slackening of vital processes is strongly marked.

Physically, these times are characterized by a lesser degree of bodily endurance, activity and dexterity; a tendency to exhaustion and *malaise*.[1] Any morbid symptoms, otherwise latent, become conspicuous, and there is greater liability to infections. Psychically, in many women, the symptoms are even more obvious. Many who are otherwise vigorous and buoyant, feel depressed and apathetic; others again are excessively irritable and excitable. Temper, hypersensitiveness, caprice, resentment, rapid changes of mood, liability to take offense unnecessarily appear, in women who are otherwise very free from these manifestations. These moods must be generally regarded as entirely normal, but they may also be accentuated to a dangerous degree or become positively morbid. Both the woman herself, her doctor, and her husband must take account of these bodily and psychic fluctuations, for they demand all possible self-control, tact, and mutual conjugal love.

Women, in the recurrent struggle with themselves which they must go through at such times, should never lose sight of the double need of taking care of themselves, physically as much as possible, and avoiding all needless exertion and strain, while at the same time resolutely mastering their tongues and tempers, for painful difficulties and dangers may arise if they "let themselves go."

And they may profitably bear in mind the underlying, unconscious physical cause of their psychic depression or irritability. When life appears unbearably dull or hard, the world hideous, and her fellow-beings hateful—or when she believes herself slighted, and is tempted to attack those she loves—let her call up the picture of the rhythmic ebb and flow, to which her life is attuned, and then she can smile a little and dismiss gloom and bitterness with the thought: "Presently I shall see it in quite a different light."

Yes—these are very difficult days for women. They are

---

[1] According to *Tobler* in 51 per cent. of women. Quoted by *Singer* in the *Monatsschrift für Geburtshülfe und Gynäkologie,* Vol. I, p. 70.

"upset about nothing." But they can prove their dignity, their intelligence, and their love, by self-control.

And men? For the husband, there are two occasions (apart from pregnancy and abnormalities) in which tact, sympathy and self-control are urgently needed, if he is to be an expert in love and life. Namely, in the first days of married life, and in the first days of the monthly vital *ebb*. The second is much the harder test—because it perpetually recurs!—but surely not any less important than the first.

Menstruation consists in a specific discharge of blood and mucus from the vagina, at regular intervals, in normal women during sexual maturity. It ceases at pregnancy. About 50 per cent. of all women do not menstruate while they are nursing at the breast (during lactation).

The average interval between periods, or menses, is four weeks from the appearance of the discharge to its reappearance. But some women have their periods regularly at twenty-six to twenty-seven days, others at twenty-nine to thirty-one days; and there is also a three-weekly type. Moreover, the interval may vary in the same woman at different times. The individual variations here are enormous. There are women who are always regular "to time"; others are never quite certain when to expect the period. Congenital, constitutional and hereditary tendencies here are further complicated by the influence of climate and way of life. And although, as explained above, menstruation is fundamentally determined by ovarian activity, the discharge can occur spontaneously, not only because of morbid changes in the organism, but also as a result of all manner of other factors, which either check and arrest it, or precipitate it: or it may be accentuated to a dangerous hæmorrhage. The most powerful examples here are (1) sudden change of climate, and (2) psychic impressions and sensations, which have special effects in disturbances of menstruation. Thus sudden shock of terror or grief—or even sudden great joy—can precipitate menstruation before it is due, or, more usually, prevent it; such psychic crises can even suddenly interrupt and suppress the menstrual discharge when it is proceeding. We do not by any means understand the precise mechanism operative in such cases; it is probably highly intricate. But even a comparatively slight nervous stimulation which causes the countless blood-vessels of the genital organs to contract or to congest can have similar results. Similar psychic causes on other vascular[1] areas produce, *e.g.*, blushes, or the sudden extreme pallor which follows contraction in terror or fear. Menstruation may also be held up through prolonged psychic states; this is shown, and not infrequently, when it is suppressed because pregnancy is either strongly desired or feared. Finally we may mention the premature appearance of the discharge on the wedding day, a phenomenon so often experienced that wise mothers, in order to avert such a particularly unwelcome accident, are careful to fix their daughter's nuptials on a day not too long after a menstruation has ceased.

The normal menstrual discharge lasts from three to five days. Here, too, there is a wide range of difference, both among women in general, and at different times in the same individual. To some extent, the duration of menstruation is affected by the woman herself, for active exertion, while it is in progress, makes the amount lost larger and the time longer. Nevertheless, many women, including medical women, have maintained that they lose less blood if they continue strenuous professional work, and even take part in sports and games, than if they lie still. On the whole, it may be said that menstruation of one to two days' duration is abnormally short, and menstruation of seven days or more morbidly long and heavy, and if such protracted menses occur more than once, a doctor should be consulted forthwith.

The discharge generally begins with an increase of mucus secretion, which becomes liquid and tinged, first faintly and then more deeply, with blood. The loss of blood is generally greatest on the first and second days, then slowly decreases, and changes to a liquid slightly blood-tinged, which gradually dries up. Not infrequently, after about three days, the discharge ceases for a day or half a day, and then continues for the same length of time.

The amount of blood lost on each occasion is generally

[1] Vascular: full of veins and blood-vessels.

much overestimated. Formerly this error was shared by doctors, who assumed a total for each period of 90 to 250 grammes, and even of 600 grammes! After the careful research of Hoppe-Seiler and others, we now know that it normally does not exceed 50 grammes monthly, and often not 30 grammes; and the daily loss is from 12 to 20 grammes. Most women, if they have not very scanty menses, are always inclined to exaggerate the amount lost, which is probably due to the fact that a very small quantity of blood can deepen the color of water in which the genitals are washed, and also of urine, considerably; and also soaks extensively into underlinen and towels, thus causing mistaken impressions about "half a chamber full of blood," and similar errors. A reliable sign of "excessive" monthly losses is the presence of clots of blood, which occasionally attain a fair size.

It is a peculiarity of the menstrual discharge that the sanguineous elements are normally kept liquid by the mucus secretions, especially from the uterus.[1] But if the bleeding is too profuse these mucus elements do not suffice to keep it liquid, and the blood solidifies, or "clots."

The menstrual discharge has a specific odor, which is intensified by the secretions of the vestibular glands; these glands secrete more profusely than usual during the period. It is, of course, obvious that the slightest neglect of cleanliness results in a most unpleasant smell, owing to the bacterial contents of the fluid, when it coagulates and dries. This also promotes local irritations and inflammations in the vulva, which may become obstinate sores, owing to the continual fresh flow of secretions and the friction of damp towelettes if these are not changed very often. Also, the outer genitalia, being swollen and congested during menstruation, are more easily injured and inflamed. The increased congestion is visibly evident at such times. The membrane of the vulva is a brighter red, and the outer labia slightly dilated and everted (or rolled back), as is the case in certain stages of sexual excitement. The vagina often has a bluish tinge. The womb feels slightly larger than usual, and laxer.

---

[1] According to *Birnbaum-Osten*, the blood circulating throughout the body is of a thinner, and more liquid consistency, during menstruation.

Both inner and outer genitals are specially sensitive and vulnerable.

There is a similar congestion in the uterine adnexæ and in the ligaments and surrounding connective tissues. This gives rise to a sensation of heaviness and swelling in the lower abdomen, pressure on bowels and bladder, and a "drawing" pain in the upper thighs. All these symptoms are more or less normal and to be expected.

The same is true of the slight pain which accompanies the uterine contractions. They are generally associated at the beginning of the monthly period, and diminish when the flow is profuse and the small lumps of mucus and clots of blood are carried out of the interior uterine orifice. Women who have experienced labor pains, described menstrual pains as identical in kind (though infinitely less), with the acute pelvic and abdominal pains peculiar to childbirth. The intensity of the menstrual pains varies greatly in different individuals, and also frequently at different times of her life, from zero to a degree which must be regarded as morbid.

The sum of all these manifestations, however, physiologically "normal," is sufficiently disabling and unpleasant to make us understand why women describe their periods as "being unwell." Nevertheless, there are women who are not "unwell" at these times, but free from any unpleasant symptoms, so that they only know they are menstruating by the flow of blood.

"Being unwell" is not a localized sensation, but general throughout the organism, even though the general effects must be regarded as *irradiations and reactions* of the genital symptoms.

We have already mentioned the typical psychic disturbances, just before and during menstruation. The feeling of lassitude and vague discomfort is very common. Headaches or *migraines* generally appear, in those constitutionally subject to them, at these times. There is an increased flow of saliva; the liver is dilated and congested (gallcolics); the digestion and appetite are upset; there is either ravenous hunger or a distaste for food; nausea and inclination to vomit, bad breath, increase of intestinal gas, frequent and profuse motions of the bowels, even diarrhœa, occur quite often, but at the end of each period there is a tendency to become constipated.   There are disturbances and irregularities in the circulation; the pulse is often uneven; there are palpitations, a tendency to varicose veins, cold feet, swollen wrists and ankles, rheumatic pains, congestion of the nasal membranes.   The thyroid gland often swells visibly, so do the vocal cords.   The vocal apparatus is impaired by the dilation and distension of the vascular and glandular posterior surface of the larynx, and in women who use their voices much, *e.g.,* school teachers, the voice becomes easily tired and changes its quality perceptibly.   This is most evident in *singing,* and causes a tendency to go flat, loss of richness and resonance of tone, and a lesser vocal range in the higher chest notes.   There are slight inflammatory symptoms in the eyes, and functional derangements; "spots," an appreciable narrowing of the field of vision, and less acute differentiation of colors.   There are similar effects on the sense of hearing.[1]   The general bodily tissues, if not swollen and congested, are relaxed.   And the picture is often completed and characterized by a striking facial pallor, a tendency to blush easily, and blue rings under the eyes.   I have enumerated these symptoms in detail in order to show that during menstruation, woman is as it were "standing with one foot in sickness": she is partly an invalid.   Fortunately, no *one* woman has to endure *all* the sufferings and disabilities described above.   In one, this manifestation appears, in another, that one.   And, I repeat, that fortunately, there are quite a number of women who do not suffer any of these things.

It has been demonstrated in detail that the *general* disturbances of menstruation—in contrast to the local, which affect the pelvic organs—are not dependent on the monthly discharge from the uterus, but are, together with this discharge, the results of a common cause.   The question is only whether all the varieties of disturbances and disability—disequilibrations of the normal bodily balance, as it

---

[1] In general I have here followed the list enumerated by *H. Schröder* in Menge Opitz "Manual of Gynæcology" (Bergmann, of Munich, publisher).

were—are due to the abrupt and rapid decline of vital processes, which we have described and delineated as the *ebb* of the wave, and in the curve in Plate V. This is partly the case without doubt, and directly so. Other symptoms are produced indirectly. For many such manifestations are due to the relaxation of the smaller blood-vessels, which is part of the *cyclic ebb,* throughout the body, and to the rapid changes in circulation; in other words, to excessive congestion in certain organs and of *defective blood supply or local anæmia* in others.

Nevertheless, there are a sufficient number of menstrual characteristics which cannot naturally or logically be classed as disturbances of circulation and attributed to irregular blood-supply. On the contrary, they give the impression of *toxic* symptoms, and are therefore attributed by some authorities to a sort of (normal and physiological) temporary auto-intoxication (self-poisoning of the system), whose exact mechanism and extent are still very doubtful.

I am fully aware that we are here in an uncharted territory, full of traps and pitfalls, and therefore shall not try to discuss the subject in detail, but do not feel justified in ignoring it.

For we have here first of all the remarkable circumstance that serious modern investigators such as Aschner[1] view menstruation as a process by which the blood is cleansed and freed from poisonous substance; and secondly the ancient belief, which women have never given up, in the "monthly purifications." And there is now no doubt whatever that the menstrual discharge is composed of secretions from the uterine membranes, mixed with blood.

Will the exact methods of science confirm the ancient belief in the temporarily "poisonous" or noxious nature of menstruation and the menstruating woman?[2] It is curi-

---

[1] *B. Aschner,* "The Excretory (Blood Cleansing) Significance of the Uterus and Menses and the Practical Results." Proceedings of the German Gynæcological Society. Innsbruck, 1922.

[2] In the year 1610, Guarinonius wrote in verse, rules and precautions to be observed by women during menstruation. They are quoted in *Ploss'* great work, "Das Weib" (Woman in biology and anthropology). They were not to attend dances or wedding feasts; wives were to avoid sexual

ous that such a belief is found in so many diverse races and religions, from the earliest times to the present day. And we should hesitate to scoff, when we remember that women themselves have never quite lost the tradition that cakes mixed and baked by menstruating housewives would not bake properly, and that even stewed fruit—not to speak of jams, jellies and preserves—were never a success if pulled, stoned and "put on" at these times. We medical men are compelled to be sceptics in so many things, and have probably acquired an excessive tendency to believe that what we cannot explain does not exist. Accordingly we have dismissed these traditions as "old wives' tales."

But in the most recent years voices have been heard to declare—as a result of systematic tests—that "there is something in it after all." They state that the toxic substances excreted during menstruation leave the body, not only in the uterine discharges, but also, *e.g.,* through the sweat glands. The question is still far from being solved, and it is peculiarly difficult to sift the possible kernel of fact from the fantastic sheaf of tradition and superstition, especially as the margin of error is great, and vitiates the statistics which hitherto have been attained.[1] Only continuous experimental research, carefully varied through diverse material and tested for sources of error, can make these points clear. Nevertheless, I do not think it is any longer permissible for an unbiased doctor to reject the existence of menstrual toxins as without foundation.

---

intercourse at such times. They were not to scold or weep or "lay about them," "or the venom would pass into their limbs and make them crooked!" They were to avoid much kissing and petting of young children; not to prepare the meals with their own hands, nor go into the cellars or to the wine vats, nor stand under young fruit trees nor vines. They were not to look into any clear polished mirror, but "sit still at home and sew." Finally they were to avoid cold and—not be sparing of the linen garments and bandages necessary at such times.

[1] *B. Schick,* in his essay in the *Wiener Klinischen Wochenschrift* (Vienna Clinical Weekly, 1920, No. 19, entitled "On Menotoxin"), describes tests and results in this connection which are undoubtedly *positive.* But the results were called in question in the "Zentralblatt für Gynäkologie," 1921, p. 819, by *H. Saenger,* who tried controlling experiments, and referred Schick's results to errors in research.

Sexual maturity lasts longer in some women than in others. Its average duration is for thirty to thirty-five years. In 40 per cent. of women it ceases between forty-six and fifty years of age; in about 26 per cent. between forty-one and forty-five; and in 15 per cent. between fifty-one and fifty-five. In the remaining 19 per cent. of cases the menses cease later than fifty-five, or, more commonly, before forty. But such very late and very early cases cannot be regarded as strictly *normal,* though they are not in any way necessarily *morbid, i.e.,* diseased; though a premature menopause certainly indicates some functional inadequacy of the interior genitals.

As a rule sexual maturity ceases earlier in women who have not borne children than in those who have; and a *late* childbirth, *i.e.,* one which occurs after forty years of age, postpones the menopause appreciably. As a rule, the end of sexual maturity (menopause) occurs early in those women in whom it began late as girls. The converse is true, though only among women of the Northern races in the temperate zone: in these cases an early puberty generally denotes long sexual maturity and late menopause. Among the colored and Mediterranean races the women, almost without exception, have an early puberty and an early menopause and cessation of active sexual life.

Thus the influence of race and climate is very great here. Also heredity: in these matters the daughter often resembles the mother (as also, *e.g.,* in fertility, in endurance at parturition, inclination to hemorrhages at and after childbirth, and so forth).

Conditions and manner of life are also important. The women of the more comfortable classes retain their youth longer than their sisters of the people. Moreover, we have here to reckon with biological strains connected with long descent and careful inbreeding.

When the regular sequence of phenomena, governed by ovulation, begins to become less regular and frequent and to disappear, the woman enters the *change of life, turn of life, climacteric or critical age.* This period is of varying durations in varying individual constitutions; it may last from one to three years, or longer, and until with the final disappearance of the monthly flow, or *menopause,* the woman enters on the years of later middle age.

Here again stress is popularly laid on the non-appearance of the conspicuous monthly flow. But we must not forget that menstruation is not the *primary* process, but an accompaniment and secondary manifestation of cyclic changes in the ovaries. Thus when menstruation ceases, in middle life, it means that the ovaries cease their rhythmic function;[1] for without ovulation—no menstruation.

The manner in which menstruation stops differs widely and individually. In some cases the stoppage is heralded by a succession of long and profuse periods. Again, the amount lost may become less and less, till it stops for a while, and then reappears. In many women the menopause occurs abruptly, "at one blow." Others, after an interval of longer or shorter duration, may again experience losses of blood.[2] In short, the "change of life" is indeed a time of change and individual variation.

As we have seen how immensely the function of the ovaries influences women's chemical processes (metabolism) and psychic states, we shall readily understand that cessation of this function must affect all the activities of the organism. The cyclic ebb and flow of maturity ceases, and the vital processes remain at a continuous level, *of a lesser degree of vigor and acuteness than the average of former years.*

One of the signs of changes in metabolism is frequently increased development of fat all over the body. Characteristic symptoms of the days of vital ebb, and menstruation, tend to appear in chronic form. The disturbances of circulation are most trying. They include sudden flushes and "waves of heat," the face becomes suddenly and deeply

---

[1] But ovarian activity without menstruation *is* quite possible, though to a diminished extent, for any length of time.

[2] But in these cases it must be emphasized that great caution is necessary. What is considered to be a return of menstruation may be a loss of blood due to serious uterine illness. In such cases immediate gynæcological examination is advisable.

flushed; perspiration is excessive and sudden, there are palpitations, dizziness, vertigo, roaring in the ears and black-
ness before the eyes; all the signs of faintness.

The psychic symptoms during the change of life may be
not only painful but much more protracted and obstinate—
corresponding to their cause—than similar disturbances just
before and during the menstrual periods. Caprice, excitability, increased impulsiveness combined with diminished
power of reason and reflection, depression with a tendency
to melancholia, are all frequent manifestations, though generally remaining within the limits of what is excusable and
endurable. But in women who before this stage in their
development have had no mental poise or stability of character, in neurotics, in hysterical cases, and those whose
heredity shows morbid tendencies—the "change" causes a
degree of psychic suffering and storm which is positively
dangerous to themselves and others.

These climacteric derangements are specially conspicuous
when the menses and the function of ovulation both cease
abruptly and at one stroke. But when the climacteric proceeds *gradually*, with slowly decreasing menses, at longer
intervals—which denotes that the ovarian function stops
by slow degrees—the general bodily and particularly mental
disturbances are much less pronounced and more easily
endured and conquered. Among these gradual climacteric
cases we find those individual women who show complete
mental and emotional balance and sweet serenity of temper
during the critical age.

When the "change" has been successfully weathered, and
the *menopause* established, even in women who have had
much to suffer during the "change," an era of mental and
psychic equanimity *should* and often *does* begin. Together
with the steady level of bodily health, characteristic of
women after middle life, this mental balance forms a well-
merited compensation of Nature for the extremely high
biological demands on women during sexual maturity. This
steadfastness and clearsighted activity enable the middle-
aged woman, especially the wife and mother, to be the center
of peace and comfort in the home, and amid all the turmoil

and vanity of worldly things. She is wise in experience and intuition; she is full of loving-kindness and knows life's difficulties and dangers and joys. She knows what her children may justly expect, and what they must be forewarned against. If she keeps her memory and sympathy young she may understand and help youth, through the knowledge the years have brought her. And she has now learned to know and understand her husband perfectly: to encourage him in his life's struggles, to forgive his faults, to meet his wishes. Thus she can richly repay the consideration a wise and just man will have shown her, and the support he has given her during the many mutually difficult days of the change of life.

And it should not be at all difficult for a woman to meet her husband's moderate sexual wishes, during the climacteric and after the menopause. On the contrary, her wishes here should blend with his—half-way. For women in their fifties, who love their husbands and have become habituated to regular sexual intercourse, have certainly—in spite of the extinction of their ovarian function[1]—no less appreciation of the joys of sex than their husbands at the same age. And the wifely appreciation is often increased by the release from the fears and trials of pregnancy.[2]

---

[1] Even though (as has been demonstrated in Part I.) the sexual impulse in both its main components is governed by the gonads or genital glands, it can persist undiminished when their functional activity ceases. This is so much more the case in women as the aptitude for intercourse is not in them dependent, as in man, on the ejaculation of the secretions of these glands. Sexual intercourse and the desire for it continue, if the mind has been attuned to its stimulation and the pleasures it brings have so valuable a part in the life that they are not willingly foregone.

[2] This fear is often extreme, during the change of life, in women who have previously gladly borne children. It is often caused by the mother's shyness and sensitiveness at the thought that her children in their teens or older, would notice that their parents still had sexual relations. This peculiar shyness corresponds to the painful embarrassment of adolescent boys and girls at the thought of such sexual relations between their parents. It is noticeable psychologically, that young people, even when they have themselves begun sexual activity, and have some realization of its importance, simply cannot tolerate the idea that their parents are still capable of such feelings. Only when they have attained wider experience and development do they accept this fact.

The fear of pregnancy during the climacteric can cause serious results, owing to the psychic instability at such times, and the irregularity of the menses. Every gynæcologist and psychologist has had experience of such cases. The converse complications ensue with women who marry late, have a fervent longing for maternity which has not been

In the pre-climacteric years—immediately before the "change"—there are usually increased desire for and enjoyment of sexual intercourse. Often this emotional and physical ardor continues throughout the change, and in rarer cases for a much longer time. But as a rule the emotional efflorescence dies down again to the accustomed level. If the husband is attentive and appreciative to his wife's needs her sexual emotions can be preserved till advanced age, and the organs remain apt for intercourse, although the years take their toll, *e.g.,* in the obliteration of the vaginal pads and folds, and relaxation of the outer labia. But if there is no sexual stimulation or gratification, the emotions decrease during the menopause and become completely extinct. And the genitals themselves shrivel or atrophy.

Let us recapitulate the contents of this chapter on the related phenomena of sexual maturity and periodicity.

The organism and functions of the sexually adult or mature woman are characterized by a recurrent increase and decrease, or ebb and flow.

This cyclic ebb and flow affects the body generally, as well as locally (in the genitals). It is governed by the activities and changes of the yellow bodies in the ovaries.

This yellow body (corpus luteum) expands, culminates and disperses as the ovum is born, or expelled from the Graafian follicle, starts, on its journey, and becomes extinct.

Thus we might alter the aphorism cited at the beginning of this chapter, "Propter solum ovarium mulier est, quod est" to "Propter solum ovulum mulier est quod est": only because of the egg cell is a woman what she is. I think, as this condenses the facts most clearly, it has many advantages for the lay student, and offers a practicable working hypothesis, both for the woman herself and the man who shares her life.

But medical men must not forget that the processes and reactions are much more complex than I have indicated.

---

fulfilled, and who, at the first cessation of menstruation are torn between hope and fear of the "Too late!" If these psychic strains and lesions are repeated more than once, there are often dangerous consequences.

The most fundamental and important have been enumerated, *e.g.,* I have mentioned that the ovaries not only secrete and produce the corpus luteum with the ova, but also an *internal secretion* of similar type, which acts *continuously* not periodically, like the corpus luteum.

I have not alluded here to the facts mentioned at length in my earlier monograph and supported by examples. Namely that by continuous feeding with ovarian extracts, as a substitute for the functional atrophy of the ovaries, the cyclic wave may be prolonged, not only at its height but also at its ebb, and if the womb is not shriveled and atrophied, menstruation may reappear.   Certainly the cyclic processes induced artificially by concentrated ovarian extract are not so intense and definite as those resulting from the corpus luteum, but they exist; and the fact that they can and do exist proves that the ebb (which preludes menstruation), though primarily due to the dispersal of the corpus luteum, must also be regarded as an essential characteristic of the adult female organism.   And this characteristic I then described as a periodically recurrent organic *relaxation* and *exhaustion.*

But this is by no means all.   Hitherto we have been treating the ovary as autonomous, *i.e.,* as an independent organ.   And so it is, to a great extent; but not wholly.   No organ of the body can be wholly autonomous.   And so the activity of the ovaries is influenced by that of other organs, both the thyroid gland (see article in the *Zentralblatt für Gynäkologie,* 1924, No. 21) and the hypophysis[1] and the pineal gland.[2]   And we must also reckon with the ovarian tension (already alluded to) and the interesting relevant experiments by *Strassmann.*

And finally: why does the cycle last twenty-eight days? Why does the ovary cease to function at a certain age? And further many other questions: and science will not succeed in giving one definitive answer to them all.

[1] The hypophysis is a gland situated at the base of the brain; it has an internal secretion, whose products have great effects, especially on the internal female genitals.

[2] The student may realize the intricate complexity of these factors by studying the Essay by *J. Hofbauer: Zentralblatt,* 1924, No. 3, "The Hypophysial Factor in Menstrual Processes and Its Relations to the Corpus Luteum."

We do not know all. We shall not know (as Dubois Rey-mond says) *all*.

But all the more reason to profit by what *we do know well*. And married couples may so profit by what I have tried to elucidate here.

And therefore they should try to understand it. At least the active partner and initiator, the husband, should try.

CHAPTER VII

ANATOMY AND PHYSIOLOGY OF
THE MALE SEXUAL ORGANS

As in the case of the woman's, I shall describe the man's genital organs anatomically and physiologically, enumerating functions together with structures.

The male genitals can be much more briefly dealt with than his partner's, for the sexual functions do not dominate and set the time to his whole life as they do to hers.

As Byron said :—

> Man's love is of man's life a thing apart,
> 'Tis woman's whole existence.

Nature has interwoven woman's life and organism throughout with sex and with potential motherhood. But man is primarily responsible for the preservation and support of the woman and children for whom he is responsible. Racially and reproductively, he has only to supply the fertilizing element to the woman. Sex is the essential element in woman; in man it is accessory.

This contrast is shown in the relative position and range of the sexual apparatus. In woman they are in the innermost recesses of the body; in man they are only an exterior limb. And this *membrum virile* is far from aesthetically attractive; in fact so little lovely that painters and sculptors habitually represent it as smaller and more insignificant than it is in reality.

We cannot subdivide the male genitals into internal and external, for the small but certainly important structures inside the abdominal cavity can best be associated with the external glands, to which they are accessory. Therefore, we shall here have no chapter corresponding to Chapter V., nor anything analogous to Chapter VI., as the male has no processes similar to menstruation, nor any cyclic crescendo and diminuendo of essential vital activities.

But we shall have to describe his specific sperm cells in greater detail than the ovum.

Plate VII. represents the male genitals and associated (urinary) organs in vertical section and drawn to scale. The bilateral organs are colored orange and not represented in section.[1] The other structures and tissues are bisected vertically, and colored differently, or simply black and white.

The duplex or bilateral organs are the testes, or testicles (No. 18), with the epididymis, in which we must distinguish the main body (No. 17) and appendage (No. 22), the vas deferens, or seminal duct (No. 15), of whose various sections we shall treat in detail, the vesiculæ seminalis (No. 8), Cowper's glands (No. 12) with their ducts. Single organs are the penis (membrum virile, or male organ), the scrotum (containing the testicles) (No. 23), and the prostate gland (No. 9). The minor accessory structures which have no *practical* significance in *this treatise* are ignored, as was the case with similar portions of the feminine genitals.

The non-sexual organs here depicted are the symphysis pubis and the bladder.

The bladder (No. 3) has a neck (No. 7), where it is supplied with a powerful sphincter muscle, which is omitted in the diagram. The neck passes into the urethra (No. 11) or urinary passage. The cavity of the bladder (No. 4) is colored blue; so is the urethra. We will assume here, and not repeat needlessly, that the male urethra is much longer than the female, and serves the double purpose of a duct for the urine and the semen.

The *penis,* whose anterior or foremost portion is between 9 and 10 cm. long, and projects or, rather, hangs loosely, possesses an invisible posterior or hind portion, the root, which runs beneath the perineal skin and the junction of the scrotum, hidden to the sight but easily felt by the fingers. The portion of the shaft of the penis, which is turned upwards and outwards, lies below the symphysis in the pubic arch, and attached by broad and firm muscles to the bony

---

[1] The plate represents the organs of the right side which should be imagined as projecting from the surface.

framework of the pelvis, which gives the organ secure anchorage.   The main portion of the penis is composed of hollow or *cavernous* tissue (corpus cavernosus), that is, of a spongy network of blood-vessels, which become stretched and tense when congested.   There are two such *corpora cavernosa* here.   All that is colored green in Plate VII. is comprised in this area.

We have already, when studying the feminine apparatus, learned to know a similar type of structure on a much smaller scale in the clitoris.

The male member contains one urethral and two penile *corpora cavernosa.*   They run parallel, but are closely connected, and may be regarded as one organ, which forms the greater part of the member when loosely suspended, *i.e.,* its dorsal part (namely, that portion in the passive non-erected penis which faces forwards, and *away* from the scrotum). The hind portion, which is tinted a lighter green, attaches the organ to the *symphysis pubis.*

The urethral *corpus* is in its longest (medial) section, a comparatively narrow column, surrounding the *urethra.*   In the loosely hanging (non-erected) penis it is the portion turned towards the scrotum (green, without diagonal lines). Behind it becomes much more massive, and forms the aforesaid *root* of the organ, which can be felt under the scrotum, and is known as the bulbus urethræ (bulb of the urethra).   Towards the extremity of the organ the corpus urethræ suddenly expands and forms the tip or gland of the penis (glans penis, green, No. 26), which extends beyond the penile corpus cavernosum and occupies the entire extremity.   The cavity here is called *corpus cavernosum glandis.*   The urethral, penile, and glandular cavities are all closely interconnected, and form a structural unity, which answers as one organ to stimulation.

Whether the stimulation proceeds from the central nervous system (brain), or is local and peripheral, the effect is the same.   The *erection of the member, that is, its enlargement, hardening and change of position* through the increased flow of blood into the veins of the corpora cavernosa, till they are congested to their fullest extent.

The corpora cavernosa are encased in powerful muscular fibers and tendons, which possess enough elasticity and pliancy to make a surprising expansion of the organ possible, but, on the other hand, to give the vascular tissue substance and support and prevent rupture of the distended blood-vessels.

The skin of the male organ is almost devoid of hair; it is thin, sensitive, elastic and dilatable. It sheathes the organs without an intermediate layer of adipose tissue (fat), but loosely, so that it can be slipped to and fro like a glove. At the extremity it forms a double fold, so that instead of being firmly joined to the *glans penis* it is attached 2 or 3 mm. behind the rim, at the upper, front angle of the shaft. This double fold of skin, depicted in the plate as No. 28, is the *prepuce,* or *foreskin.* In young children and immature boys it extends beyond the *glans* and covers it, like a miniature *trunk.*

In adults the *glans penis* is generally just visible as it protrudes in the aperture of the foreskin. This aperture is normally wide enough, and the foreskin sufficiently elastic, to be easily pushed back. Then the exact shape of the *glans,* hitherto indistinct, is revealed as a blunted or truncated cone, which is longer and thicker at the posterior than at the scrotal side of the penis. In consequence, the slightly prominent hind rim of the top, the *corona glandis,* is not circular, but an oval, whose plane is at an angle to the axis of the penis itself.

Thus the preputial sack or sack of the foreskin (colored red, and numbered 27 in diagram) is deeper and roomier on the dorsal side of the penis than on the scrotal side. On the scrotal side in the center is a tiny strip, which connects gland and prepuce and prevents too deep an exposure of the gland. This is called the *Frenulum preputii* (No. 24). Its analogue in the womanly organs is the *Frenulum clitoridis.* Indeed, all the other parts of the clitoris (tip, shaft, cavity, foreskin and sack) correspond to those of the penis. Thus the clitoris is to be regarded, both biologically and anatomically, both in function and structure, as a miniature penis, without the combination of the male organ with the urethra.

As we have mentioned the typical secretion or *smegma,* and the need for sedulous care in its removal, when treating of the clitoris, we do not need to repeat ourselves here. Although the production and accretion of this tallow-like substance behind the *corona glandis* is not as a rule so conspicuous as in the analogous female organ,[1] either in amount or odor, on the whole, the warning we gave to women holds good for their husbands too. Especially to avoid inflammations, I urgently repeat that there should be regular and thorough cleansing of the preputial sack, and the corona and frenulum.

It is generally believed that the Oriental ritual custom of circumcision (in Jews, Moslems, etc.) derives from this hygienic need. For removal of the foreskin, which is also often practiced in modern surgery, is an effective prophylactic against the accretion of *smegma* (smegma preputii), as well as possible infections through coitus, and greatly facilitates cleanliness.

The *glans penis* is covered by a continuation of the inner preputial lining, *i.e.,* a membrane which does not resemble the epidermis. At the edge of the *ostium urethræ* this merges into the mucous membrane. The skin of the glans has very sensitive neurons, of different types, bound together by numerous reticulations, so that a close network of the most delicate sensory apparatus is constructed, and is peculiarly adapted to receive even the slightest mechanical stimuli and transmit them to the brain, which feels them—if they are not so violent as to cause acute *pain*—as specific sexual pleasure (*voluptas* is the technical term).

The exact area of maximum sensibility for sexual pleasure is the lower surface of the *glans* (especially the band or *frenulum*), which even surpasses the upper (posterior) rim or *corona*—also a highly charged and susceptible nerve cluster. Here, too, we find a strong similarity to the clitoris, having learned that the *band* (frenulum) and lower surface of this female structure are its most sensitive areas.

The foreskin is also rich in neurons, which subserve the same purpose, as is also the whole skin of the penis, though

---

[1] Or anything like so great as in some male animals at the breeding season.

the sensation attained here is less acute than at the extremity.

Mechanical stimulation of these neurons causes a reflex congestion of the corpora cavernosa, and the organ becomes *erect*. This may also and equally be caused directly from the brain through psychic images and impressions. Indeed, the latter type of stimulus is probably the more frequent; direct mechanical excitation comes into play after the erection has begun.

Moreover, erections may be caused by reflex action from the other pelvic organs. I refer to the stiffening of the organ in the early morning which is so often noticed on awakening from sleep, and is due to reflexes during sleep from the pressure of the full bladder. During certain illnesses erections may be produced directly from the spinal centers, and be obstinate, prolonged and painful. (The so-called *priapisms*.)

Nevertheless, the most recent research has not confirmed the opinion favored by the laity, that the "center" governing erections is situated in the spine. Although the reflex must pass through the lower extremity of the spinal column, its center is situated in the sympathic nervous system of the pelvis.

The process of erection transforms the soft, small, drooping penis, which in its passive state could not possibly perform the sexual act, into a stiff, firm, yet elastic instrument, perfectly adapted for pouring out its seminal liquid into the furthest recesses of the female parts, for in full erection against the man's abdomen it lies at an angle and with a slight backward curve, which exactly *fit into the normal vaginal angle and curve forward.* Moreover, in normal cases, the length and circumference of the erect male member completely fill the vagina (which is distended lengthwise in coitus) if penetration is not quite up to the "hilt" or root. Nevertheless, there are considerable individual differences here, of which we shall treat, in detail, when describing the sexual act. The length of the visible shaft of the penis in erection, according to *Waldeyer,* is between 14 and 16 cm.; its circumference in the middle 12 cm.

When the stimuli causing the erection have attained their

summit, they relax and decline, and the erection subsides as the extra blood supply leaves the corpora cavernosa.

The *urethra* or *urinary passage or duct* is the long, curved *conduit* which passes from the bladder and cuts through the penis.   Its uppermost portion, *i.e.,* that directly in touch with the bladder, serves solely for the passage of urine.   But from the point where the seminal ducts (*vas deferens*) join it on either side (as indicated by No. 11. in Plate VII.) it also receives and conducts the spermatic secretions.

The urethra may easily be divided into three portions, according to the bodily areas through which it passes.   The first, or uppermost, is within the pelvis; when the man stands upright on his feet, the direction of this part of the urethra is almost vertical, and directed downwards, as depicted in the Plate.   It is mainly surrounded by the *prostate* gland; (No. 9, reddish brown) and separated from the bladder by a powerful sphincter muscle.

Below the symphysis, in the part left *white* in the Plate, between the prostate and the (green) corpora cavernosa, the urethra changes its direction, and passes through the muscular tissue of the *pelvic floor* and enters its *perineal portion.*   This second urethral region, which lies beneath the pelvic floor, ends in the roots of the penis, and has the same horizontal direction and slight upward slope.   At its second, downward curve, where the loosely hanging exterior portion of the penis begins, there begins also its third (or penile) region.   The second and third portions are shown in the diagram, within the corpora cavernosa.   In medical practice they are together termed the *anterior* (*or front*) *urethra,* while the short, vertical portion within the pelvis is called the posterior (or hind) urethra.

The length of the anterior urethra, when the penis is in its normal slack and pendent state, is about 15 cm.   When the penis rises in erection, it lifts the urethra, whose slight downwards curve can be obviated at other times by lifting it with the hand, as in urination.   The urethra stretches itself elastically when the penis becomes erect, and its direction becomes vertical, though still with a slight curve. The urethra expands when passing through the glans, or penile tip, and at once contracts at its external orifice into a tiny vertical slit, its narrowest portion throughout the whole of its length.

In the anterior urethra are a good many very small glands, which, together with *Cowper's glands*—bilateral structures as large as small peas (No. 12 in the Plate)—secrete a small amount of transparent, thin, alkaline and very slippery fluid. This substance has the same practical significance as the secretion from the glands of Skene and Bartholin, in the woman. They too function under influence of sexual excitement, and are instrumental in making the *glans* slippery and facilitating its insertion into the vagina. The secretions of Cowper's glands help to make the urethra more suited to receive and transmit the semen, for they counteract the effects of the distinctly *acid* urine, by their own *alkalinity*. I consider this latter function less important than *lubrication*, however, for there can only be very slight traces of urine in the urethra during the passage of a much greater amount of *semen,* and this passage is extraordinarily rapid. The mucus secretion of Cowper's and the urethral accessory glands, may appear *after* the local excitation and erection of the male organ, and thus form, as it were, a second stage in the process of preparation for union. Or it may appear while the member is still slack, or at least not in full tension. The latter is especially the case if sexual excitement is produced through solely psychic impressions such as thoughts, books, pictures, without direct female agency, or if the *psychic* influence and contact with a woman who is desired, much precede physical contact: as they should do in what we have termed the prelude to sexual communion. (See Chapter VIII.)

Inexperienced youths, who are anxious about their mental and physical health and their virile potency, still often mistake this normal *lubrication* for *loss of semen. It is nothing of the kind.* It is a distinct process, which *prepares* the bodily organs for coïtus and at the same time expresses the soul's desires.

The old Catholic moral theologians (*e.g.,* Sanchez and St. Alphonso de Liguori) knew it well, correctly appreciated its mental reactions and importance, and gave it the term "distillation" (or *destillatio*) as distinct from *pollutions* or loss of semen, apart from coitus.

We may finally note that this distillation sometimes does not occur at all; more especially when the erection is due mainly to external (mechanical) stimuli, and the psychic emotions are only slight or even reluctant. If, in such situations, the woman has been inadequately prepared on the psychic side, and her vestibulary glands have not functioned, the sexual act may be very difficult and painful, *for both partners.*

The *testes* or *testicles* (singular, *testis*) are two oval bodies, enclosed in a sack or bag, the *scrotum.* The left testicle is generally slightly the lower of the two, and the whole structure has thus an asymmetrical look, which is not æsthetically pleasing. In normal proportions, the center of the scrotum should reach lower down than the tip of the slack penis. The skin of the scrotum is darkish, and thickly covered with hair; there is no adipose (fatty) layer. Under the skin are thick layers of smooth (involuntary) muscular tissue which contract in response to various stimuli (*e.g.,* extreme cold) and turn the loose scrotal pouch into a firm one, with a somewhat wrinkled surface. As this aspect is considered the more attractive (or the less unattractive), plastic artists, especially in classic antiquity, have always chosen to perpetuate it in their marble statues. In so doing, they have made many living men liable to comparisons much less than favorable to flesh and blood!

The scrotum is divided by a partition, in which the sinews are conjoined, and each division contains one testicle and one epididymis. The partition is continued externally in a sort of *seam* or fold, which runs backward into the perineum, and forward on to the lower surface of the penis.

Testicles and penis are close together, and functionally interdependent. In the testicles the spermatozoa, or male life seeds, are formed; through the penis they are transferred from the body. But in order to pass into the penis, the spermatozoa have to go a long way round, through the pel-

'vis. This is due to biological evolution, for the testicles were originally contained in the pelvic cavity, and only descended into the scrotum at a comparatively recent stage. In many species of animals this process is repeated in the individual, for the testicles normally repose within the abdomen, and only descend into the scrotum and become visible during the breeding season (time of sexual activity, or *rut*). There are certain morbid conditions and peculiarities of structure among men which recall this ancient stage of evolution (rupture, hernia, cryptorchism).

The path taken by the testicle in its primeval descent from abdomen to scrotum is traced for us still in the convolutions of the *spermatic cord*. This consists of the ducts (vasa deferentia), with a network of nerves and blood-vessels, and runs through the hollow of the groin, above the symphysis, down to the back of the testicle.

Testicle, epididymis and cord are—on either side—surrounded with muscles and membranes corresponding to the layers of the abdominal wall. Parallel are clusters of sinews which can lift the testicles (the *cremaster* muscle). This lifting occurs together with a contraction of the scrotum. It can be exemplified, by a typical reflex action, if the inner surface of one of the thighs is rubbed with vigorous, short strokes, for the friction visibly moves and raises the testicle on the same side.

The mature testicle is from 4 to 4½ cm. long; at the utmost it does not exceed 5 cm. It is from 2 to 2 4/5 cm. broad and thick. The weight runs from 15 to 26 grammes. The testicle on the left side is larger than on the right. The nerves and blood-vessels enter the organs from behind. Besides this each testicle is joined and clasped from the back by the *epididymis*—an oval pad or cushion. The head of the epididymis (No. 17) is fastened to the upper pole or extremity of the testicle (18), and the two structures are closely interconnected, as the testicular tubules extend into the epididymis, whose base or lower extremity at the lower pole of the testicle becomes the *vas deferens,* or seminal duct, and curves sharply backwards.

The testicle is divided internally by a regular pattern of

partitions into pyramidal *cups* or *cells*. In each of these is a cluster of very minute, curved, and intertwined *tubules,* in which are formed or secreted the spermatozoa, or sperm cells, containing the male reproductive element. These tubules are so narrow that a coarse hair could only just pass through them. Towards the apex where the cells converge, the tiny tubules straighten themselves, and join, and finally emerge from each cell as *one* tube, which passes into a net-work of similar tubes, still contained in the testicle, but continuous with that of the head of the epididymis. This set of tubes is again convoluted and intertwined. They unite to form a single duct, which curls and twists as it forms the main portion of the epididymis, continues into the extremity, and then becomes the spermatic duct, seminal duct, or *vas deferens*. This is also convoluted, but much less intricately. These structures are represented drawn to scale in Plate VIII. (A).

The formation or production of semen, seed or sperm-cells, goes on, in man, from puberty to advanced old age. Microscopic research has enabled us to find, in the convoluted testicular tubules, sperm cells in the most various stages of development—a process which appears to take a comparatively long time. In accordance with the ground plan of this book, we shall not discuss the extremely intricate manner in which sperm cells are produced, but it is most essential to describe the complete and functional male reproductive cell in detail in spite of its microscopic size.

These cells are termed seminal cells, semen (Latin for *seed*), sperms or spermatozoa (a Greek word, whose singular is spermatozoön) ; they are the living and active ingredient in the male sexual discharge. They are among the *smaller* types of sperm, *i.e.,* they are smaller than the spermatozoa of many species of animals which are themselves smaller than man! In fact, human spermatozoa are between 50 microns and 60 microns in length.[1] They consist of head, neck and tail (Plate VIII. B). The head is flat and somewhat pear-shaped; the outer circumference is thinner and

---

[1] Micron $= \frac{1}{1000}$ part of a millimeter, hence quite invisible to the naked eye; and the ovum is *only just* visible.

forms a sort of rim. It forms the essential portion of the
cell, the fertilizing agent which transmits the qualities of
genus and individual. Its proportions are as follows: 4·2
microns long, 3·1 microns broad, and 2 microns thick—at
the edge only ·2 microns thick.

The neck unites head and tail, which is relatively long
and acts as oar or rudder; it sweeps the spermatozoön
forwards, by a series of vigorous twists and writhing movements, strongly suggestive of the swimming eel, or the
strokes of a whip lash. But this characteristic motion only
begins when the sperm cells meet the secretions of the
vesiculæ and the *prostate gland*. So long as they remain
enclosed in the testicle and the head of the epididymis, the
spermatozoa are motionless, and apparently mostly immature. They fully evolve and mature as they pass into
the efferent ducts of their parent glands. In the innumerable
twists and turns of the epididymis, which is a sort of special
receptacle for them, the sperm cells are probably blended
with a liquid secretion from the membranes, which forms a
fluid more of the consistency of the discharge at ejaculation.
(We must assume something of the kind, for in the secretion
extracted from the extremity of the epididymis the sperms
are no longer packed together in clusters, but float
separately.)

Apart, therefore, from the independent motion of the
individual sperm cells, we must assume that they are driven
forward and onward in the testicles by the accumulation of
secretion, and gradual muscular pressure. The same factors
are operative in the epididymis, but here they are assisted
by the incessant action of the tiny fibers which line these
ducts[1] and keep up a capillary current towards the *vasa
deferentia*.

Once within the *vasa deferentia* the transport of sperm is
effected by contractions of the powerful muscular apparatus
of these ducts. And these contractions are probably
rhythmically followed by expansions, which act as pumps
and draw or suck more sperms out of the epididymis. The
last stage of their appointed way through the urethra is

---

[1] *Cf.* the similar capillary current in the oviducts.

traversed with lightning speed and impetus in the *ejaculation* or *emission.*

The topics just alluded to have practical as well as scientific importance.   This practical importance may be great, as *exact knowledge* here prevents mistaken deductions and conclusions.   Thus we can understand why, after several rapid and successive ejaculations, *i.e.,* in repeated coitus at short intervals, the amount of seminal fluid decreases, and is found microscopically to contain few normal and active sperms, and more that are extinct or immature.[1]

The motion of the sperms continues automatically in the seminal fluid and the normal secretions of the womanly parts.   It is still an open question whether they are occasionally immobile and passive during their progress through the woman's organs, or continuously in motion; and also whether they are able to draw nourishment and stimulant either from the other male secretions or the female secretions (Skene's glands, Bartholin's glands, vaginal and cervical passages), which preserves them and enables them to retain their mobility in spite of the comparatively enormous distances traversed.   We cannot deny the possibility of such local sustenance and refreshment.   A pause or temporary cessation of movement is also not by any means improbable; we have seen already that they are first stimulated to active advance by mixing with the product of the prostate gland, although they have inherent power of independent movement.   We know that, *e.g.,* among *bats,* which have connection in the autumn, the sperms can remain dormant in the uterus throughout the whole winter and impregnate the

---

[1] As a young medical practitioner, I had an experience in this department which was an unwelcome surprise, both to myself and my patient. It was my duty to examine and analyze a specimen of fluid from a gentleman of "fast" life, who had formerly suffered from epididymitis (inflammation of the epididymis).   This specimen was abnormally thin and liquid, much too small in amount, and containing *no* mobile (active) spermatozoa, but only immature cells, such as, at that time, doctors *erroneously* regarded as extinct or deformed.   I reported that spermatozoa of that type were very inapt for fertilization; he chose, for his own convenience, to take this diagnosis as an absolute guarantee that he could have connection, but not procreate, and on the next occasion he made his partner pregnant.

ova in the spring. On the other hand, if we microscopically
examine spermatozoa contained in seminal fluid which is
preserved at mean bodily heat in incubators, where it cannot
dry up, we may observe that they remain alive under these
conditions for eight days, and are in constant motion,
whenever observed. So it is quite possible that they continue moving from the moment of ejaculation till fertilization within the feminine organism.

This period of time is very variously estimated. Some
authorities think it is only from twenty-four to thirty-six
hours. Others assume eight or even fourteen days. Taking
into consideration the analogy of various animal species and
practical experience rather than experimental research, I
am inclined to believe in a long continuance of seminal
vitality.

These sperms move forwards at a rate of speed which,
under the microscope, appears about 3 mm. a minute. This
means that each spermatozoön moves its own length forward in a second. They are propelled onwards with enormous force, obstacles are thrust aside or cloven through, and
the advance is steadily *upstream*. And, as I have mentioned,
a capillary current downwards and outwards, towards the
vagina and introitus, is always operating in the woman's
oviducts and uterus; so the invaders must swim against
the stream to attain their goal. Probably their extreme
rapidity is slightly diminished by the capillary current. At
least, it is assumed that they only advance 1 to 1½ mm.
every three minutes, so that as they emerge from the *liquid
ejaculate* at the external *os uteri,* they only reach the cavity
of the uterus *in two to three hours.* A few more hours and
they will have entered the oviduct or tube, and in its lateral
portion they meet the released ovum. One of the spermatozoa darts forward and plunges into the ovum, its head
becomes merged with the ovum, and fertilization has taken
place. *Fertilization* or *conception* thus cannot take place at
earliest—if we accept these calculations—before eight hours
have elapsed after coitus.

And what is the latest possible date? Of course we
assume there has not been another coitus in the intervening
period! This is very hard to decide. But various circum-

stances lead me to assume that we must allow for considerable time here. In more precise terms: I consider it probable that from eight to ten days after a coitus a spermatozoön ejaculated on that occasion may fertilize an ovum. But, in opposition to some authorities, I am of the opinion that spermatozoa received by the female organs during a coitus before a menstrual discharge have *not much* chance of surviving the menstruation, and remaining hidden in the tubes, to fertilize the product of the next ovulation. But I will not pronounce this to be impossible, especially if the ovulation occurs prematurely.

Finally we must learn what happens to the many spermatozoa which do not meet and merge with the ovum. Only *one* is so fortunate as to be functional, when it has conjoined with the ovum no others can penetrate. And as in every coitus (unless it follows too quickly after a preceding ejaculation) *between 200 and 500 million spermatozoa are flung forward into the vagina—myriads must perish for each one that survives.* What happens to these myriads? Many ebb again out of the vagina in the liquid secretions ejaculated with them. Another portion, certainly proportionally large, are dissolved and neutralized fairly soon by the local (vaginal) secretions, which are too acid to suit them as a medium.[1] The slight acidity of the vaginal secretion at certain periods of the cycle, and the distinctly alkaline spermatic fluid and uterine and tubal secretions, on the other hand, are very congenial to the sperm.

The extinct sperms decompose and disintegrate (fall apart). The remains are carried out of the vulva with the urine or by douches and ablutions.

On the other hand, some of their chemical ingredients, together with those of the accessory glands, are absorbed into the vaginal membrane and incorporated in the blood.

A small number reaches the uterus. Most of these perish on the way to the Fallopian tube or oviduct. But the uterine lining is more absorbent of spermatic substances than the vaginal. And many still active sperms actually pene-

---

[1] The enhanced acidity of these secretions during pregnancy destroys them very soon.

trate this mucous membrane, and have been microscopically discovered in and among the epithelial cells in all stages of disintegration.   It is obvious that their chemical components are thus all the more thoroughly absorbed and assimilated by the whole body of the woman.

Only a very few sperms enter the oviduct.   There the same fate as met their fellows awaits all *but one,* which is destined to transmit life.   But we have not succeeded in tracing their presence here as in the uterus.   Possibly the capillary current wafts them back to the uterus.

Only a very small number, which have the toughest vitality and most active mobility, reach the abdominal cavity itself.   Here, as shown by *Hœhne's* experimental injections into the peritoneal cavity,[1] they are attacked by the phagocytes (white corpuscles), which are the scavengers and cleansers of the human organism, and exterminated within twenty hours.

The *prostate gland* is shaped like a horse-chestnut, and surrounds the posterior urethra, so that its longer section lies behind, but a small portion before, the urinary duct. The anterior or front surface of the prostate approaches the lower rim of the symphysis; the neck of the bladder is embedded in the upper prostatic surface.   The hindmost portion, as shown in Plate VII. (No. 9), slopes lightly downwards, and lies contiguous to the enlarged portion of the bowel which we described and depicted when treating of the female genitalia.   The prostate can be felt by the finger if inserted into the rectum.   The lowest extremity of the prostate is supported on the muscular pelvic floor, just above the juncture of the urethra with the corpora cavernosa of the penis.

The prostate is a cluster of glandular cells, separated by connective tissue, provided with smooth (involuntary) muscles, and sheathed in an outer wall of similar muscle. This powerful muscular apparatus is able, during its spasmodic contractions or convulsions at the moment of sexual congress, to squeeze and force the secretions it contains into the urethra.   The ducts in which these secretions are formed are about *thirty in number,* and open close together

---

[1] Described in the *Zentralblatt für Gynäkologie,* 1914, No. 1.

at the same place in the urethral wall where the two seminal
ducts also join the urethra, that is, on the *urethral crest*
(No. 10).

The urethral crest is an oval elevation, about 3 mm. high
and the same wide, in the middle of that section of the
urethra which passes through the prostate gland; it
protrudes from the posterior wall into the duct itself.   Its
length is not exactly measurable, as it merges into a sort of
longitudinal fold of the mucous membrane; but it is approximately between 7 and 8 mm.   It consists mostly of erectile
tissue, like the corpora cavernosa and the female clitoris and
bulbi, and is interwoven with elastic and smooth (involuntary) muscles.

The specific secretions of the prostate gland form a milky-
white, thin, alkaline fluid containing the special chemical
substance—called spermin—which gives the seminal discharge its characteristic odor.[1] For these prostatic
secretions are forced into the urethra together with the
secretions from the testicles (sperm), and thoroughly intermingled in the convulsive contractions of the sexual act.
Prostate secretions form a large proportion of the *ejaculate,*
or discharge, and, as we have seen, their alkalinity preserves
the spermatozoa and stimulates their mobility.

We have already mentioned some significant facts regarding the spermatic ducts, seminal ducts, or *vasa deferentia.*
I shall here allude chiefly to their association with the
reservoirs and vesiculæ, or vesicles.   The ducts themselves
are decidedly long—about 45 cm.—which derives biologically from the descent of the testicles out of the abdomen
into the scrotum.   They ascend on either side, out of the
testicles, and intertwine with nerves and blood-vessels to
form the bilateral *spermatic cords,* close under the skin, to
the outer extremity of the groins.   On this section of its
length the spermatic cord can be easily felt with the fingers.

If the contents of the scrotal pouch, on either left or right
side, are moved between the fingers, between groin and
testicle, one can feel a hard, round cord of about the thickness
of a narrow pencil.   After having passed through the groin[2]

---

[1] Spermin is more fully described later in the text.
[2] It does not enter the abdominal cavity proper.

it descends into the lesser pelvis, covered by the peritoneum, and skirts the base of the bladder. At this point it becomes enlarged and forms a spindle-shaped cavity, the *seminal reservoir* (bilateral).

The extreme length of the spermatic cord is of as much importance from a practical as from an evolutionary point of view. For this length makes it a much more effective suction-pump for the testicular products. This length also makes it able to contain a large amount of such secretions, so that throughout it serves as a *reservoir,* as well as a *conduit* or *duct.*

But the reservoirs *par excellence* are the two enlarged portions below the bladder. They look like lumps or protuberances, and are divided internally into tiny compartments by the web-like folds of the mucous membrane, forming deep and irregular interstices. In these cavities, which are between 3 and 4 cm. long, and almost 1 cm. broad, the seminal fluid from the epididymis collects. The automatic involuntary contractions of the muscular walls spray the fluid through the tiny passages which form the terminal section of the spermatic cord into the urethra. And at the same time, by the same muscular spasms, the contents of the *vesiculæ,* or seminal vesicles, are also flung forward into the urethra.

The vesiculæ (No. 8 in Plate VII.) are two flat, oval bodies, 4 to 5 cm. long, 2 cm. broad, and only 1 cm. through, which lie between bladder and rectum. They resemble the *reservoirs* in their internal structure, with the difference that each vesicle consists of a *twisted* or *convoluted* main duct, with several branches ending in culs-de-sac; they open into the main duct, and this again into the lower extremity of the reservoir, so that the vesicle may be considered an oval *annexe* or extension of the reservoir.

For a long time medical science considered that the vesicles themselves served only or mainly as *reservoirs,* and it is certain that some sperm cells are always to be found in the vesicles of sexually adult men, and that any liquid injected into the *vas deferens* fills both reservoir and vesicles before it streams through the tiny aperture into the urethra. But all test experiments of this type have, of course, been made post mortem, so that we cannot be equally sure of their validity for the living.

It seems to me most likely that the main storage of semen takes place in the reservoirs, and that when these are over-full the vesicles act as safety-valves and extra containers.[1]

But the main office of the reservoirs is to secrete special ingredients which are mixed with the seminal fluid. The vesicular product is a tough, yellowish, and sticky substance, which can be distinguished in perfectly fresh ejaculate, in the form of tiny *grains* (like frog's eggs but without the core) and serves to make the consistency less fluid and more gelatinous. But these grains very soon dissolve and the ejaculate becomes wholly liquid.

We have already mentioned the stimulating effect of the vesicular secretions on the spermatozoa. Moreover, the increased amount of substance serves to disperse these cells. It is not yet known whether the peculiar consistency of this substance has any particular value for the preservation of the sperms. The final sections of the *vasa deferentia,* which pour the contents of reservoirs and vesicles into the urethra, are both only between 2 and 2½ cm. long. They intersect the prostate gland, from either side, converging diagonally, and open into the urethra, very close together, at the summit of the *urethral crest.* At first they are 2 mm. in diameter, but they contract to a quarter of that width[2] (½ mm.), so that the spermatic substance is squeezed and pressed into the urethra in superlatively thin spray and with great force. This is essential, as we shall explain later on.

Through *ejaculation,* or *emission,* the male sperms are finally ejected from the body. Ejaculation is the aim, the summit and the end of the sexual act. We shall discuss it

---

[1] It is significant that animals with ample *reservoirs* (cattle, sheep, stallions) perform coitus very quickly, as does *genus homo.*
Dogs, cats, and others who have no reservoirs, and are thus compelled to depend on the vas deferens for their seminal supply in coitus, take a comparatively long time.

[2] To form an idea of these proportions, we may say that the tuyere-aperture in the carburetor of a medium-sized automobile is twice as wide across!

in detail, as such, in the following section, especially in connection with the impressions and sensations accompanying it.

But we shall deal here with the *mechanism* of ejaculation as the accumulated spermatic fluids may be evacuated, automatically in men and boys, *without sexual intercourse, and even quite apart from erotic stimulation or sexual thoughts or wishes.*

When the accumulated tension or *summation* of stimuli—whether these are external and mechanical, *i.e.,* peripheral, and/or solely psychic and imaginative, *i.e.,* central, or exclusively the result of brimming seminal fluid in the reservoirs and vesicles—has passed a certain limit, the smooth involuntary muscles of these four organs contract automatically in strong spasms, and drive their fluid contents in tiny columns of spray against the anterior urethral wall. At the same time, the prostatic muscles contract, and project the special secretions of the prostate into the urethra. These various secretory substances are thoroughly intermingled because of the extreme tenuity of the vesicular streams and the impetus with which they are ejected and rebound from the urethral wall to meet the prostatic secretion as it pours out of its numerous apertures. (See under the description of the structure and functions of the prostate.)

Thus it will be seen that the mechanism of this intermingling of secretions is complex.

And the whole process is completed (at least in normal individuals) by the *erection* which precedes these reflexes[1] and causes the urethral crest to swell and protrude. This makes the diagonal forward direction of the two terminal sections of the *vas deferens* steeper and more closely convergent, so that the various fluids are more thoroughly mixed, and the whole amount directed towards the penile portion of the urethra. And at the same time, this swelling acts as a stopper to or *occludes* (shuts off) the posterior urethra—which is, as it were, also *locked* by certain pro-

---

[1] A reflex is the involuntary reaction of stimuli applied to a certain nerve or nerves, on other nerves, and the resultant action without participation of the cerebral centers. This is important.

state muscles, which form a ring round the urethra and spasmodically contract.

Thus it becomes impossible for the seminal fluid to flow away inwards in the direction of the bladder. Its only available egress is towards the outer world. And simultaneously it becomes impossible for the urine to pass with and mix into the sperms. So long as the penis is in erection, the occlusion by the urethral crest makes it impossible to "pass water" or urinate.

The blend of liquid secretions, formed in the prostatic portion of the urethra, into what we know as the semen or seminal fluid, is instantly ejected from the body. This, too, is a purely reflex action. Therefore it is totally impossible, when the ejaculation has once started, to inhibit it by any effort of consciousness. It occurs spontaneously and inevitably, even though in this case, through the action of muscles of the ridged and voluntary type, which are otherwise controlled by the conscious will. The reflex is set in motion by the projection of the liquid semen against the internal urethral wall; its *sensory* result is the feeling of ecstatic pleasure (even in emissions during sleep). Its *motor* result is an immediate succession of rhythmic or spasmodic convulsions of the powerful muscles around the root of the penis, and of the whole pelvic floor. The most active muscle, in ejaculation, is one which encloses the *bulbous urethræ* and lies close under the perineum. Its paroxysms can be clearly felt by the finger on such occasions. It is indicated in Plate VII. by No. 14, and colored bright red. (Musculus bulbo cavernosus.)

The rhythmic spasms of ejaculation fling forth the semen from the external orifice with an impetus which may be perceived if the emission takes place *in vacuo*. The seminal stream usually covers a distance of from 15 to 20 cm., but has been known to exceed 1 meter.

Probably, in the first coital spasm, while some of the seminal liquid is discharged outwards, some also passes into the posterior urethra. And when the paroxysms subside, more flows back, so that the alternate muscular tension and relaxation act here, too, as a suction pump.

In a few convulsive forward thrusts, the bulk of the semen is ejaculated, a few further slighter and gradually decreasing contractions dispose of what remains in the urethra, and the reflex is at an end. Presently the tense erected penis grows smaller, and slacker, and resumes its normal position —unless further stimulation persists and causes a renewal of the process—and the erection and ejaculation are at an end.

It is difficult to ascertain exactly whether vesicles and reservoirs are entirely emptied when ejaculation occurs. But when it is found possible to repeat coitus almost at once, we may safely assume only a partial emptying of these organs, although we must concede that both during the first emission and in response to the stimuli preceding the second, wave-like successive contractions of the *vasa deferentia* rapidly provide further seminal fluid. Perhaps complete or partial discharge is a matter of individual idiosyncrasy. Some authorities accept the possibility of a *unilateral* (one-sided) evacuation. Individual idiosyncrasies here would explain why one man can only have *coitus* once on each occasion, and another several times in rapid succession. Moreover, this facility (or potency) certainly depends less on the amount of testicular secretion than on increased activity of the accessory glands. When ejaculations occur in rapid succession, only a thin fluid is finally discharged, which contains mostly prostatic secretion but no sperms, or at most very few.

The *pollutions* or involuntary seminal losses to which young men who are sexually abstinent are peculiarly liable owing to the accumulation of sperms, can take place every fortnight or three weeks and sometimes every eight days. In later years they occur less often. They usually take place only during sleep and in association with erotic dreams, and the ejaculation is accompanied by deep pleasure and satisfied relief.

As regards the interaction between the local processes in the genital organs and the psychic images and feelings, it is just as likely that the tension in vesicles and reservoirs causes the motor reflexes of erection and emission, and that the dream passes through the mind concurrently, as that the local tension causes the dream and the dream the ejaculation.

In any case, erection and ejaculation during sleep give us the most arresting, simple, and purely physical example of the "urge to relieve tension" or "urge to relax," so that *in such cases* we may accurately apply the term *"urge of sexual evacuation."*

But *how* complex is the psychic response, in waking hours, to the tension of the seminal reservoirs! Even if the psychic unrest is the direct result of the physical tension, the resultant impulse and desire are consciously aimed much more at satisfying an emotion than at relieving a physical need! So that we can no longer here speak of "evacuation" only, or even predominantly.[1]

What wondrous interplay of stimulation and inhibition, excitement and restraint! And especially of inhibition and restraint. For the motor reflex of ejaculation which derives *solely* from the seminal reservoirs and causes the *unconscious* discharge—only happens during sleep! And this proves conclusively that when consciousness is awake, the process of ejaculation is inhibited and controlled from the cerebral cortex, *i.e.,* through the active co-operation of the soul.

And similar inhibitions of erection and ejaculation, through the higher nerve centers of the brain, may prevail under various other circumstances; a fact which many men have great reason to be thankful for—and not a few, the reverse.[2]

A few more details are appropriate with regard to the sperm, or semen, although the main facts have been stated above.

Human semen is discharged on each single occasion to the amount of between 5 and 10 c.c., each cubic centimeter containing about *sixty million* spermatozoa. When emis-

---

[1] The *urge to relieve tension, i.e., to attain sexual satisfaction,* is completely separated from the urge to *evacuate,* in the countless cases where there is no bodily pressure of accumulated semen but only psychic longings and impulses.

[2] *Cf.* the Fourth Episode in Schnitzler's "Reigen."

sions occur in rapid succession, both quantity and quality
diminish. When first exposed to the outer air, semen
appears as a glutinous fluid containing tiny lumps or
granules; its color is a faintly yellowish white, its chemical
reactions alkaline, *and it has a very distinctive odor, which
increases under the application of heat or washing with
warm water.* Very soon the granules vanish, and the semen
liquefies completely, but tends to *shred* itself. When it
dries up it first becomes very sticky, and then leaves on
woven materials (clothing and sheets, etc.), *hard white
marks,* which can be washed out with cold water, but are
very hard to remove if hot water is used. It is of importance in forensic medicine that the sperms are distinguish-
able in laundry-water.

Under the microscope we may distinguish in normal
semen not only the countless lively active spermatozoa, and
few abnormal (or immature) forms, but also various other
cells and micro-organisms which have no practical importance for this treatise.

Peculiarly striking crystals are formed in the semen if it
is frozen or precipitated. They are almost the length of a
spermatozoön. In spite of their great diversity of shape,
these crystals (first discovered by *Böttcher* in 1865) all
consist of the same substance, a composite of *spermin.*

In the last ten years of the nineteenth century *spermin*
was exhaustively studied, chemically and biologically, by
A. von Poehl, of Petersburg. He succeeded in producing
spermin by chemical synthesis.

He was able to demonstrate (among other phenomena)
that the characteristic odor of semen is exclusively due to
its content of *spermin.* So this odor does not come from
the testicular secretion, which has hardly any spermin, but
from the *prostatic fluid.* Therefore the seminal secretions, if
obtained straight from the *vasa deferentia,* do not smell of
spermin, although such testicular secretions are the main and
most important ingredient in the ejaculate.

Moreover, chemically pure combinations of spermin[1] can

---

[1] I use the term spermin for the sake of simplicity. But really this
substance is combined in diverse manners, *e.g.,* the spermatic crystals are
formed by a combination with phosphoric acid; Poehl also experimented

exhale the unmistakable seminal odor, even in extremely weak solutions.   This circumstance enables us to understand its transmission to the breath of some women after coitus.

Poehl's researches proved also that spermin, when introduced into the bodily organism, accelerated metabolism and generally quickened vital energy.   And this explains in itself the tonic effect of coitus on women, for it is beyond question that the seminal fluid is partially absorbed by the tissues of the female organs.   Of course, we may at once admit that this exhilaration and invigoration may not be wholly due to spermin, but partly also to other seminal ingredients.   Equally we recognize the possibility, or, rather, probability, that sexual union refreshens and strengthens the woman in other ways as well, *e.g.*, through increasing the amount of her own internal secretions and through psychic channels.

The internal secretions of the male genitals (endocrines, hormones) are certainly very important, as we have mentioned in our earlier section.   In the adult man they promote general bodily vigor, mental initiative and capacity, and sexual emotions, especially in their preliminary stages.

Unlike the woman's ovarian products, the man's internal secretions do not show any cyclic variations, but continue at a steady level, throughout maturity.   And they have not the same decisive influence on the whole individual existence, in his case as in hers.   Man is not subject to the recurrent alternate ebb and flow of all vital processes, which characterizes woman.[1]

But at a certain age, the external and internal secretions of the testicles diminish, gradually.   This is one of the symptoms of senescence (advancing age).   But it has special significance, for when the testicles begin to atrophy, their

with muriatic acid.   Poehl's solution does not smell in itself.   The highly characteristic odor only becomes apparent after certain definite chemical changes.

[1] *Cf.* Ralph Cheyney, the American poet:
   "You move with the moon, dear, breathe with the tide,
   In fellowship to me denied."

internal hormones no longer exercise such powerful stimulus on the general individuality, and the functions of separate organs, and so the atrophy of the testicles emphasizes and promotes the ageing of the whole body and often of the mind, as well. Thus, there is formed a *vicious circle,* an unbroken chain of unfavorable effects, whose main link is the decreased production of testicular hormones.

Modern scientific research has brought proof of this theory in two independent ways, and has based its conclusions also on earlier observations. The experiments of *Steinach*[1] have shown that the *ligature* of the *vas deferens* (vaso ligature or vasectomy) does not only arrest senescence, but can even cause existent symptoms to disappear, to some extent.[2] And the work of *Voronoff,* who has replaced the failing internal secretion of human testicles by transplanting interstitial tissues of anthropoid apes, has had similar results.

Of course, it is intended, in such experiments, to help men who are affected with premature exhaustion and senility. We are not yet in a position to speak authoritatively about the final consequences of such operations, from the point of view of practical everyday life.

In our present state of uncertainty, it seems advisable for a healthy man in the fifties and sixties to prevent, so far as possible, the atrophy of his organs, by exercising them *regularly and appropriately, i.e.,* not with excessive frequency, but also not too seldom. *I assume, of course, that he will have always preserved them from morbid infections!*

For every organ atrophies, if it is not used at all, or used very little. We doctors meet this symptom everywhere, and we always warn against it. So why should we not point out that inactivity of the testicles helps to bring about premature senility and degeneracy, and thus depresses and debilitates the whole individual; whereas moderate and suitable use of the sexual function—which is possible up to a very great age—keeps the whole organism comparatively vigorous and efficient. Of course, there can be

---

[1] Published, William Heinemann (Medical Books), Ltd.
[2] It would take far too long to explain the causes and processes at work here.

risks and drawbacks, physical and moral, in advising elderly men to have sexual intercourse. *But let no man take my words in this sense!*

But I take the responsibility of advising regular conjugal intercourse, in the fifties *and sixties, unless specific morbid symptoms counter-indicate.* In this respect, too, domestic life, viewed and practiced in the light of *Ideal Marriage,* can bring health and happiness to body and mind, and soul.

SECOND INTERMEZZO OF APHORISMS

1.

In order to perform coitus according to Divine Law, complete knowledge and full mastery is needed of all things concerning Man and Woman.

Omar Haleby.

2.

Of all vital questions, none is more important than understanding of the acts and processes which ensure the perpetuation of life.

Camille Mauclair.

3.

There is no topic whose interest is at once more humanly universal and more acutely personal; and at the same time, none on which wise advice is more needed: especially in view of the appalling blunders and follies he has committed in all times and lands, under the pitiless sway of the little blind wanton god.

L. de Langle.

4.

If men would give to their married life one-tenth of the trouble and thought they give to their business, the majority of marriages would be happy.

Robert Haas.

5.

He who maintains that he loves without desire is incapable of experiencing desire.

W. T.

6.

Sensuousness is no sin, but, on the contrary, an adornment to life, a gift of God, like the sweet winds of spring and summer. We should enjoy it, with clear conscience and gladly, and should wish it to all healthy full-grown men and women who want it and need it.

Gustav Frenssen.

7.

It is better to marry than to burn.

I. Corinthians vii. 9.

8.

If genuine and profound love prevails in married life, and the wife, when youth and health were hers, has met the husband's wishes without selfishness and caprice, we surely should expect that the man will not grumble at difficulties which are inevitable if he is to show proper consideration for her welfare.

S. Ribbing.

9.

Everyone whose heart beats truly and with goodwill,
Reverences his wife, and tends her carefully.

Achilles.
Homer's "Iliad," Book IX., 341.

10.

In sooth a godly man is he,
That cherisheth her carefully.

Luther.

11.

We know for how brief while
In woman's heart the fire of love can burn,
If eye and hand 'plenish it not, afresh.

Dante.

12.

The woman whose husband is steadfast and of good grace,
Shows forth his troth and love, in her happy face.

Goethe. (Proverb.)

13.

All things in woman are a riddle: and all things in woman have one meaning: pregnancy.

Nietzsche.

14.

In man, prudence.
In woman, patience.

Old Italian Proverb.

15.

Women of active brain and balanced personality, who at the same time know how to remain essentially *feminine; i.e.,* women who understand their own nature, their real superiorities and their defects—are very rare.

Jules Huret.

16.

Love covers a multitude of sins.

I. Acts Apostles iv. 8.

17.

Behold what love can do!
Cripples it maketh hale,
Brings Peace the world into,
Hushes the slanderous tale;
Fills up the home with joy,
And tranquil blessedness.
And though the world annoy,
    Love's name is steadfastness.

J. Cats.

18.

How long does youth last?
So long as we are loved.
    From the Golden Book of Countess Diana.[1]

19.

Love does not count the years.

Stendhal.

20.

What does age matter, if we meet it together?

Stendhal.

21.

Love extends the Ego, to include Thee.
Love refines the Ego, to embrace Thee.

W. T.

---

[1] "The Golden Book of Countess Diana" summarizes and records "questions and answers" of a distinguished group of men and women.

PART III

SEXUAL INTERCOURSE

ITS PHYSIOLOGY AND TECHNIQUE

"Every natural faculty—and every organic function is such a faculty—by means of exercise, evolution and inheritance, can become an Art."

H. Vaihinger.
"The Philosophy of As-If." [1]

CHAPTER VIII

DEFINITIONS, PRELUDE, AND LOVE-PLAY

By the term sexual intercourse, we herewith designate the full range of contact and connection, between human beings, for sexual consummation. But let us first of all make unmistakably clear that by "sexual intercourse," unqualified by any adjectives, we refer *exclusively to normal intercourse between opposite sexes.* If we cannot avoid occasional reference to certain abnormal sexual practices, *we shall emphatically state that they are abnormal.* But this will only occur very seldom, for, as postulated above, it is our intention to keep the Hell-gate of the Realm of Sexual Perversions firmly closed. On the other hand, Ideal Marriage permits normal, physiological activities the fullest

---

[1] "Philosophie des Als-Ob": Popular edition. Chapter II., p. 8. (Publisher, Felix Meiner, Leipzig.)

scope, in all desirable and delectable ways; these we shall envisage, without any prudery, but *with deepest reverence for true chastity.* All that is morbid, all that is perverse, we banish: for this is Holy Ground.

In order to obviate confusion, let us first define what we regard as normal sexual intercourse. It is not altogether easy. All rigid definitions and sharp distinctions are particularly difficult in sexual matters. I think the most comprehensive and exact definition is as follows: That intercourse which takes place between two sexually mature individuals of opposite sexes; which excludes cruelty and the use of artificial means for producing voluptuous sensations; which aims directly or indirectly at the consummation of sexual satisfaction, and which, having achieved a certain degree of stimulation, concludes with the ejaculation—or emission—of the semen into the vagina, at the nearly simultaneous culmination[1] of sensation—or orgasm—of both partners.

Complete sexual intercourse comprises: the prelude, the love-play, the sexual union; and the after-play or epilogue (postlude). Its summit and its purpose alike blend in the *third stage.* The accepted technical term for this third stage is *coitus;* but I shall call it *communion.* This has the associations of union, consummation and copulation: and has the further advantage that it does not emphasize the activity of the man and the passivity of the woman, which in Ideal Marriage should merge into a melodious *mutuality* of interaction and response. Communion-mating— merging together—implies *equal rights and equal joys in sexual union.*

This mating or communion—which may also, in the narrower and more precise sense, be termed sexual union— begins with introduction of the male organ into the vagina, reaches its summit in the twofold *acme* and its purpose in the outpouring and reception of the seed of life. It concludes, strictly speaking, when the phallos is withdrawn from the vagina. Its *biological purpose* is attained in *fertilization* or

---

1 The term *culmination* or *acme* is used preferably to *orgasm.*

impregnation, but impregnation is not necessarily a part of the process of sexual union, nor is sexual union always an indispensable preliminary condition for impregnation.[1]

At the conclusion of sexual union or communion, begins the *after-glow,* the epilogue, which may, however, be completely omitted by couples who do not truly understand or feel love for one another. In such cases, having attained satisfaction, both man and woman turn away from each other, if only for a time. But when love is both intensely passionate and delicately considerate, such after-play becomes an important phase of sexual life; it is all too often ignored or neglected in ordinary married life today. In Ideal Marriage it must attain full recognition and appreciation.

It is not possible to set a definite time limit to this epilogue. It dies away like the final chords of a melody. It should echo, and vibrate, and reawaken in the preliminaries of a new act of sexual communion.

Thus couples may achieve that *continuity of communion*

---

[1] *Note on pregnancy without previous coitus.* There are numerous though, of course, exceptional instances on record of impregnation or conception following the penetration of sperm-cells into the female genitalia without complete *immissio penis* or entrance of the male organ. Such cases are of great practical importance. They plainly prove two things. *Firstly,* that under certain circumstances impregnation can result if the seminal fluid is deposited in the external genitals or *vulva* even when the *hymen* remains unbroken. And *secondly,* that a spermatozoön can reach the female organs indirectly, *e.g.,* through the contact of a finger, and preserve sufficient vitality to be able to make the long ascent, *from the vulva to the ovary,* without the impetus of ejaculation, and to penetrate and fertilize the egg-cell in its inmost sanctuary; a supreme proof of the incredibly concentrated activity and force of these primordial life seeds.

Peculiarly significant, on the practical side, are such cases in which there has been a *transmission* of sperm-cells from a residue deposited in the *male urethra,* and carried from thence, in the act of urination, to the *preputial gland,* where they may also remain for a while in a state of suspended activity. To be then, through renewed sexual contact, whether by insertion *without ejaculation* or more superficial contact introduced into the female organs.

Other cases are still more complicated and instructive. In these, sperm-cells deposited in the vagina or outer sexual organs of one woman, may be transmitted to the vulva of a second woman or girl, who becomes pregnant as a result, while the first woman escapes. These extraordinary cases have been observed and established beyond any doubt. They prove the extreme ease with which impregnation can be effected, and the care which is necessary in dealing with either the seminal fluid or specimens of sperm-cells. They also illuminate and explain certain impregnations in spite of "the utmost precautions" from an unsuspected angle.

which I consider one of the most beautiful results of Ideal Marriage, and at the same time one of its most reliable foundations.

As soon as the first stirrings of the impulse of approach are perceptible, the prelude to sexual union begins. It continues at an unfaltering *crescendo,* in some cases slowly, in others rapidly, and in exceptional instances with the speed and certainty of lightning.

And where does it end? It ends as the love-play begins.

Surely it is not necessary to observe that we cannot fix on any one instant of time as terminating the prelude and initiating the second stage? It is obvious that they merge into one another in delicate gradations, that sometimes acts and responses characteristic of love-play appear in the prelude, and that, on the other hand, especially on the woman's side, a timid reserve and elusiveness manifests itself, even when the second fuller erotic chords have sounded.

Nevertheless, it seems most helpful to indicate a dividing line, a natural Rubicon, between these two phases of the love drama. And it is not difficult to recognize: for the *erotic kiss* or *lover's kiss* is the prototype of all erotic contact, and initiates a new grade of tension, for which reasons I consider it belongs definitely to the second stage.

This second stage is enacted from the erotic kiss to the beginning of *erotic communion.* It is a preliminary to such communion, and is *indispensable* if both partners are to be able to attain such communion in complete harmony of body and soul.

This particular stage in sexual relations is of special significance for the hitherto inexperienced and "unlessoned girl"; for an expert and delicate art in love-play on the man's side is generally necessary in order to excite her fully and make her ready for, and receptive to, consummation.

In practiced lovers, especially between partners who have become thoroughly adapted to each other's individualities, both preliminary prelude and love-play may be "got through" in one brief gesture, or wholly dispensed with.

ok, a word of invitation and suggestion suffice—espe-
after prolonged abstinence from one another, to prepare
for the supreme act and initiate it.

But this lightning love contact can only occur very seldom
and on exceptional occasions, between persons of finer feelings, and only such are capable of Ideal Marriage; and
when it does occur, there must be complete mastery of
intimate æsthetic technique.   Otherwise it is essentially
gross and must have severe psychic consequences.   For the
man who neglects the love-play is guilty not only of coarse-
ness, but of positive brutality; and his omission can not
only offend and disgust a woman, but also injure her on the
purely physical plane.

And this sin of omission is unpardonably *stupid*.

For love-play, as an art, gives a profusion of pleasures
which are certainly not inferior to those of communion
itself.   In Ideal Marriage this second phase in the drama of
sexual relations should be as much appreciated and culti-
vated as the third.

If we consider each phase separately and in detail com-
mensurate with its importance, we need not spend too much
time over *preliminary technique*.   It is simply the translation into tactful and skillful actuality of the principles
enunciated in our third chapter on general sexual physiology.

Looks and words have the main *rôles* in the prelude, for
they can best utter the feelings at this early stage when the
soul is more stirred than the body.

But even the minor *rôles* here are important: see all that
has previously been said about the association of the sense
of smell with sex; see also Rousseau's dictum on the power
of "le doux parfum d'un cabinet de toilette." [1]

And we may also refer, in this connection, to *dancing*,
which has certainly lost a portion of its primeval significance
as a sexual ritual,[2] but, nevertheless, in modern civilization
retains much force of erotic symbolism and suggestion.   This
is especially the case with certain folk-dances, *e.g.,* the

---

[1] Cited in the nineteenth aphorism of the First Intermezzo.
[2] See among others, Ploos-Bartels' "Das Weib in der Natur" and
"Völkerkunde."

Russian Trepak, the Sicilian, and Tyrolese (Schuhplattler), which are obviously pantomimic courtships. They attain their effect not only by the play of gesture, but also through the power and vivacious grace of movement, and generally also by the musical accompaniment, the strongest factor here being *rhythmic*.

In the *prelude* the impulse of approach works through the three senses of sight, hearing, and smell. Taste and touch come into play at closer range, and it may be said that *touch*, once in action, soon becomes paramount.

There are two main types or, one might say (to continue the musical analogy), *motifs* in the prelude: *coquetry* and *flirtation*.

If I make use here of the first word, I do not wish to emphasize the associations of vanity and frivolity which attach to it in its original form and language.

What I mean in the erotic prelude to Ideal Marriage by the term *coquetry*, corresponds, if I am not mistaken, to the true original meaning of the word, and implies the interplay of alternate approach and retreat, attraction and defense, which by the resultant accumulating tension and summation constitutes one of love's strongest spells on the psychic side.

Coquetry, if employed by a woman of sensitive feeling and artistic taste, with delicate gradations and due discretion in its more defensive aspects, can be one of the most graceful erotic manifestations, for there is peculiar charm in a retreat followed by a renewed advance. We realize this general rule of æsthetics in music, where it is most effectively used; in the drama, where a short interval enhances interest in the action when it recommences; and in the erotic art, through coquetry. And we shall find this deliberate momentary retreat and reserve as a subtle relish in the more intimate stages of the love-play, and even during the summit of sexual intercourse.

But, let us not forget: every stimulant in overdoses is poison; just as poisons in minutest doses on appropriate occasions act as stimulants.

Even so in art; in the fine arts, musical, literary, plastic, pictorial; and equally so in the finest of all, the art of love, intentional and conscious reticence must be most carefully and discriminatingly used. Those who know not how to employ such methods at the right moment in the right manner and with complete proficiency—*had best leave them quite alone!* Or let *him* (and not less *her!*) beware of over-dosage! For too little can at most here simply fail of special effect—but *too much reserve,* too strong accentuation of the defensive, the independent, causes not stimulation but paralysis; it paralyzes human sympathies in the one partner, specific sexual desires in the other.

And the piquant relish of coquetry, excessively used, does not only inhibit and paralyze. It tastes sour and repellent; arouses distaste, and is abjured!

Lovers—beware!

We must define the sense in which we use the term *flirtation.* In dictionaries we find translations and definitions which lay stress on *dalliance,* on the playful elusive flutter of attraction. But we do not require a special term for this, we have a full vocabulary of our own.

Neither do we require to make "flirtation" synonymous with "courtship" or "wooing"—as some sexologists do—in the fullest sense. And finally, as we aim at serious clarity and precision here, and a responsible scientific treatise need employ no *doubles-entendres,* we have no use for the term "flirtation" to designate sexual relations outside marriage, in which the partners go more or less far—generally more so—without complete coitus. Certain modern fashionable circles find it convenient to understand by "flirtation" everything except the one coital act; to make *"flirtation"* synonymous with the whole of erotic love-play and specific local stimulation, but we need not use the term in this sense, for it is not only linguistically incorrect, but also superfluous. We face facts, and have an arsenal of terms which express them, with dignity and lucidity.

But we cannot dispense with the concept of flirtation if we retain what I believe to be its original sense: *the performance and experience of the prelude to erotic relations in the definite intention of not going beyond this preliminary stage.*[1]

In this respect, flirtation, especially between married couples, may beautifully refresh and renew erotic feeling. Thus, like coquetry, if used at appropriate times and amounts, it should not be omitted from the technical side of ideal marriage.

The most important instrument in the prelude to sexual intercourse is—conversation; the exchange of impressions and ideas. Its most effective subject is—Love. Its effects are produced by suggestion: auto-suggestion and mutual.

The best realization of what this prelude *means* may be formed if we consider its bodily influence. I am not now alluding to the *general* organic effect shown by more rapid heart action (tachycardia). The *local* sensations prove clearly that the erotic prelude of contemplation and conversation is—a *preparation.* For, if conducted according to the rules of this oldest human art, *through purely psychic stimuli, it produces an unmistakable physical symptom in both man and woman—at least in the normal erotically experienced woman.* This symptom is *distillation* or the lubrication of the genitals which physically expresses the desire for closer contact and forms an indispensable condition to such contact, or at least to fully and mutually satisfactory communion.[2]

The second stage or act in love's drama—love-play—

---

[1] I think the proviso essential; for otherwise flirtation would only mean a prolonged and refined preliminary stage and there would only be confusion if we employed the term as synonymous with *prelude.*

[2] Distillation or lubrication is the secretion of mucus from the smaller genital glands, as described in Chapters VI. and VII. As physiology has not replaced the term distillation (originally invented and circulated by moral theology) with any other, I prefer to use it, instead of a paraphrase. The other local manifestations which often appear during the prelude (erection and swelling of the clitoris in the woman) are less frequent than lubrication, and generally belong to a later stage of love-play.

In the second stage, without sufficient prelude, on the contrary, the genitals expand and become turgid before lubrication.

arises from the impulse for sexual gratification in its widest sense.

Among the Western races—for whom these suggestions are intended—it almost always begins with the kiss—with the lover's or *erotic kiss,*[1] *bien entendu.* There are, of course, kisses that have nothing to do with sexual love. It would be quite indefensible to assume the contrary, as kisses are often given and received which are wholly formal and conventional, or actuated by affection other than sexual. But this second category is much less numerous than simple-minded folk suppose, or than they wish to believe, and/or pretend to believe. For the sexual emotions have a much wider range and more complex *rôle* in life than people generally venture to realize, or at least to express in words.

In any case "just an innocent little harmless kiss" is often far less *"innocent"* in the accepted sense of *sexless,* than it is conventionally (or conveniently!) assumed to be. For many adults, of otherwise open mind, who attempt to be honest with themselves, have found that the "innocence" of a reverent or pitiful kiss on brow or hand, has proved quite fictitious!—whether the fiction was profitable or harmful in its further stages.

And there are other kisses, more or less distinctively sexual, which are given and received with such haste, embarrassment and awe that they belong rather to the *prelude* than to erotic play itself. Such are, for instance, the kisses exchanged as part of certain games, and those

---

[1] Japanese, Chinese, Annamese do not *kiss* as we understand the term. Instead of the mutual contact of mouths, there is a *nasal contact,* with delicate, deliberate inhalation.

A report from Tokyo which appeared in the Press, in September, 1924, was typical of the difference in Japanese ideas and feelings; of the indecency, even obscenity, of the mouth kiss, in their eyes. In an exhibition of European works of art, a reproduction of Rodin's group, *"Le Baiser,"* was concealed behind a bamboo screen and not open to the public.

And it is known throughout the world that the erotic technique of the East has not been impaired by omitting the mouth to mouth kiss. Both Near and Far East value and practice erotic technique, as a rule, far more highly and generally than the Western world, and we can learn much from them in this art.

And the olfactory, or nasal kiss—the sniffing or inhalation of each other's skin and breath, is much more practiced in the Western world than is commonly supposed. I shall refer to this later on.

which adolescent young people venture on, largely in a spirit of curiosity and experiment.

All these *varieties* of the genus *kiss* lack the typical characteristic of the erotic kiss.   For the erotic kiss is mutual; it is given and received *from mouth to mouth with mutual pressure.*

This is its signature and its significance.

The erotic kiss itself is rich in variations.   It may "brush the bloom" like a butterfly's wing by a light stroking of lips with other pursed lips; be, as it were, an "effleurage," to use the technical term of massage therapy for gentle stroking, and of poetry for fleeting, hardly perceptible contacts.   From its lightest, faintest form, it may run the gamut of intimacy and intensity to the pitch of *Maraichinage,* in which the couple, sometimes for hours, mutually explore and caress the inside of each other's mouths with their tongues, as profoundly as possible.[1]   But it is indisputable that the greatest penetration in kissing is not for *all* lovers the same as the maximum pleasure and stimulation.   Mastery of this art is a matter of delicate differences rather than of *one* limited and sharply defined style.

But the *tongue* is indispensable in the erotic kiss; and "plays lead" in its most important variations.   This may take the form of vigorous and pronounced penetration, but in a much more subtly differentiated manner than among the primitive peasantry of the Vendée.   Indeed, the tongue-kiss is most captivating when the tip of the tongue very lightly and gently titillates the beloved's tongue and lips.

Three senses are blended in the kiss: touch, taste, and smell.   *Sound* should be conspicuous by its absence!   The sense of smell is important here.   There are differences and

---

[1] The name "Maraichinage" derives from the Maraichins or inhabitants of the district Pays de Mont in the Vendée (Brittany), where this form of love-play is extremely popular among young unmarried people. The publicity of its performance in the Pays de Mont, does not seem to detract from its enjoyment in the least.   This is perhaps because *Marcel Baudouin,* medical man and local mayor, has been cited as recommending Maraichinage as "a real antidote against depopulation," in an essay submitted to the Parisian Académie de Médecine, by no less a personage than *Debove.*

Incidentally, those who wish to give a learned name to this practice should not talk of "Cataglottism" but rather "Kataglossism."

blends of the personal odors from the skin around the mouth aperture, from the cavity of the mouth and from the breath. We have mentioned these above in treating of the erotic influence of personal odors. Probably the special scent of the *skin* is more important than is generally supposed. In any case there is much foundation to the derivation of kissing from the mutual nosing and sniffing of animals.[1] In those human races who *inhale* or *sniff* instead of *tasting* when they kiss (or as we call it "rub noses"), the scent of the skin is probably felt as the predominant attraction, though the breath is also perceived.

And no doubt also the sense of touch receives impressions, though probably less finely graduated and intense than in the kiss from mouth to mouth.

And one sensory element of the mouth and tongue kiss (*buccal* or *bucco-lingual*) is absent in the nasal kiss: the factor of *taste*. This is a factor which most people fail definitely to perceive, and there are only very few connoisseurs who can discriminate and describe the individual flavor of their beloved's kisses as the Ancient Romans could.[2] But there is a faint yet undeniable difference in the kisses of different individuals or of the same individual at different times: a difference perceptible to the sense of taste, though hardly definable in words. It probably arises from the natural moisture of the mouth and the salivary glands. We know that the composition of the saliva varies; we have tested this by physiological chemistry (apart from morbid states) in strictly normal processes, such as pregnancy, and we know that various substances, introduced into the body through the veins or vagina, become incorporated in the saliva.[3]

All this suffices to give a certain individual flavor to the moisture of the mouth and throat, and we must remember that flavor and odor are not ever *entirely* separable;

---

[1] See *Archiv für Kriminalanthropologie,* 1908, and the learned periodical *Sexualprobleme,* 1908, p. 430.

[2] For instance, the kisses of *Poppæa,* Nero's second wife, are described as tasting of wild berries. *Cf.* "Song of Solomon."

[3] Why should there not be differences here during menstruation, and the phases of the cyclic ebb and flow? Or under psychic influences? *Cf.* the transmission of the smell of semen, mentioned in Chapter III.

and this gives individuality to kisses.   For the erotic kiss, at least the longer and more fervent erotic kisses between lovers, is essentially, and in contrast to the formal, conventional kiss, not dry, but moist.   The moisture passes from each mouth to the other, even if in a very small amount. And many lovers, perhaps most, prefer an amount that is not very small.   The poets who rhapsodize, "And I will drink thy kisses, as oft, of yore," are literally correct, as a matter of erotic technique—for erotic kisses are drunk, or, at least, *sipped*.

I need not here repeat what has been said of the tactile sensations conveyed in kissing by the stroking (friction) and titillation of and by the lips and tongue.

Here I will only emphasize two contributory factors, which have been ignored in Chapter III.   The first is the peculiar tactile sensation afforded in kissing by *suction,* which is generally present, in greater or less degree, and which may be modified and varied, according to whether it is *actively exercised, passively experienced,* or *a blend of both.*

The second factor, unmentioned till now, is the use of the *teeth* in the kiss.   They not only support the lips, but in the more passionate kisses they are often active agents.

Indeed, both the active and the passive partner feel a peculiarly keen, erotic pleasure in the tiny, delicate, gentle or sharp but never really painful nips man and woman exchange as the love-play quickens, especially when such caresses are applied in rapid succession and in adjacent places.

I have tried to show how manifold and especially how multiform are the components whose *tout ensemble* is the erotic kiss.   It is self-evident that there are innumerable possibilities of variation, shading, diminuendoes and crescendoes here.

The love-expert knows them and uses them.

The novice should learn them here, for they will be all needed in Ideal Marriage.

Balzac says: "If a man cannot afford distinct and different pleasures to the woman he has made his wife, on two successive nights—he has married too soon."

And the husband has indeed married too soon, if he does not know how kisses may vary between those who love each other—or cannot make use of this knowledge, in practice.

Love-play knows not only the erotic kiss from mouth to mouth; kisses on various parts of the body are also appropriate and acceptable at this stage of approach.

Such kisses can be graduated, primarily, according to the place to which they are applied—mouth and breasts are specially *erogenous areas,* but apart from them, it may be said that erotic sensibility increases, from the periphery towards the center; from forehead and temples downwards over the cheeks and throat; from finger-tips along the palms and arms; from the insteps and ankles, up the calves and thighs, steadily increasing as the genital organs are approached. For details we may refer the student to what has been said at the conclusion of Chapter III., on "Erogenous Zones." A further diversity may be introduced here, in *intensity of degree,* by alternating light, stroking or "tickling" kisses with strong suction and pressure with the teeth. But, in contrast to the play of sensation in kisses from *mouth to mouth,* in which active and passive tactile feelings are *reciprocal,* the bodily kiss gives a very different kind of pleasure, according to whether it is given or received. Both feelings can be erotically delightful, and the more so if each partner can be, simultaneously, kisser and kissed.

In analyzing these caresses it is evident that the stimulations received by the partner who is kissed are wholly tactile, whereas the partner who kisses receives through lips and tongue-tip and transmits to the conscious nerve-centers in the brain sensations both of touch and scent.

In fact, the body kiss gives play to a distinctly primitive *olfactory* or *inhalation* method—far more so than the typical mouth to mouth kiss of the West; and not only for the active partner but for the passive as well. For the peculiar sensations which the nerves of the outer epidermis receive (from the current of air which varies in temperature from cool to warm, as it is inhaled or exhaled, and which almost resembles an irregular intermittent pneumatic massage, and is certainly the chief agent here), are felt as extremely agreeable by many persons, and apparently consciously registered as such—by women, especially.

For the active partner the type of olfactory sensation received varies, of course, according to the kissed place. This needs no further proof.   Equally, there is no need to enlarge on the influence the sense of taste can exert, in certain circumstances, individuals, and bodily areas.

I have mentioned the part the *teeth* can play in erotic kisses, both in those from mouth to mouth and on other parts of the body, and have emphasized the entire normality, in love technique, of slight, gentle bites, or rather *nips,* which do not break the skin.   But, of course, this does not mean that even these playful bites are exchanged in every erotic kiss; far from it.   Nevertheless, when the love-play culminates and the greatest possible intensity of feeling *is expressed in kisses, both partners tend to use their teeth, and in so doing there is naught abnormal, morbid or perverse.*

Can the same be said of the real love-bite that breaks the skin and draws blood?   Up to a certain degree—yes. But then there comes a limit beyond which lies—pathological and perverted sexuality.   And yet it is very difficult to decide exactly where this border-line lies.   As in all departments of emotional life, the stages from the normal to the morbid, from the intense to the bizarre are so gradual that they can hardly be delimited by any hard and fast frontier.   Does not every devoted lover prove himself, in a sense, "as one of unsound mind," whose aim is abnormally limited, whose field of vision is absurdly narrow?   And yet there must be some rule, some guiding sign, some boundary! And I think we are justified in drawing the line, both in the love-bite and wheresoever else sexual pleasure is stirred at the infliction or endurance of pain (bodily or psychic), and of drawing it clearly and firmly at the first signs of cruelty.[1]

---

[1] We are not called here to discuss the interrelations of cruelty to the sexual sphere. But it must be fully and frankly admitted that these in-

The *normal love-bite* generally occurs at the more intense moments of erotic play or during actual coitus, whether in the swift crescendo of sensation or the supreme moment. The most favored places in the man's body are the shoulder, especially the left shoulder, or the space just below the collar-bone; in the woman's the neck—again on the left side —and the flanks of the abdomen. This selection depends probably in part on relative bodily stature and positions in coitus, but also on obscure atavisms which we have not yet traced or understood. Women are conspicuously more addicted to love-bites than are men. It is not at all unusual for a woman of passionate nature to leave a memento of sexual union on the man's shoulder in the shape of a little slanting oval outline of tooth-marks. The bite occurs almost without exception *during coitus* or immediately afterwards, while the generally gentler, slighter, or at least less noticeable love-bites given by the man to his partner, are part of the erotic play before, or the final stage after, coitus.

But does this mean that the male partner is so much gentler and tenderer than the woman? That he holds himself back, even in the supreme ecstasy? No! far from it; that would be a poor and disappointing experience for the woman. For there can be no doubt that women would not and do not believe themselves really loved unless they feel that the man is completely carried away by his emotion at the appropriate time. And many blue marks of bruises on women's arms are witnesses of the man's *"tourbillon."*

To quote from Dr. Havelock Ellis's "Love and Pain," Vol. III. of *Studies in Psychology:* "We have to admit that a certain pleasure in manifesting his power over a woman by inflicting pain upon her is an outcome and survival of the

---

teractions are manifold and extremely powerful. Nevertheless, they are pathological—for practical everyday life, at least—and belong to that type of sexual abnormality which, in its pronounced form is most hideous, devastating and inhuman. While avoiding these horrors, in thought and deed, let us remember that like most other forms of moral insanity these too have their roots in perfectly normal natures and conditions. That is, tendencies in this direction exist in every normal person, and can especially be observed in children, but fortunately also can be successfully transmuted and overcome.

primitive process of courtship, and an almost or quite normal constituent of the sexual impulse in man.   But it must be at once added that in the normal, well-balanced and well-conditioned man, this constituent of the sexual impulse, when present, is always held in check.   When the normal man inflicts, or feels the impulse to inflict, some degree of physical pain on the woman he loves, he can scarcely be said to be moved by cruelty.   He feels, more or less obscurely, that the pain he inflicts, or desires to inflict, is really a part of his love, and that, moreover, it is not really resented by the woman on whom it is exercised.   His feeling is by no means always according to knowledge, but it has to be taken into account as an essential part of his emotional state.   The physical force, the teasing and bullying, which he may be moved to exert under the stress of sexual excitement are, he usually more or less unconsciously persuades himself, not really unwelcome to the object of his love.   Moreover, we have to bear in mind—a very significant fact from more than one point of view—that the normal manifestations of a woman's sexual pleasure are exceedingly like those of pain. 'The outward manifestations of pain,' as a lady very truly writes, 'tears, cries, etc., which are laid stress on, to prove the cruelty of the person who inflicts it, are not so different from those of a woman in the ecstasy of passion, when she implores the man to desist, though that is really the last thing that she desires.'   If a man is convinced that he is causing real and unmitigated pain, he becomes repentant at once.   If this is not the case he must either be regarded as a radically abnormal person, or as carried away by passion to a point of temporary insanity."

What both man and woman, driven by obscure primitive urges, wish to feel in the sexual act, is the essential force of *maleness,* which expresses itself in a sort of violent and absolute *possession* of the woman.   And so both of them can and do exult in a certain degree of male aggression and dominance—whether actual or apparent—which proclaims this essential force.

Hence the sharp gripping and pinching of the woman's arms and sides and nates.   Hence too, the significant fact that this masculine erotic manifestation belongs to the moments of coitus itself, and not to its preliminaries.[1]

Contrariwise, the peculiar violence of the *love-bite* is seldom used by the man during the sexual act. This is in itself remarkable, for his forefathers in the dark ages of our semi-anthropoid and animal evolution, might be supposed to have bequeathed to him the imperious instinct of fastening himself on to his mate with teeth and jaws, during the act. Perhaps there are atavistic reasons why the relatively few and slight love-bites given by the man during coitus are, almost without exception, on the left side of the woman's throat. Or it may simply be because of the relative mutual attitudes during the act.

And the origin of the love-bite is quite different from that of the pinching, gripping and thrusting forms of violence alluded to above.

I think there can be no error in assuming that the feminine inclination to bite during the sexual act[2] arises mainly from the wish to give a kiss more intense than is humanly possible.[3] This leads to *strong suction* and to sharp use of the teeth, and thus to a feeling of satisfaction on the part of the biting woman, and of strong exultation of the bitten partner. This feeling of the bitten man is complex, interwoven of joy and pain. Of joy, physically through the strong stimulus to the nerves, and psychically through the consciousness or semi-consciousness of the beloved woman's need to give her love the supreme expression. And of pain—which in a state of acute sexual excitement is hardly felt as such—and in most cases would be only very slight, as the "normal" love-bite does *not* break the skin. It cannot therefore break a small vein, or draw blood, for the slightly blood-tinged

---

[1] Hence, also, *the intentionally violent specific movement in coitus,* to which many men sometimes resort, during the act, and which are even more appreciated by their partners than by themselves! This savage thrusting movement does not proceed from the conscious wish to heighten sensation by friction, for the special stimulus of friction is often keenest when the pressure is slightest.

[2] We have already seen that this inclination is greater in woman than in man, who has his muscular power, and uses it wildly, as a vehicle for the expression of his sexual ecstasy. Ellis and other authorities agree here.

[3] Another theory of the origin of kissing derives it from the biting of our animal ancestors during coitus. According to this view, the *bite* is the original manifestation, the *kiss* the secondary and derivative.

moisture on the bruised place is, as a rule, only saliva with a slight admixture of blood from the pressure of the woman's gums; it makes no real wound, only a bruise which for a few days, or at most weeks, turns from purplish to greenish-yellow and vanishes without a scar. Such cases as those of Edith Swanneck, immortalized by Heine,[1] and famed in Old English tradition, are so rare that they cannot be regarded as "normal" actions, though such actions are not necessarily committed by *"abnormal"* persons.

For such a love-bite as Edith Swanneck's, the previous explanations seem superficial and inadequate. It almost suggests an association of the two primitive urges of self-preservation through attack, and reproduction through sex; such as is found as the rule in some species of the less evolved animals,[2] and can be recognized in some forms of mental derangement.

And this strange momentary merging of two primeval forces may also account for some of the "normal," gentler love-bites.

And the same may be true of another motive which un-doubtedly can inspire the *coital bite*. It can be given out of *concentrated sexual hatred:* not out of any degree of sexual love. Only a very superficial observer can miss the primitive repulsion and antagonism between the sexes which are as real as and more permanent than the attraction. The attraction may, and often does, prevail for a time; but the antipathy is there, and its expression is much wider and often quite as vigorous. Underneath love there always lies in wait hatred.[3] And surely this is one of the profoundest causes of the tragedy of humanity! It is this possibility that gives such a sinister suggestion to the love-bite; and to the trium-phant slap with the open hand on the nates which many a

---

[1] Heine's poem: *"On Hastings' Battlefield"* :

> And on his shoulder she beheld three scars,
> And kissed them once again: wounds of no wars,
> No foeman's brand had smitten—
> Three little scars, her own white teeth had bitten.

[2] Certain spiders and insects (mantis).

[3] We shall devote special study to the combat against this sex antag-onism and endeavor to illuminate the problem of preserving married happi-ness from a purely psychological aspect.

man either gives his partner, or feels an impulse to give her, at the conclusion of coitus. For these manifestations are quite "normal," both in the sense of frequency and of fundamental unconscious motives.

But do not let us dwell longer on this tragic note. It is one of the main objects of Ideal Marriage to make the love-motive soar and suffuse and triumph over its ugly elemental foe. Let us also remember, in the sense of Ellis's great chapter on *"Love and Pain,"* the words of Matilda Wesendonck's poem:[1]

> "If only Pain brings ecstasy
> —Thanks, thanks to Nature, yet again,
> For having given to me such Pain."

Love-play should and does not only express itself in kisses, but in touches and manual caresses in all degrees, from gentlest titillation and lightest stroking with the tips of the fingers, to gripping and pressing with the palm and fingers together, though here, too, it may be enunciated as a rule that the lightest touches are the most effective.[2] The stimuli given by manipulation are about equal for the active and the passive partner, although different in color-tone as it were. They are strongest when activity and passivity alternate, and, above all, when they are simultaneous. And, of course, for both modes, *psychic preparedness* is absolutely essential: the consciousness must receive these impressions without reluctance or resistance.

For the passive partner, the exact bodily area manipulated makes a great deal of difference. In this connection, we may refer to what has been said, in Chapter III., about the sense of touch; we may re-emphasize the importance of the *erogenous* zones, while remembering that these are not identical in all individuals—or, at least, do not possess identical degrees of sensibility. Finally, we may urge the marriage partners to explore and study each other's idiosyncrasies in

---

[1] Set to music by R. Wagner.

[2] A similar gripping and kneading movement of the hand is known in therapeutic massage as *pétrissage.* Moreover, another method of massage, the *tapotement,* quite light, elastic tapping or patting, may be used with distinctly strong erotic effect, especially on the loins and pelvic region, where it is even more stimulating than "pétrissage." But it is rarer in conjugal relations, as it is not so obvious and needs some skill in practice.

this respect, and to make frequent and fervent use of such knowledge.

For the active agent in these caresses, the particular place favored has importance, because it is in itself stimulating and delightful to know, feel and see the delight and stimulation one can give. And in these matters pleasure shared is double pleasure indeed. The particular structure, and particularly nerve supply, of the place caressed, is the determinant of the degree of pleasure received.

And, of course, the specifically sexual organs and their environs are the main focus of attraction.

Love-play reaches its maximum in contact with the *external* sexual organs: for only these *external* organs are *normally* in question at this stage of the love-drama.

We must speak of this in detail, but must first mention the breasts and nipples, which are also sexual organs with high erotic value. We may again stress the extreme sensitiveness of the nipples (including the *areolæ*) to contact by tongue, or finger, or by definite suction. These caresses give special delight when a certain degree of excitement has already been reached. And this effect is further enhanced when the nipples themselves have become *erect*—for they are just as capable of erection (proportionately) as the clitoris and penis.[1] Erection of the nipple (*mammillary erection* or *congestion*) can occur either as a result of direct mechanical stimulation (touching, sucking) or by reflex action, in harmony with the congestion of other sex organs, especially of the clitoris; or, more rarely, and in women of extremely ardent temperament, in response to purely psychic influences. Apparently, frequent mammillary erection develops increased mammillary sensitiveness. The sensation afforded is strongest if it coincides with stimulation of another erogenous zone. When the nipple and the clitoris are simultaneously and delicately caressed, they mutually enhance each other's stimulation, and this double contact gives to many women the maximum of possible pleasure outside coitus.

The man's nipple is built on the same plan as the woman's,

---

[1] But these processes come about in quite a different way, as the structure of the nipple is different.

but is a much more rudimentary organ.   Therefore it is much less sensitive sexually.   But it is capable of receiving sexual sensations and becoming erect (or turgid or tense).

Mammillary stimulation is agreeable to the stimulator as well as to the passive partner, but generally to a lesser degree, and in a predominantly *psychic* mode, through the consciousness of conferred pleasure.   For the structure and appearance of the nipples are not, *per se,* calculated to rouse strong erotic excitement.

The breasts, on the contrary, are erotically very conspicuously attractive.   If there is any psychic inclination to approach, the mere sight or outline of the bosom is somewhat exciting to men; and to touch this portion of the beloved woman's body increases desire.   For the woman, too, this kind of caress—which must not be too rough—is full of sexual delight.   Women desire their breasts to be admired and fondled, and often seek such endearments or suggest them, more or less clearly.   Nevertheless, speaking generally, the active man seems as a rule more excited by this kind of caress than the woman who receives them.

In any erotic play executed with delicate reverence and consideration—and, above all, when the lovers have not become quite accustomed and attuned to one another—a considerable amount of time should be given to kisses and manual caresses before the genitals are touched.   After gentle strokings and claspings of the accessory organs the hand should lightly and timidly brush the abdomen, the mons-pubis, the inner side of the thighs; alight swiftly on the sexual organs and pass at once to the other thigh.   Only by a cautious and circuitous route should it approach the holy place of sex and tenderly seek admittance.[1]

At this point begins the stage in the love-drama which I have termed "local stimulation."   If the seeking and stroking hand was the husband's, the thighs of his wife will have slightly separated at his touch, and her special organs have become more accessible.   And if his previous caresses have caused a certain degree of excitement, these feminine organs will have received a larger blood-supply and begun

---

[1] In what follows it has been our effort to attain perfect clearness, while preserving the dignity of science.

to expand. The outer lips pout and part, revealing the clitoris and inner lips. And the glands of the vestibule moisten the vulva with their special clear and slippery secretion.

Thus the husband's caressing hand has no difficulty in finding the vulva, and continuing its gentle endearments. These will be chiefly bestowed on the *Glans clitoridis,* the tiny organ which projects in the center; all the more so, as excitement will have already congested the clitoris, leading to its expansion and the *retraction* of its prepuce. Thus the finger cannot miss the most sensitive spot of all (where the *frenulum* or rim is attached), and this sensitiveness is multiplied by the erection of the tiny organ. This form of contact—almost inadvertent at first—is acutely delightful to the wife and increases her desire, incalculably. And the man's increases in response, as he feels her pleasure at his touch. And then there follow spontaneously and as a matter of course, the prolongation of clitoridal titillation and friction, and of the adjacent structures: the inner lips, the orifice of the introitus vaginæ, and the whole shaft of the clitoris; but the main focus of pleasure is in the Glans clitoridis. And this local (genital) stimulation, to the accompaniment of kisses and words of love, with a crescendo of emotion, whose most effective instrument is the *exchange of manipulation,* continues and accelerates itself till the male member, or *phallos,* is introduced into the vagina; and with this, the aim and *finale* of the love-play is reached, and merges into the beginning of sexual communion, or coitus.

We have stressed the charm of *reciprocity* in this local stimulation. But the manipulation of the male organ by the wife is not such an obvious and inevitable phase as the active *rôle* of the husband. Nevertheless, it is very valuable and significant. A woman who has been fully initiated and possessed by the husband she loves, invariably, almost automatically, tries to touch and fondle his genitals with her hand as soon as the erotic love-play—both general and particularly *local*—has stirred her sexually, to a certain degree of ardor. The objective realization of his excitement (for he will be, by that time, in full erection, or if not, will become so, at her touch) is a supreme psycho-erotic joy to her. And she expresses this joy by extending her clasp and casual stroking of the phallos, to a systematic stimulation. She tries to find the most acutely sensitive spots, or if she has knowledge and experience of them, she applies what she knows. And the man's lightning response, his "yes, yes" and cries of pleasure, the crescendo of his whole organism, teach her, without delay.[1]

Nevertheless, she will do well to observe a certain diffidence and economy of direct *penile* stimulation. And this, not only or mainly because extreme *directness* in the woman's sexual manifestations is apt to repel her husband; on this subject we shall have more to say later. But, above all, because *in general* women require *longer time and a wider range of stimuli* than men do, in order to attain to the culmination of pleasure, or *orgasm*. If the man receives too many powerful sensations before actual *coitus* begins, then only a very little more is needed to bring about his *ejaculation* and *orgasm*. And it is more than probable that this "little more" is not adequate to give the woman what she, too, requires. Thus she fails to attain satisfaction owing to her own mistake in erotic technique. And it goes without saying that *local stimulation* can only be *occasionally* necessary in the man's case, *e.g.*, when he is, for some reason or another, less than normally excitable, below par in virility or just after previous coitus.

It will be equally clear from the preceding remarks that for many women the exact reverse holds good. At least so long as and until they are erotically experienced. Such women, in order to attain the mutual simultaneous culmination of perfect coitus, require both extensive and intensive initiation and preparation, including not only an artistic prelude and a finely planned and progressive love-play, but

---

[1] If slight stimulation is sought, the front surface of the organ should be stroked, specially in the urethral area and rim of the glans or tip. Stronger sensations are caused if the shaft is clasped from above and encircled with palm and fingers; and by a definite rotary friction of the glans. But the latter portion must be sufficiently lubricated by the thin mucus discharge or pain and inflammation will ensue, not pleasure. Or, the shaft can be encircled as though by a ring. The most acute and subtle stimulation is caused by slight friction of the frenulum preputii or band of the foreskin.

also and especially local stimulation, tactfully and considerately begun by the husband, and executed with persistence and insight, even at the cost of considerable self-abnegation and passional restraint on his part.

And this local stimulation is often far from being so easy as I have indicated above in describing what happens in normal satisfactory love technique.   The wife does not always give access to the husband's caressing hand.   And if, when gentle pressure and words of reassurance and entreaty on his part have succeeded here, there is not the necessary excitement and desire on her part, to cause swelling of the labia, dilation of the vulva, and erection of the clitoris— then, as these manifestations are normal and desirable *before coitus, it is both stupid and grossly selfish of the husband to attempt it, if they are absent.*   For it means that he will leave her ungratified.   Prolonged local stimulation is the only means to save the situation here, for it is the only way to give the wife the requisite degree of local congestion and expansion and psychic readiness.   "Praeterea censeo, vulvam sacratissimæ Majestatis, ante coitum, diutius esse titillandam."   (*I.e.,* "Furthermore, I am of the opinion that the sexual organs" [*i.e.,* in this case the clitoris] "of your Most Sacred Majesty should be titillated for some length of time before coitus.")   Thus ran the concluding sentence and substance of the diagnosis received by the Empress Maria Theresa from her celebrated Imperial physician, the Dutchman *van Swieten,* when she consulted him about her early sterility.   History has testified to the efficacy of his prescription in the Empress's sixteen children!   We will not here further deal with the connection between dyspareunia (scientific term for inability of husband and wife to achieve the acme of sexual pleasure at the same or approximate moments) and sterility, however interesting and important the topic undoubtedly is.   We will only repeat, with all possible seriousness and emphasis, that much marital unhappiness, attributed to the apparent sexual frigidity of the wife, could be avoided and prevented if the medical profession had not allowed themselves to be deterred from explaining many technicalities of a normal married life, owing to a mixture of false modesty and professional reserve and did not still often prudishly abstain in appropriate cases (and such are not rare!) from repeating the advice which that wise expert in medicine and human nature gave to his ultra-chaste and moral Empress.[1]

And we shall, in the course of this study, prove that they would not only be disciples of the famous Viennese clinician, in so doing, but of the leading Christian moral theologians as well.

Local specific stimulation may be retarded and impaired by inadequate amount of mucus secretion in the wife, owing to poor reaction of the vestibular glands to previous bodily or psychic excitations. For if lubrication is not ample, any continuous friction of the vulva, clitoris and introitus vaginæ, whether during manipulation or—more vigorously —in coitus, causes pain instead of pleasure, and makes these tender tissues so irritable and inflamed that, if the contact persists, any sexual activity becomes impossible[2] through the pain it causes. Therefore the *natural lubricant* must be —as soon as it is evident that distillation is delayed or insufficient—replaced by some artificial preparation which will make the parts slippery without in itself conducing to irritation.

The greasy ointments frequently in use for this purpose[3] do not fulfill either requirement. They do set up irritation because they are not soluble in water, and thus cannot be entirely removed by the most vigorous ablutions. They ferment, become rancid, and promote irritation. The same is true of vaseline, although this does not become rancid. Its indissolubility and the consequent impossibility of washing it completely away, make its application to the vulva seriously unwise. The medical and pharmaceutical preparations used in gynæcological practice to facilitate the insertion of a finger or surgical instrument, are also unsuitable for

---

[1] *Cf.* her "Morals," Commission and its Laws.

[2] The same is true in the man's case, as we have said. We will only add here, that "dry" friction can easily lead to inflammation of the glans and especially of the prepuce.

[3] The purpose is, as a rule, only to ensure that vulva and penis are slippery enough to make insertion feasible.

coitus, because they contain soap, glycerine, or stronger antiseptics, and the necessary protracted friction causes them to inflame the mucous membranes.

So the most suitable genital lubricants are vegetable (herbal) preparations which are soluble in water, and contain very few irritants. They most resemble the natural secretions which they replace.

But the most simple and obvious substitute for the inadequate lubricant is the natural moisture of the salivary glands. It is always available; of course it has the disadvantage of very rapid evaporation. This makes it insufficient in cases where actual communion is prevented by lack of distillation. And during a very protracted local or genital manipulation, this form of substitute must be applied to the vulva, not once, but repeatedly. And this may best, most appropriately, and most expeditiously be done without the intermediary offices of the fingers, but through what I prefer to term the *kiss of genital stimulation,* or *genital kiss:* by gentle and soothing caresses with lips and tongue.[1]

This type of stimulation has many advantages. First of all the lack of local secretion ceases to be a drawback, and even becomes an advantage. Secondly, the acuteness of the pleasure it excites and the variety of tactile sensation it provides, will ensure that the previous deficiency is made good; *i.e.,* that sexual excitement and desire reach such a point that—either by these means alone or aided by other endearments—distillation takes place, heralding psychic and bodily readiness for a sexual communion, successful and satisfactory to both partners.

The genital kiss is particularly calculated to overcome

---

[1] As all expert readers will easily understand, I have intentionally *not* employed the more or less technical terms for the attainment of orgasm through bucco-lingual contact with the genitals, for *this* reason: I refuse to use these expressions which almost always refer to pathological practices, when I treat of manifestations which are, in their present context, *absolutely unobjectionable and legitimate,* ethically, æsthetically and hygienically. (Of course, their hygienic and æsthetic value depends entirely on the spotless cleanliness and wholesomeness of the bodies of both husband and wife.)

frigidity and fear in hitherto inexperienced women who have had no erotic practice, and are as yet hardly capable of specific sexual desire.

But—the husband must exercise the *greatest gentleness, the most delicate reverence!* The old proverb says : from the sublime to the ridiculous is but a step. In the lore of love, this proverb means that *supreme beauty and hideous ugliness are separated by a border-line so slight that our minds and senses may transgress it, unawares!*

We may assume that it is unnecessary to describe the technique of this form of genital stimulation. It may be constructed from what has already been said in detail, about the kiss in general, and about the special structure of the feminine organs.

The same obtains as regards the *analysis* of this procedure. I will only emphasize that the sensations of taste and smell are more likely to be of greater importance here than in the mouth kiss! Therefore, and as the special situation and secretions of the genital organs present difficulties in this respect, let the passive partner take care, to prevent repulsive and unfortunate impressions by the most scrupulous and meticulous personal cleanliness! We have indicated some special precautions in Chapter III.

For the *active* partner, the pleasures of the genital kiss are *wholly psychic.* They center round the joy of giving joy to and rousing desire in the beloved, and the imaginative realization of this pleasure and desire. (Of course, this psychic and emotional pleasure may be intense, and transmit itself to the *periphery,* in the form of increased tumescence.) The feelings of the passive partner, on the other hand, however strong their emotional undertones, are predominantly peripheral, *i.e.,* physical.

The fact that in this particular form of caress more than any other, the man is generally the active partner, is because of his naturally greater initiative, and also because of the difference in the *tempo* of the respective erotic reactions, which is usual while the woman is still a novice.

On occasions when the man's reactions are less rapid, the woman may with advantage take the more active part during the second act of the love-drama, and *herself, most successfully, give—instead of receiving—the genital kiss.*

Is it necessary, however, to emphasize the need for æsthetic delicacy and discretion here? To advise her to abstain entirely from such contacts during the early stages of married life, and only to venture on them later, and experimentally? To remind her that she runs greater risks than he does, in approaching that treacherous frontier between supreme beauty and base ugliness? I think there is *no* need; for she knows this intuitively, she feels it with all a woman's instinctive modesty.

But, of course, the psychic situation is very different when, through mutual memories of joy and love, a happy adaptation has been achieved, and given her the artistry of experience.

Then a certain feminine initiative and aggression brings a refreshing variety. Let her be the wooer sometimes, not always the wooed. She can be so while quite retaining her distinctive dignity and sweetness. This *rôle* of wooer can express her love in a very desirable way, and be intensely gratifying to the husband, who feels that he not only feels desire, but inspires it, too.

In this more evolved and richer harmony of relationship, the use and enjoyment of genital stimulation and the genital kiss, will depend wholly on inclination, temperament, individual sensibility and practice of both partners. They may be enjoyed alternately or sometimes simultaneously.

For in every form of sport or art, every adept makes full use of every aspect and possibility, in order to perfect and vary his achievement. He neglects neither the grand effects nor the delicate details. And so, how should it be otherwise in the art of love which is the richest and subtlest of all?

CHAPTER IX

1. *Physiological and Technical Considerations*

IN *union* or *coitus,* prelude and love-play attain their goal, and sexual relationships their culmination.

In its ideal form, husband and wife take a fully equal and reciprocal share in this most intimate merging; their souls meet and touch as do their bodies; they become *one.*

And fortunately this ideal is not unattainable; it may and sometimes does become actual.

This full equivalence and mutuality obtain in Ideal Marriage, even though the man is the transmitter and the woman the receiver. Even though he is certainly, and must be, essentially active, she is quite as certainly not the purely passive instrument which she has been so long considered, and still is considered, far too often. And in any case she *ought not* to be a purely passive instrument! For sexual union only takes place *physiologically* (*i.e.,* according to the laws of Nature), rightly and suitably, if and when both partners fully participate and feel supreme sexual pleasure and complete relaxation or relief. If, anywhere and in any circumstances, the demand for equal rights for both sexes is *incontestable,* it is so in regard to equal consent and equal pleasure in sexual union, and in the interests of *both.* Therefore in Ideal Marriage, the man does not perform the act on a passive woman, but they *both together* achieve *sexual communion.*

Sexual communion (coitus, copulation, the sexual act, or connection, or intercourse) is the third act in the love drama. It begins with the insertion of the male penis (or *phallos* as the Greeks termed the erect and active organ) into the female vagina (*immissio penis*); and reaches culmination in the ejaculation of semen into the vagina, and in the approximately simultaneous orgasm or summit of enjoyment in both partners. Communion ends when the phallos is removed from the vagina.

The accumulation or *summation* of excitement necessary for both the male and female organism, in order to reach the *acme* of pleasure, is achieved through a succession of stroking or thrusting movements (friction). As the phallos is rubbed and pressed against the folds and pads of the vaginal walls (especially of the anterior surface) the nerves of the male organ, and especially of its tip or glans, become so stimulated that tension is finally relieved in the sympathetic-spinal reflex discharge or ejaculation. Concurrently, the increasing and overwhelming sensory impressions received by the cerebral cortex (higher nerve centers) are felt psychically as acute pleasure. These feelings increase in force till they attain their summit in the second in which ejaculation begins. When ejaculation occurs, the pleasurable sensations continue in the form of satisfied relaxation and relief. When it ceases, the *orgasm* or physical discharge is at an end. The psychic and physical sensations die away, into gratification (*bien-être*), a sort of drowsy bliss.

The stimuli of the penile nerves may differ in degrees of intensity and shades of quality; and there are corresponding diversities in the sensations of pleasure they bestow. It is of much importance in determining these sensations: whether the stimuli are localized mainly in the *frenulum preputii* or the posterior rim of the *glans;* whether the vagina is a trifle wider or narrower; whether it is smooth or delicately folded and crinkled; whether the *introitus vaginæ* fits the shaft of the penis closely, or hardly clasps it at all; whether the tip of the penis touches the *Portio vaginalis* or cannot reach it. Thus it will be readily understood that a certain correspondence or *congruence* of the sexual organs of the partners is essential for ideal communion. A normal penis can no more be perfectly stimulated by (and/or afford perfect stimulation to) an unusually wide vulva and slack vagina than can an abnormally undeveloped or inadequately erected penis attain satisfaction by, or give it to, normal female genitalia. If a strong desire for sexual satisfaction has been aroused, minor stimuli certainly suffice to cause ejaculation and a *relative* culmination of pleasure or, at least, relief. But the glorious consciousness of having tasted the supreme pleasure, and the soothing, complete relaxation are lacking, and with them the psychic effect, at once tender and triumphant, of an ideally successful *coitus*.

Therefore, for the man as well as the woman—and even from his wholly egotistic point of view—it is anything but a matter of indifference whether she is "cold" or responsive, actively engaged or passively submissive. And the many men who "have connection" or "copulate," regardless of their wives' participation in pleasure, are not only callous, coarse and inconsiderate, but certainly also and equally *stupid*. For the physical stimulation given to the male organ by the contact of the female genitalia is considerably increased by sexual excitement and desire on her part. Quite apart from the lubricating secretions of the vestibular glands which counteract pain in both partners, the woman's excitement and desire congests the *bulbi,* clitoris, and the vaginal walls, slightly contracts the latter and draws the mouth of the womb downwards, thus producing an elastic tension throughout orifice and passage, which cling closely and with a velvety softness to the male organ, and give the best conditions for further successful stimulation. This vaginal clasp, in its pillowy softness and delicacy, its intense warmth, is in itself a delight. A further delight, very acute and individual, is given by the occasional undulations or contractions of the vaginal muscles which occur in some women (not by any means in all) during strong sexual excitement. Finally, a most important factor is the involuntary convulsion of the muscles of the pelvic floor in the last stages of excitement and during the actual orgasm; and equally so, the conscious and voluntary rhythmic contractions of these muscles (particularly of the *Levator vaginæ* and *Constrictor cunni*), which can be operated in order to increase the pleasure of both partners. The acutest stimuli are afforded by the reciprocal pressure and friction of the phallos and the vulva and vagina. It is obvious that this pressure must be intensified when the female organs are sufficiently congested and, as it were, erected, to clasp and grip the male organ as closely as possible.

In a later chapter we shall enumerate the various ways in which this friction may be applied, and explain their technique, which has great importance.

Generally, the active agent in genital and coital friction is the husband; the woman may participate with the most intense appreciation, but her *movements* are as a rule much slighter. But there are variations and permutations, many shapes and colors in love's kaleidoscope, and the partners may exchange *rôles* in this respect.

When the partners are well adapted to one another the woman may often share the specific coital *movements,* by bringing her pelvis forward at the right moment and then swinging it back, thus increasing both rhythm and friction. But there is risk of too vigorous motion, whereby the intromittent organ slips out of the vagina and does not immediately find its way back, and this is a most jarring and unwelcome interruption. Or it may be difficult to "keep time" correctly with one another, thus diminishing instead of enhancing pleasure. To be forewarned against such disturbances and disharmonies is surely to be forearmed.

Let us recapitulate what we have just explained—we have emphasized the value of sexual desire and sexual pleasure in the woman—we have pointed out that they greatly enhance the stimuli the man receives, and the sensations and emotions he experiences, so that ideal communion brings him far greater and keener satisfactions than the poor substitutes of one-sided, mean-spirited sexual indulgence. But—we must not omit the chief factor of all: Love.

Psychic love, *bien entendu*—and this is no flight of fancy, or poetic license of speech! And even less a moral sermon! I speak as, and only as, a physiologist with some special knowledge of sex. And as such, I can have no doubts whatever. Normal human beings cannot be emotionally and psychically happy in their love unless it has bodily realization and consummation, and equally there can be no ideal communion on the physical side without mutual communion of souls.

For sexual pleasure—and the sexual *act* itself—are largely subordinated to mental and psychic functions. Psychical response is *indispensable* to sexual connection. Without it the man does not even get an erection; and though it is possible for a woman to submit to coitus against her own wish and inclination, it is impossible for her to *participate* in what she only *endures* and does not *enjoy*.

A perfectly performed *communion* demands from both partners a psycho-erotic approach such as is only possible *where Love is.*

Only where Love is can the sexual pleasure be at its height, the orgasm ecstatic, the relief complete, and the drowsy, dreamy relaxation which follows communion, a *perfect peace.*

A certain degree of sexual tension in the husband is indispensable for *coitus,* as otherwise *immission* is impossible. If *absolutely necessary,* the woman can, on the other hand, begin the coital act without special preparation. But if she is temperamentally ardent, or completely attuned to her husband, by experience and practice, she can make up for her initial placidity and attain the orgasm together with him. (Cf. Curve B on p. 185 of text.) She can do this by conscious intention to enjoy all the stimuli received; a psychic process in which both the active will and the unconscious and subconscious factors of experience and practice co-operate, under the scepter of sympathy and love.

The man, when he begins the act in an advanced state of tension,[1] can help his wife to "keep pace" with him by *so far as possible* suppressing his own consciousness of local stimulation. Thus the amount of friction necessary to induce ejaculation is increased. As each movement to and fro means additional excitation for the wife, she is enabled to "catch up" with him and reach the goal simultaneously, without excessive overstrain. I have here intentionally used a figure of speech which clearly depicts what should occur in

---

[1] As may happen, for instance, when he awakes from an exciting, erotic dream, and forthwith translates it into reality.

coitus. The phrase is Kehrer's,[1] and is used in his monograph, "Causes and Treatment of Sterility." [2] He com-
pares the relation of the partners in coitus to that between
the runners or horsemen who "start at the same moment,
and wish—at equal and not too rapid pace—to attain the
goal side by side." But the comparison only fits a couple
who have mastered their technique and are reciprocally
adapted; a point which is also stressed by Kehrer himself.

If the wife is still inexperienced—and it takes rather long
before a woman who has neither a strongly sexual temperament nor previous experience can be educated to full erotic
efficiency—she will soon be left far in the rear, and never
attain the goal, because his orgasm, in these circumstances,
must necessarily occur first.

When the two participants in the act are so unequally
equipped, the more apt and active must do what the superior in a contest of speed or skill does. He handicaps
himself in order to preserve the woman's interest and ensure
her pleasure in coitus. I have endeavored to visualize this
in Curve C, and to explain methods fully in the preceding
chapter.

For a normally *potent* man (*i.e.,* one of average sexual
constitution and disposition) has *no other* means of equaliz-
ing matters. He can, through his own control of consciousness, somewhat postpone his reflex of ejaculation; but only
within very narrow limits.

The woman has greater adaptability. *Granted experience
and practice,* she can either accelerate or prolong her own
reactions, in harmony with his, to a considerable extent.
And this adaptability is made possible because the strongest
stimulus that ushers in the woman's orgasm is given when
the man's ejaculation begins.

But before considering these stimuli, we must turn back
to the phenomena which precede them, on the wife's side.

---

[1] And was originally used in Ovid's *Ars Amatoria,* lines 722-3, quoted
in the Intermezzo at the end of this portion of the book.
[2] "Ursachen und Behandlung der Unfruchtbarkeit," von L. Kehrer.
Publisher, Th. Steinkopff, Dresden, 1922.

We have described them in previous chapters at length, and need only recapitulate as follows. Under the influence of specific sexual excitement, caused either by bodily contacts or psychic and mental impressions, or both, and more especially in response to tactile stimulation of the vulva, clitoris, vagina, and portio (or vaginal portion of the womb), an increased local blood supply, with resultant dilation and partial erection (or stiffening) of these structures, ensues, which enhances their sensibility and makes them *fit more closely* to the intromittent phallos, and clasp and pillow it in a soft yet springy sheath. This further increases mutual stimulation. The male and female organs both dispense and receive further stimulation through mutual friction, as they are moved to and fro, by his coital movements and occasionally by hers also. *These stimuli are reciprocal,* and are intensified for both partners by involuntary or wholly or partly intentional *contractions* of the muscles of the female pelvis and genitals. In addition to the stimulation the phallos affords the *introitus, vagina* and *portio* it may also specially excite the clitoris and frenulum as it brushes against them.

It *may* do so. For this type of coital stimulation depends very much on individual structure. For example, on the size of the clitoris, on the development of the frenulum, on the position of the clitoris (and there is considerable diversity in these respects, especially in *position, i.e.,* whether the little organ is situated higher up on the front of the symphysis pubis, or almost below it). It depends also on the pelvic angle, on the circumference of the phallos, the attitude of the partners, and the kind of movements they employ.

We are probably right in believing that the clitoris was meant to be stimulated in coitus together with the vagina. The fact that this superlatively sensitive and excitable organ protrudes downward in erection, and seems to urge and press towards the phallos, tends to prove it.[1]

---

[1] There is an interesting and instructive anatomical representation of this by *Kobelt-Rieffel.* I do not know where the original is to be found but there is a copy in Luciani's *Physiologia,* Fourth Edition, Vol. V. Plate 69. (Publisher, Soc. Editrice Libreria, Milan.)

But unfortunately, often and perhaps even generally, this does not happen in modern women of our race; partly, or principally, because of insufficient development of the clitoris, of its relatively high position on the symphysis, and because of very slight pelvic inclination. These symptoms are often found together, and are due to a certain degree of *arrested development or genital infantilism.* Slight degrees of such genital infantilism are so common nowadays (in Western Europe and America) that they can hardly be considered morbid. And more pronounced cases are not by any means rare, but should be considered and treated as definitely *pathological,* as they cause numerous vital disturbances and disharmonies. As regards the genital function in women, pronounced infantilism is probably the most frequent cause of *sterility.* And even the extremely slight arrest of clitoridal development, cited above, is so far *pathological* inasmuch as it often accompanies a sub-normality of sexual emotion. The small size and high position of the clitoris which prevent its full stimulation in coitus have therefore special significance. Even though this sexual subnormality is *not incurable,* it often causes lack of mutuality, at least in the beginning of married life, and demands all the husband's knowledge and skill in his *rôle* of sexual initiator and educator. Here he must show the art commonly attributed to the seducer. Otherwise he runs the risk of leaving his wife permanently cold, frigid and indifferent or averse to his sexual attentions.

But the infantile type of clitoris—like the whole female genital structure but to a greater degree—may grow larger if there is an active sexual life during several years. In this respect, as in many others, "practice makes perfect."

We will now consider the special stimulation the woman receives during sexual union or coitus. We must clearly understand that the sensations caused by stimulation of the vagina are quite distinctive and dissimilar from those due to stimulation of the clitoris. In both cases there is pleasure,

Cf. also Dr. R. Latou Dickinson's pamphlet, "Average Sex Life of American Women," 1926. Reprinted from Journal of the American Medical Association, October 10th, 1925, Vol. 85, pp. 1113-1117. (A. M. A., 535, N. Dearborn Street, Chicago.)

and characteristically sexual pleasure, or *voluptas*. But the sensations differ as much between themselves as the flavor and aroma of two fine kinds of wine—or the chromatic glories and subtleties of two quite separate color schemes. And even the orgasms induced by clitoridal or vaginal stimulation respectively are curiously, though not widely, *different,* although the internal mechanism, the reflexes, the local and cerebral discharges, and the ensuing relief may be equal and identical—as can, in fact, partially be proved.

Thus we perceive that the woman has a potential range of permutations and variations in sexual pleasure which are not possible to the man; and that within each main group of genital stimulations, clitoridal or vaginal, there are many possible semitones of pleasurable sensation.

Perfect and *natural* coitus would give the woman a blend of both types of stimulation. Such a blend would involve supreme pleasure and probably very rapid orgasm. The indications and contraindications here may be deduced from what has been said. Technique is often difficult, however. When the clitoris is set very high the woman must take an attitude which accentuates pelvic inclination, or both partners must adapt themselves. The special contact may be made if the phallos leaves the vagina completely and brushes and strokes the clitoris with the *glans* or tip. But there is the risk of missing the tiny target and breaking the current of sensation. Finally there is the obvious method of combining vaginal friction by the phallos with simultaneous clitoridal friction by the finger (genital stimulation).

But in ideal communion the stimulation will generally be focused on and in the vagina, including *introitus* and *portio*. And this will be fully adequate for such a variety and intensity of sensation as will culminate in the orgasm.

In normal and perfect coitus, mutual orgasm must be almost simultaneous; the usual procedure is that the man's ejaculation begins and sets the woman's acme of sensation in train at once. The time it takes for the sensation received by the woman to reach her central nervous system and

translate itself into supreme delight *is less than a second.*
Such is the marvelous rate of nervous transmission.

If we analyze the process of sexual communion into its
components and stages, we may best do so by means of a
diagrammatic curve. This aims at showing the manner in
which tension accumulates in both partners, and its diminuendo after the acme is attained.

This double diagrammatic curve visualizes the summation
of sexual desire and pleasure, bodily and psychic (both are
interwoven), during normal ideal sexual union. The thick
line represents the man's reactions, the slender line the
woman's.[1]

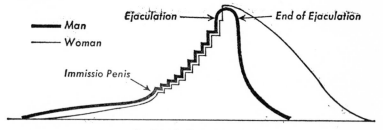

A. Ideal Communion.

Up to the moment of *immission* which begins actual coitus,
during the gradual *crescendo* of prelude and love-play, the
parallel lines will move forward, as a rule in the manner
indicated in A. A harmonious and mutually adapted couple
begin communion in a state of approximately equal exaltation and excitement. From that moment the stimuli
intensify and accumulate—owing to the half-involuntary
characteristic coital movements—not in an upward slope
as before, but in lightning leaps, and in perfect *unison,* until
the ultimate threshold is crossed by the man, and sets in
train the reflex of ejaculation. Now the curves diverge.

From the moment that the accumulated stimuli release
the mechanism of ejaculation—and thenceforth *no* effort of
the will can stay it—and the seminal fluid is flung in the

---

[1] Earlier authorities, *e.g., Kehrer,* have also reproduced such curves.
My estimate approaches Kehrer's and, on the whole, our diagrams correspond. But the careful observer will distinguish differences which are not
unimportant.

tiniest yet most vehement jets against the anterior urethral wall—from that moment, the man's sexual pleasure soars suddenly into the culmination or *orgasm,* while simultaneously his reflexes continue, in the interjection of the seminal fluid from the urethra into the vagina, through powerful spasms which cannot be inhibited by the conscious will, although they are executed by rigid (*i.e.,* voluntary) muscles. At the same time the combination of liquids forming the semen pours into the urethra from prostate and vasa deferentia until the supply is exhausted or the reflex at an end.

The beginning of the reflex—*i.e.,* the impact of the first jet of life-giving fluid against the urethral walls may give the signal for the orgasm and even intensify sexual excitement. But the real *core* of the orgasm and its summit occurs somewhat after its onset, when the motor-reflexes are in full force, and the stimuli the man receives are heightened by the responsive movements of the woman.

Then—the force of the seminal jets suddenly drops, owing to the diminished supply of fluid. The reflex declines in force, and the ecstatic pleasure fades, slowly at first and then rapidly, till both are at an end. Thus the normal orgasmic curve in the man is in the shape of a *high and narrow arch,* almost a peak, corresponding to the ejaculatory movements which consist, as a rule, of from five to seven muscular spasms, beginning vehemently, and then after a second or third superlatively intense movement, rhythmically dying away, into a profoundly pleasant repose and relaxation. That is—unless new excitements supervene. The *erection* subsides rather quickly, although for some time the penis may remain perceptibly larger than in its normal state. It depends very much on individual inclinations and special circumstances, whether the organ is retained in the vagina for a while, or retracted (withdrawn) immediately after ejaculation. We may, however, observe that on the woman's account, a needlessly abrupt conclusion of the act is to be avoided.

The processes and sensations of the orgasm are much less easy to describe in the case of women than of men. The physical mechanism is more complicated, and the processes, even within the limits of *physiological normality,* have individual variations, such as are excluded in men, and can only be directly observed in very exceptional circumstances.

Let us postpone for a while the consideration of what exactly *happens* during the feminine orgasm and concentrate first on the mechanism of its reflexes. We must quite clearly realize and remember, however, that the woman's orgasm with all its bodily symptoms and psychic concomitants, can occur *without any preceding male ejaculations:* and in very passionate and excitable women it may have been experienced several times before the man's discharge.

Although this is indisputably true, it is equally certain that in normal communion the man's ejaculation gives the signal for the woman's orgasm as well as his own.

But this again may happen in two ways. The final reflex in the woman may receive its signal from her realization of the muscular contractions of the man's orgasm; or from the impact of the vital fluid.

In any case the significance of the second is very great: and the greater the more tender and fervent the woman's love. It forms a fit and perfect final link in the wonderful chain of love processes. Those who forget or ignore it have an inadequate and distorted view of this phenomenon.

But only women themselves can declare which of the two —orgasm convulsion or ejaculation—is the talisman which heralds their supreme ecstasy.

And here, individual differences become apparent at once. There are women who decisively affirm that they only experience the orgasm if and when they feel the impact of the seminal fluid against the *portio vaginalis.* But they are in an unmistakable minority. And it is possible to prove this, for the fact that—in adequate and satisfactory conditions— the feminine orgasm almost always occurs immediately after the man's ejaculation, even when this cannot be felt as focused on the portio,[1] or when the fluid is very slight in

---

[1] *E.g.,* owing to occlusion by pessaries and other apparatus, or to removal of the *portio* in operations.

amount[1]—shows that the particular type of sensation is not by any means necessary or universal.

But, of course, it would be a decided error to deny any importance to the fluid impact. But with the majority of women the psychic response is different. We must admit that only few women are at present capable of observing and recording their own sensations, and then subsequently of analyzing them; and a certain practice is necessary. In cases where it is possible to question and receive a coherent answer, we find some individual instances of orgasm in response to the gush of semen. The majority of women who can be articulate on this subject express themselves in this sense: "After the accumulated tension of the preceding contacts and stimuli has brought me to a state of intense anticipation and excitement, I feel the onset of the orgasm at the precise instant that I perceive the first convulsive contractions of the phallos in the vulva and vagina, and simultaneously the orgastic spasms of my husband's whole body.[2] The ecstasy of this supreme moment is such that its increase by further stimuli would be impossible and beyond my power to endure. Then—I feel the liquid torrent of the ejaculate—which gives a perfectly distinct sensation—as *gloriously soothing* and refreshing at the same time. It enables me to receive unimpaired delight and benefit from the concluding rhythmic ejaculatory movements, without over-strain. These stimuli, afforded by the masculine spasms, and the soothing libations of the seminal liquid are so complete and harmonious that my enjoyment remains at its summit, until my husband's orgasm ceases, when mine also very gradually and slowly subsides."

The *gradual* nature of this subsidence, and its extreme slowness in comparison with what she observes in her partner, are feminine characteristics, which *all* women would probably confirm. But we must note that the objective (physical) phenomena, especially the tense expansion of the erectile tissues, diminish much more rapidly than their subjective accompaniments, so that the genital organs have

---

[1] *E.g.*, after repeated acts, or even before ejaculation occurs.
[2] Here is shown the significance of the purely psychic factor mentioned above.

already returned to their normal passivity long before the
emotions and sensations have died away.

In Curve A we have attempted to represent, geometrically, what we have just described. In any case, it may serve
to elucidate the course of excitement and gratification during
sexual communion, and their comparative conclusion in man
and woman respectively.

I add, further, a Curve B, representing the course of
events described on p. 176 (of the original text), namely,
when communion between a mutually desirous and harmonious pair has begun without special preparation (*i.e.,*
prelude and intensive love-play), but where this is made
good by the previous erotic experience of the wife. We may

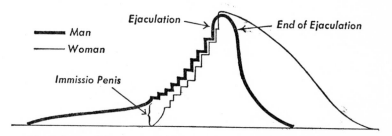

B. Coitus with an experienced woman without preparation.

point out that this curve would show some alterations if we
bore in mind the necessary conscious retardation and prolongation of the man's excitement.

Finally, we have Curve C, which depicts what we considered on p. 177, namely coitus with an inexperienced
woman, after excitation by genital contacts and love-play.
In all three diagrams, the section before the point indicating
insertion is too short in comparison with the rest. The duration of prelude and love-play can vary infinitely.

It is thus evident that a complete and satisfactory sexual
communion must meet all the erotic demands of both body
and soul, and should not in any way be neglected or impaired.
At the same time, as Curves B and C show us, sympathy,
control and skill may do wonders to overcome difficulties and
disparities.

Among other possible difficulties is the risk that the man's orgasm may not[1] be accompanied by the soothing contact of the seminal fluid on the womanly organs; and this may lead to excessive local irritation and congestion for his partner. One method of obviating this bad result is by psychic effort on the part of the woman, as by conscious contemplation of some other object. But if she neither can nor will do this she runs some risk in the long run, and in frequent intercourse, of local congestion and unrelieved tension, which is far from negligible, whether physically or psychically, especially if there is an individual tendency to neuroses.

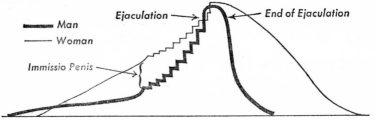

C. Coitus with an inexperienced woman after genital stimulation.

And the psychic effort necessary in order to distract the attention in such circumstances—especially if it is made often—together with the loss of specific pleasure, and the slight and inadequate orgasm, are certainly calculated to cause psychic and mental disturbances in women of sensitive nervous organization—and, as is well known, there are many such women. This must have deleterious effects on marital happiness. It is, at the present time, impossible to estimate how much *unbalance* of mind and nerves, and *misery* in marriage, are due to this check and deprivation of *complete relaxation* in coitus. But I am as profoundly convinced of its frequency and importance as of the underestimate (or neglect) of this factor by doctors and laymen alike.

But there are other interruptions and impairments to the normal act, far more serious than such diminutions of complete feminine relief as are usually the result of attempts to

---

[1] As in coitus condomatus and use of rubber caps.

prevent conception. These much more fundamental and injurious cases are those in which the wife attains a considerable degree of tension, reaching in fact the state which normally ushers in the orgasm. But—there *is no orgasm,* owing to either absolute or relative cessation of contact, and therefore no gratification and relief. The normal reactions, bodily and psychic, are suspended, and the vehement desire, unrest and local congestion continue indefinitely.

This may, of course, be a symptom of certain morbid conditions. But to deal with such would be much too lengthy and outside the scope of this book. If we confine ourselves to strictly non-pathological cases we shall still find them deplorably frequent, and we shall also find that they are due to the inadequate technique of the husband, or to his absolutely unfair and fraudulent[1] behavior in coitus.

His inadequate technique may be quite involuntary, and may affect the woman alone, as the whole processes and reflexes in the man are successfully achieved but do not afford the necessary degree of stimulation to the woman, who is *anæsthetic* (deficient in special sexual excitability) owing to ignorance, inexperience, or temperamental coolness; the partial and unintentional nature of this failure of technique does not *modify its deplorable results, immediate and permanent.*

And as to the stupid and cruel selfishness of such men as really think *only* of their own gratification—as only too often happens—this has been suitably characterized at the beginning of this study.

It may be worth while to look at the *graphic* representation of such a one-sided *copulation*—for we cannot call it *communion.*[2]

Such a representation as the above is significant when compared with C, and the "ideal" A. The differences then become extremely marked.[2]

---

[1] The term fraudulent is deliberately chosen. The man's actions represent a fraud against his wife, even if she is a consenting party. For she little knows the full effects of what she allows—or even sometimes exacts!

[2] In all these graphs, the thick line which denotes the man's sensations is exactly similar. This is done for the sake of simplicity and force, without taking into consideration the influence of the different feminine states on the man in the various circumstances.

A similar unsatisfactory (and, if habitual, painfully injurious) effect on the woman is produced, though she is of warm temperament and prompt susceptibility, in cases where the man is "below par" and manifests this by too early emission (*ejaculatio præcox*), as, *e.g.,* is often found in neurasthenic subjects (if I may be permitted to employ this old-fashioned term and concept!). These cases are on the borderline of *disease,* and require medical attention if the partners are not able to achieve by means of careful and skillful *compensatory* technique.

I have tried in Curve D to represent, as exactly and effectively as possible, the progress of sexual excitement in women who only reach a certain pitch without orgasm.

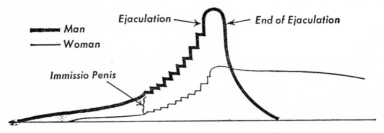

D. Coitus with an inexperienced woman without adequate stimulation.

We must bear in mind that the thin delicate line in these graphs represents not only local (genital) congestion, but psychic and mental tension as well. And that these—in the Graph D—do not relax and subside, after an ecstatic culmination, but remain for a considerable length of time, at a high pitch—though without the pleasure and benefit of the orgasm.

This means for the genitalia, the indefinite prolongation of a state of nervous stimulation and extra blood supply which is only natural for comparatively short periods at a time. And for the mind and soul: the continuance of extreme tension without corresponding relaxation, of an expectancy with no likelihood of fulfillment, of a profound *unrest.* The position of the feminine line in the latter (right side) portion of Diagram D has a very different meaning to the ascending lines in the left side portion of A, B and C. For these latter show a summation or accumulation of desire and pleasure, and then, in their descending portion, a satisfied and delighted *relaxation;* whereas in D the disappointed anticipation must inevitably pass into ungratified jarring, nervous anger, fatigue, *malaise* and pain. If this occurs by some mischance once in a while it will not necessarily do harm. The disappointment will not be insurmountable, and the mind regains equipoise in the prospect of another and happier occasion.

And the genitalia recover from their irritation, and return to wholesome normality. But it is very different if and when the same disappointment is incessantly repeated. The congestion of the genitalia becomes chronic; frequently morbid discharges are set up; the functions of ovulation and menstruation become irregular, profusely painful or suppressed. In short, we have that well-known (though strongly idiosyncratic, *i.e.,* individually varied) state of persistent genital irritation and hypersensitiveness, with its vague or definite localized or wandering pains, that occupies so many hours of gynæcological consultation. And the attempt to treat these distressing symptoms leads to many fruitless and complicated prescriptions, and often to equally vain surgical operations—vain because the same cause of all the damage is ever at work anew, and more widely, and is neither dreamed of by the unhappy patient nor alas! diagnosed aright by the doctor, who is still too often afraid to ask about such things, because he is ignorant or inappreciative of their true value.

So, above all, I would impress on all married men: *every considerable erotic stimulation of their wives that does not terminate in orgasm, on the woman's part, represents an injury, and repeated injuries of this kind lead to permanent—or very obstinate—damage to both body and soul.*

These peculiar dangers to the wife's physical and mental health are great if the man's technique is poor; but greater by far if he practices so-called "conjugal frauds," or *coitus interruptus,* or "withdrawal." This method is often employed to prevent conception.[1] The man rapidly draws back the phallos from the vagina, at the moment he feels the ejaculation commence, or knows that its onset cannot be postponed. The ejaculation therefore occurs—outside the vagina. And with the *ejaculation* there also occurs *orgasm* —*for the man.* Even though the intensity and *abandon* of his pleasure is diminished and impaired, to some extent he attains relief and relaxation. And accordingly coitus interruptus is not so harmful to him as to the woman, although it is *certainly not* wholly innocuous, especially for persons of delicate nervous organization, and many neurasthenic manifestations must be attributed to this practice in their inception.[2]

But for the woman the effects of this practice are infinitely serious; unless, indeed, she is without any sexual sensibility and remains "cold" and passive throughout the performance —which in *such* circumstances, can only be considered fortunate. Should she be endowed with average emotional or physical susceptibility, the subjoined Graph E shows to what she is subjected.

At the moment of maximum anticipation, when local and general tension and excitement have all but reached their summit—the normal course of events is abruptly checked, and—as orgasm does not ensue—congestion and nervous stimulation, after a short drop, remain at a high level for an indefinite time. Again, let us remember that physical and psychic influences of sexual desire differ *toto coelo,* according to whether this desire culminates in gratification and relief, or represents only a vain, unsatiated, unrelieved longing, which becomes a positive *malaise* and pain.

I ask my readers' indulgence for the frequent reiteration of these facts. But I consider this emphasis necessary, because of their intrinsic importance and the neglect they still

---

[1] Which it notoriously often fails to do.
[2] Morbid local conditions as a result of frequent sexual excitement without natural relief are far less often observed in men than in women. This is partly because men—sexually normal men, at least—have their orgasm much more in their own power, and are not wholly dependent on their partners. But certain illnesses, such as, *e.g.,* hypertrophy of the prostate, are attributed by many authorities to chronic irritation and congestion, due to imperfect relaxation of sexual excitement.

so often meet. It is obvious that the woman's tension after
the man's ejaculation is much greater than before. It is
also much greater than (as in Graph D) after coitus with insufficient love-play and an inexpert woman, and it takes a
far longer time to revert to the normal level. Thus there is
great and ever-growing danger of new psychic lesions and
physical strains of the same kind accumulating and accentuating chronic congestion and ungratified sexual desire;
with all that these imply.

I have treated coitus interruptus in some detail (although
its *abnormal and anomalous nature* puts it, strictly speaking,
outside the purview of physiology) for this reason: that it
is absolutely typical in essentials and results of *what definite
sexual excitement without gratification means for a woman.*

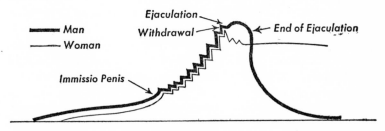

E. Coitus Interruptus.

And also in order to warn against it *with all the emphasis at
my command.* Some persons will, of course, reply that a
great many married people practice coitus interruptus without, in their opinion, suffering harm therefrom. The answer
is: that can only be possible if the wife remains totally
indifferent and sexually anæsthetic; if the man has very
blunt nervous sensibilities, only cares to relieve his own genital tension, and cares nothing for *his wife as an individual,
or a mate;* and even then only if this anomaly is seldom
practiced. But all such conditions are incompatible with
the "adequate and harmonious sexual activity" which we
have accepted as one of the corner-stones of marriage, and
the edifice must totter to its fall, or is already in ruins.

*For sexually adequate, sensitive and vitally vigorous peo-
ple, systematic coitus interruptus means not only a degrada-*

tion but also an extermination of the marital relationship: a
danger to the husband's health, and a crime against the wife.

Let us finally glance at the category of cases diagramma-
tized in D. We have already suggested means to prevent
inadequate sexual gratification of the woman, *i.e.,* by appropriate introductory love-play and genital stimulation. Here,
as everywhere, it is true that "prevention is better than
cure." But the cure, or rather the successful treatment in
such delicate cases, is no easy matter. The suitable prescription consists in applying prophylaxis when the injury has already happened! Or, to be precise, *if after immission the*
man has had his ejaculation without producing orgasm in
his partner he should immediately caress and stimulate her
to "concert pitch," by genital friction and manipulation;
unless indeed he should have inclination and potency to start
afresh, on a new love-play, communion and orgasm. But,
of course, genital stimulation is more appropriate and effective as preventive than as therapy! It is more easy as well
as delightful for the man, and more æsthetic, for as an epilogue it is apt to assume a certain *constraint* which impairs
both ethical and æsthetical value.

Therefore here, too, prevention is better than cure. But
cure is better than neglect of ills.

If the man should be unable to produce his wife's orgasm
by genital friction, *autotherapeutic measures* are probably
better than none at all, although the objections, on many
counts, to such expedients, are far from trivial.

The matter has been much more widely debated, and of
more ancient existence than our modern recognition of the
injury done to women by lack of gratification in sexual intercourse: a recognition which has not yet become part of
the civilized conscience. The older school of Catholic moral
theologians discussed the "moral conflict" it entailed. And
the new school were also obliged to consider it. The Vicar-
General, D. Craisson, in his authoritative work "On Sexual
Matters for the Guidance of Fathers Confessors" ("De rebus
venereis ad usum Confessariorum," Paris, 1870) on p. 172,
remarks: "The fourth question is as to whether, if the husband should withdraw after ejaculation, before the wife has

experienced orgasm, she may then lawfully at once continue friction with her own hand, in order to attain relief." The answer is that "certain moral theologians deny this, but the greater number permit it, because," and so forth. "In the same manner it is lawful for the woman to prepare herself by genital stimulation for sexual union, in order that she may have orgasm more easily,"[1] and so on.

Luciani, the eminent Italian physiologist who prints this extract, adds this justified comment: "What profound practical wisdom is embodied in these concessions, which are destined to reassure hypersensitive consciences among the faithful!" ("Quanta sapienza pratica in questi concessioni, dirette a tranquillizare le timorate coscienze religiose!")

---

[1] I have not been able to find an authorized translation of Craisson's book. I therefore have made my own, using the terms already familiar to my readers instead of such as science now discredits (*e.g., seminatio* or ejaculation of seed by the woman!). Here are the Latin quotations: "Quær. 40. An viro retrahente post propriam seminationem sed ante mulieris seminationem, possit illa statim tactibus se excitare ut seminet? Resp.: Sententiam negantem a quibusdam quidem tenere, communnis vero affirmatus, hoc esse licitum, quia . . . etc. . . . imo mulieri permittitur se excitare ad congressum, quo facilius in coitu seminet, etc."

CHAPTER X

11. *Physiology and Technique* (cont.)

LET us now inquire what *exactly happens to and in* the female *genital organs*: (*a*) *in coitus, and* (*b*) *especially during the culminating orgasm.* We may profitably confine ourselves to the second point, for the former has been dealt with at some length in Chapters IV. and V., as well as in the immediately preceding chapter. We are aware, then, of the increased flow of blood to the entire genital tissues, the tense swelling and expansion of the *Corpora cavernosa* (bulbi), the erection of the clitoris, the secretion of the vestibulary glands, the opening of the vulva, the contractions of the vaginal walls, and of the whole musculature of the pelvic floor.

We know from observations during gynæcological inspection of women of very warm constitution, that even before the orgasm begins, the uterus contracts and changes position,[1] and it is extremely probable, as deduced from comparative study of animals, that the muscles of the oviducts share this *movement of approach.* We may also assume that there is additional fluid secretion in uterus and tubes, and in the cervical glands.[2] We have, in short, of late returned to the opinion that a Graafian follicle in an advanced stage of evolution may be ruptured in coitus and release the ovum.

Thus, in woman equally with man, the whole muscular and secretory (glandular) structure of the genitalia participates individually and collectively in sexual intercourse. This is a confirmation (as are also our latest acquisitions of

---

[1] *Cf.* among other authorities, H. Freund's Address in the 1922 Assembly of German Naturalists and Doctors "On the Physiology of Generation, and the Problem of Sterility."

[2] *Cf. Sellheim* in the discussion following *Freund's* lecture.

knowledge on menstrual phenomena) of the ancient and
popular theories, based on modern scientific knowledge and
freed from irrational superstitions—after a period of negation.   Simultaneously, we have passed out of and beyond
the era in which the wife was considered *sexually as a passive
implement, receptacle and incubator,* and have recognized
and accepted her as *an active, adult and equivalent sexual
being.*

But are we to react against ancient errors, and in our
equal consideration and respect for the woman, so far as to
talk of a *semination* by the woman?   (*Cf.* Craisson's words,
quoted at end of last chapter.)   For there can obviously be
no question of a *seminal* discharge on her part.

But what of "ejaculation"?

Here the matter is still uncertain and very difficult,
especially because of the extreme individual diversity
among women.   There can be no discharge of *spermat,* as
in man; but "ejaculation" is often used as synonymous with
"orgasm," and without clear understanding whether anything is ejaculated, and if so, *what.*   So far as I can form
an opinion on this subject, it appears that the majority of
laymen believe that something is forcibly squirted (or propelled or extruded), or expelled from the woman's body in
orgasm, and should so happen normally, as in the man's case.

I cannot venture to decide whether it *should* so happen,
according to natural law.   There is no doubt that it *does*
happen to some women.   But whether these are a majority
or a minority, I am unable to determine.   The only substance
which can possibly be *forcibly expelled* (squirted or ejaculated) is the thin fluid mucus which fills the *Glandulæ vesti-
bulares majores* (Bartholin's glands) at the onset of orgasm.
We have seen that these glands begin to secrete immediately
sexual excitement manifests itself.   Skene's glands do the
same, but are far too small to furnish enough secretion for
an "ejaculation."   We also know that the mucus secretion
flows into the vulva (lubrication or *destillatio*) and is most
beneficial or, indeed, necessary in preparing the *introitus
vaginæ* to receive the phallos without pain.   And this secretion will accumulate during the movements of coitus, so
that a certain amount is present in the glandular ducts.   And

the distended glands are, of course, subject to strong pressure during the powerful spasmodic contractions of the pelvic muscles in the orgasm, while the tense *bulbi vestibulæ* serve as cushions or supports. Thus, the secretion collected in Bartholin's glands may, under certain pressure, be squeezed out and forcibly ejected from their orifices.

The process may, in fact, be occasionally verified *when the orgasm follows clitoridal friction alone*. But of course, we cannot draw valid conclusions as to its frequency. Similar verifications in *coitus* are totally impossible. Even if the woman declares that she has "ejaculated," that means that she has experienced a complete orgasm. It is not possible for her or her partner to distinguish any mucus secretion which may have been ejected from her vestibulary glands, from the overwhelmingly larger amount of male ejaculate.[1] Teleologically, there is no purpose in an ejection of vestibulary mucus during the orgasm, though much reason for its exudation beforehand. *Finally, it is at least just as certain that such an "ejaculation" does not take place in many women of sexually normal functions, as that it does take place in others.*

Any other feminine discharge (not *ejaculation* which means squirting or very vehement expulsion) during the orgasm can only be possible from the womb itself. And it is not antecedently unlikely that the thick mucus clot, exuded by some women subsequent to coitus, has left the uterus during the orgasm.[2] But it is equally probable that in these cases there has been a morbid increase of secretion, for the mucus substance is generally yellowish and glutinous instead of transparent or faintly milky, as is normal. Moreover, the typical and essential uterine action in the orgasm is somewhat different, and we shall now deal with it.

It need hardly be explained that it is absolutely impossible to observe or verify this process during communion. Thus we are compelled to refer to and rely on observations of the

---

[1] In theory it might be supposed that during *Coitus condomatus,* where the secretions of the two partners are separated by the appliance, this difficult point might be settled. In practice there has been no elucidation.

[2] This can only be observed in *Coitus condomatus,* as otherwise the secretions mingle and the seminal fluid overwhelms the other.

uterus, and especially the *portio, during orgasms produced
by intensive stimulation of clitoris, vagina,* or *portio, without
actual coitus.* There are only rare opportunities for such
observations. Nevertheless, in the course of years sufficient
data have been collected from various sources to enable us
to form an idea of the uterine action and response in
the orgasm.

We have already established the fact of the uterine contraction and, so to speak, *erection* during sexual excitement. We will now cite a passage by J. Beck (one of the
first authorities, I believe, to record this phenomenon, in
medical literature), describing his observations on the *portio vaginalis* and especially the *ostium externum,* at the
inception of the orgasm. The woman in question had prolapse of the womb, which made the portio vaginalis
accessible to sight; and she was extraordinarily susceptible to erotic excitement, especially if the *portio* were
touched. Definite stimulation here produced the orgasm at
once.

"The vaginal portion of the womb was at first tense,
motionless, and apparently quite normal; the orifice was
closed and no instrument could have passed. Almost immediately after contact, the ostium opened and closed spasmodically, five or six times in succession, whilst the outer
border was drawn sharply inwards towards the cervix. This
lasted about twenty seconds, then all reverted to its former quiescence. The aperture closed, and the portio resumed its former position." [1]

There is every reason to believe that in women of normal
erotic potentialities, and normal uterine position, the orgasm
would show identical processes. And that these would be
the same, whether produced by vaginal or clitoridal contacts. But, *Nota Bene,* of very unequal intensity, in different women, and also in the same woman on different
occasions. The decisive factors in these variations are at
present beyond our ken.

Further individual idiosyncrasies exist in the amount and

[1] Not having the original text available, I have translated from Luciani's version; he quotes Beck in his "Physiologia."

alkalinity of the mucus secretions in the cervix.   Modern
sexologists[1] have maintained that the mucus plug called the
"Kristeller" (see p. 75) *is extruded or expelled during the
uterine spasms in orgasm.*   But, owing to its thick, firm,
adhesive consistency it remains attached to the lining of the
cervix.   It dips or plunges into the seminal liquid, loads
itself with spermatozoa, and is then reabsorbed into the
womb, in the relaxation following the orgasmic contractions,
for the uterine cavity expands and acts as a suction pump.
Many eminent gynæcologists have accepted this hypothesis,
apparently oblivious of their own professional daily experience, of the wide individual variations of amount in this
cervical mucus, and certainly without having been privileged
to observe the orgasmic phenomena in this sense; for they
are by no means so simple as the sexologists suppose.   Even
though there are occasional facts which indicate movements
on the part of the Kristeller, such a regular fishing for
spermatozoa by the uterus, through its adhesive mucus
tongue (the comparison with an ant-eater is irresistible!)
cannot actually take place.

But we must realize and accept the active reception of
sperms by the uterus in orgasm, through aspiration or suction, *i.e.,* contraction followed by expansion, and generally
also by more or less vigorous independent motion of the
ostium or mouth of the womb.   And this is of the utmost
practical importance.[2]   Its change of position or *descent,*
owing to the contractions of the vaginal muscles, and the
orgasmic spasms of the abdominal wall, both contribute to
bring the aperture nearer to the seminal fluid.[3]   Finally,
the cervical mucus can aid the spermatozoa in their upward
advance, by providing an accessible, favorable protective
element.[4]

We have now, I think, exhaustively treated the physiology

---

[1] Sexologist is the term for doctors who specialize on sex matters, but
who are generally originally nerve-specialists or venereologists and not
gynæcologists.

[2] Here we have the modern scientific version of the ancient proverb:
"Uterus est animal sperma desiderans" ("The uterus is a creature that
desires or drinks the seed").

[3] The elastic muscular tension of the Ligamenta sacro uterina restores
the organ to its normal position.

[4] We must also assume a stretching or extension of the posterior vaginal
vault in orgasm. But I have never seen it recorded.

of the woman in coitus, according to the best of our knowledge at the present time; and simultaneously we have also dealt with a considerable amount of essential technique.

In Chapter VII. and Chapter IX. we have discussed the man's rôle in coitus so fully that we need only touch a few isolated points.

And first of all, with the *prolonged erection following ejaculation,* which may sometimes occur owing to the close constriction of the vulvo vaginal muscles, especially when a passionately responsive woman has a somewhat late or very long orgasm.

In such cases, the vulvo vaginal rim, through the operation of the *Constrictor cunni* muscle, can compress the base of the male organ so firmly as to prevent rapid subsidence. This is, of course, specially advantageous for the woman. But, if this muscular constriction lasts too long, or is too violent, it may cause painful disturbances, unnatural swelling of the phallos, and difficulty in leaving the vagina. The same can be said of the Levator vaginæ, the upper encircling muscle, of the female passage. Its operation is physiologically attractive and enhances the pleasure of both partners. Its efficient tonicity can prolong full erection and facilitate complete womanly enjoyment and relief; and both by voluntary and intentional contractions and reflex (involuntary) spasms. But in the latter cases *cramp* may be set up, which is positively painful for both partners, and may even *catch* the glans penis. ("Penis Captivus" or *vaginism. Cf.* the normal process of coitus in the canine species.)

Circumcision in man appears to have strong effect on efficiency in the sexual act. Not, that is, in altering or increasing *potency* but in affecting the sensitiveness of the *glans.* It is not quite easy to be certain, here, as among nations who practice ritual circumcision, all men are circumcised. But some primitive races circumcise frequently, but not as a matter of religious and social *mores,* and here comparisons are possible. An interesting account by Frederici,[1] runs as follows: "The native 'boys' who collect together in the stations and plantations, discuss

[1] Contributions to "Anthropology and Philology of German New Guinea," Berlin, 1912.
Documents about German Protectorates, Supplement 5.

sexual matters constantly among themselves and it is well-known *that those who are circumcised have much less tactile sensibility in the glans than those who are not. The circumcised men admit frankly that they take longer before ejaculation than their fellows."* And *Fehlinger,* in his "Sexual Life of Primitive Peoples" [1] suggests that *"the purpose of circumcision is probably the prolongation of coitus, as the exposed glans takes longer to reach the summit of stimulation than the covered."*

It is obvious, from what has been already said, that such prolongation is highly favorable to the majority of women. So we need not be surprised that both ancient and especially modern literature contain female characters who have sought in vain to match their sexual gratification with their sexual desires, in relationship to various men, and finally turned to members of circumcised races.

It is extremely difficult to determine whether the lessened susceptibility of the glans means diminished sexual enjoyment on the man's side, or whether his enjoyment is increased through the prolongation of the act. But both primitive races and more especially Oriental civilizations regard the removal of the prepuce as sexually advantageous, for they greatly value the utmost possible *prolongation* of the act. This is doubtless partly due to the universal human wish to taste every joy to the full, and particularly to increase the intense pleasures of coitus which always seem, in retrospect, tantalizingly brief. This is in my opinion a perfectly normal and physiologically justified desire which is operative, whether consciously or unconsciously, in every sexually healthy and vital person, and certainly in every man. An even more significant factor, however, is the primitive "barbarian's" appreciation of the woman's desire and pleasure; even though in other departments of life, he despises his partner, overworks her like a beast of burden, and disposes of her as a piece of property, he is, on this point, much superior to the average man of Western civilization. The primitive is not satisfied with an act of coitus, or proud of himself, if he has not gratified the woman

---

[1] "Das Geschlechtsleben der Naturvölker." (Publisher, K. Kabitzsch, Leipzig, 1921.)

who has shared it. He is glad—like a true "Don Juan contemporain"—in the joy he has given.[1] So the wish and pride of being desired sexually is not the least of the motives which make men seek and practice circumcision.

But—the desire to prolong the act may lead to excesses and abuses. Both in a positive sense, in the form of too often and rapidly repeated orgasms, but negatively, as well, in that the coital stimuli are intentionally and consciously reduced to such a level that there are finally *no* stimuli at all, and *no coitus in any tolerable sense.*

In my opinion such abuses have begun, when the man *has recourse to artificial means of distracting his attention, such as eating, drinking, smoking, etc.* (as well of course as consciously directing his thoughts away from his sensations, and thus diminishing the cerebral stimuli which contribute greatly to the orgasm).

This *psychic* postponement of culmination and prolongation of excitement, even though it may have certain æsthetic risks for the man, may so help and delight and appeal to the woman, physically and psychically, that it constitutes a most intimate erotic bond, and more than outweighs any disadvantages. Therefore I have not hesitated to recommend the occasional use of such methods, in order to equalize the delay in the woman's sensations. But its habitual employment has great drawbacks, and its advantages may be found equally in other directions.

And does the habitual exaggeration of prolonged coitus by the Hindoos, Javanese, and other Orientals, *really give the woman the fullest extent of pleasure, from phallic friction in the vagina?* I am inclined to doubt it, *because such deliberate distraction of the man's attention would probably imply some degree of local passivity—or at least much less frequent and vigorous phallic motions.*

And in any case it is fairly certain that *prolonged passivity in coitus* is out of the question for men of white Western

---

[1] *Marcel Barrière:* "Essai sur le Don Juanisme contemporain" (Paris, 1922), describes the emotional attitude and the technique of the modern erotic expert, with masterly knowledge and great charm of style. He omits to compare the modern Don Juan (who does not systematically desert and "throw away," but concentrates on awakening and enrapturing his "victims") with the primitive Oriental. But the student of sex matters at once sees the resemblance.

races in modern civilization, on purely æsthetic grounds—
except occasionally and in modified form at the close of
communion.

Æsthetic objections cannot be raised against the most
conspicuous excess in the method of *deferred ejaculation;* but physiologically, it must be regarded as a real *abuse,*
though in a negative sense.   It consists in *insertion* (*Immissio penis*) *without ejaculation.*   In other words: communion that is no communion; coitus that is no coitus.   I
am not aware whether this practice also originates with
the colored races, but am under the impression that
I have read somewhere of its popularity among the
Japanese.

Havelock Ellis gives an account of its *ritualization* by
certain communities in the United States of America.   Alice
Stockham[1] made propaganda for it in her book "Karezza,"
and Marie Stopes has given a detailed description of it under
the same name, though without urging its practice indis-
criminately.   She writes: "The idea being, that after
mutual passion has been roused and union effected,[2] instead
of encouraging the excitement by movement and so on, an
attempt to reach complete calm, both mental and physical,
should be made.   This is achieved by the cessation of
physical movement, and *the centering of thought on the
spiritual aspect of the beloved"* (p. 190).   (I have italicized
the last words, which confirm my view that there is nothing
psychically unlovely in this procedure—on the contrary!)
"Extremists in the practice of this idea would go so far as
to prevent ejaculation on all occasions, but others use it

---

[1] Dr. Marie Stopes, in her book, "Married Love," refers to Dr. Stockham's book, which is out of print. Dr. Marie Stopes herself is D.Sc. and
D.Phil. Her book, "Married Love," is often attributed in lay circles to
a medical woman, and references to the book which appear in certain
newspapers give color to this mistake.   This is regrettable, for the well-
known and widely circulated book has valuable and courageous ideas, but
at the same time gives currency to views, which a doctor or at least a
gynæcologist recognizes at once as impossible from a medical man or
woman.   The layman, on the other hand, attributes undue weight to them
because of the supposed professional knowledge of the authoress.

[2] I have quoted verbatim in order to prove my point and in order to
show that I do no injustice to Dr. Stopes.

Dr. Alice Stockham was a professional medical woman with a large
practice in the U.S.A.   She was prosecuted under the Comstock Law in
the early 1900's (beginning of this century).

only to increase the length of time between the occasions when ejaculation takes place" (p. 191). "There are . . . marriages in which the husband is so undersexed that he cannot have ordinary union save at very infrequent intervals without a serious effect on his health. If such a man is married to a woman who has inherited an unusually strong and over-frequent desire, he may suffer by union with her, or may cause her suffering by refusing to unite. It is just possible that for such people the method of Karezza (see Dr. A. Stockham's book 'Karezza' on the subject) might bring them both the health and peace they need; conserving the man's vital energy from the loss of which he suffers, and giving the woman the sense of union and physical nerve-soothing she requires" (p. 85).

On principle I have avoided mentioning views and quoting statements in this treatise, in order to confute them, for this would bewilder and mislead many lay readers. But I have made a point of citing Marie Stopes in such detail, in order to demonstrate, out of her own mouth, how an able—even an eminent—person can arrive at absurd conclusions, when venturing on territory in which she is not at home.

For, quite apart from other turns of phrase in the final quotation, which make a specialist shake his head—this explanation of Dr. Stopes' *culminates in a contradiction in terms* which must be immediately evident, even to a non-medical reader, who has understood and assimilated the lessons of the present monograph.

To expect a "physical nerve-soothing" for the woman "after mutual passion has been roused and union effected" *without* the attainment of the natural culmination of orgasm, with all its infinite liberation and relief, is *physiologically quite senseless,* and no normal person, man or woman, can be "soothed" in this manner.[1] On the contrary, the employment of such an expedient, especially if it becomes habitual, must lead to a perpetual and increasing dissatisfaction and unrest, an accumulating genital congestion

---

[1] Careful and prolonged analysis of the expression "physical nerve-soothing" would be necessary in order to discover the exact sense in which it is used. Perhaps the authoress herself is not quite sure. We may, however, assume that a sort of satisfaction and relief of tension is meant.

and profound emotional irritation and exasperation, of whose dangerous results we have already said enough. Therefore I *must utter an urgent warning against Karezza,* and have only given so much space to its consideration, because it appears to be occasionally tried by married people who wish to avoid impregnation, and because Dr. Stopes' book is well-known, both in the English original and translations.[1]

My warning loses none of its validity if and though I admit that this sort of communion which is not communion, may occasionally take place without risk or damage between a very sexually *anæsthetic* man and his equally *anæsthetic* wife (whether this mutual tepidity be constitutional or the result of extreme fatigue)—when their affection craves a close bodily contact, without any explicit sexual need.

We have a further point to discuss, which is important from the *technical* point of view. That is to say, the comparative size of the organs in the two partners.

The empty vagina, in a state of sexual repose, has an average length of 7½ to 10 cm.; 7½ for the length of the front or anterior wall from *introitus* to *portio,* and 10 for the posterior wall up to the *vaginal vault or fornix.* For purposes of insertion or intromission, we may reckon the vaginal passage as 10 cm. long. But the length of the axis or medial line of the erect penis on the dorsal side is 15 cm. Thus, assuming average or medium proportions in both partners, we find a considerable disparity in the length or depth of phallos and sheath. How is this compensated?

Firstly, by the fact that, as a rule, penetration does not take place up to the root. This only occurs in certain special positions and attitudes.

Secondly, by the elasticity of the vagina. This flexibility varies very much as between one woman and another, but is generally quite considerable. Of course, the contractions of the vaginal muscles, especially the longitudinal sinews, have a contrary—*i.e.,* telescoping—effect. But, normally,

---

[1] In order to be quite fair to her, I repeat that Dr. Stopes *does not recommend* Karezza, but neither does she condemn it; and this latter omission, together with the tone of the passage quoted, I consider dangerous for many of her readers.

the natural flexibility prevails. But when the internal muscles are powerfully developed, and the excitement extreme—especially at the onset of orgasm—and when the phallos penetrates to its full length, there can be acute disparity and difficulties, even with organs of average proportions. *If the profoundest penetration is a violent internal thrust, such disproportion may cause a laceration in the vaginal vault.* This only happens very rarely under average conditions, but its *possibility* even then should not be forgotten. And it becomes even probable when the genitals are abnormal. When such abnormality has an *infantile* trend, we must reckon with diminished pliability and flexibility of the vagina, such as is also a symptom of senescence (advanced age) and of certain diseases. We must also bear in mind the peculiar vulnerability of the tissues during pregnancy, and especially shortly before and after giving birth. And finally there are cases of marked physical disproportion when a very large phallos is mated with a normal vagina, or a normal penis with a very short vagina. The first possibility materializes oftener than the second, but even then it does not often make mutually satisfactory coitus out of the question.

However, we must not ignore the serious danger of a combination of circumstances, *i.e.*, absolute disproportion, vehement excitement, rough invasiveness, and above all, special vaginal vulnerability—leading to a rupture of the vagina, which endangers the woman's life. This peculiar peril is partly because of the strong hæmorrhage which ensues, and partly because of the likelihood of peritonitis; for the rupture, if any, generally takes place in the fornix and involves the delicate peritoneal membrane (see Plate II.).

It is an interesting and well-established fact that it is hardly possible to draw any correct inferences from the general bodily build and stature of man or woman, as to the size of either phallos or vagina. There have been intimately painful cases when after the marriage ceremony, the couple who appeared so well matched, find that they are quite incompatible and incommensurate. On the other hand, it is really remarkable how often a marriage between a tall and powerful man and a small woman is as successful sexually as in every other way.

Of course the protective instinct of the man may express itself in such marriages in the erotic relationship, as well as in the whole field of life, and lead him to exercise especial forethought, caution and tenderness. But it is also noticeable that women of short stature and small bones can often meet all requirements in the flexibility and capacity of their vaginæ. And their sexual vigor and efficiency are also conspicuous, not only in coitus, but in their buoyant reaction to the mental and physical stress and strain of menstruation, pregnancy and parturition, their fine flow of milk, and easy and frequent conception.[1] In short, little women approximate most often to the *typical womanly ideal*. But of course this is only the case when this small stature is perfectly proportionate throughout and when the sexual development is adequate. When the small stature is due to some form of abnormality, it is more than likely that the genitals will show serious defects structurally and functionally, in one way or another.

This is especially true in cases of the form of arrested development which we have learnt to know as *infantilism*. Infantilism is by no means necessarily associated with short stature or delicate proportions. Tall persons and even giants are particularly liable to slight or severe degrees of infantilism. Nor is infantilism confined to women, but exists in either sex.

For sexual functions infantilism is an even more serious defect than for other activities of mind or body. In women it may coincide with or imply menstrual disturbances, difficulty in conception, tendency to premature miscarriages, sterility and inability to feed at the breast. Psychically it can manifest in abnormally slight inclination to sexual intercourse, and frigidity in actual coitus. And also, though less commonly, in a narrowness and inelasticity of the vagina which may make coitus difficult and even impossible.

The various grades and stages of genital infantilism in

---

[1] *Cf.* the saying among the English common people: "Little women— big breeders."

women are so numerous, that it is not true that all girls who suffer from some of these symptoms are fully inapt for married life. That would be too sweeping an assumption. I have professionally known not a few women, who at the beginning of their life with their husbands, had much to contend with, owing to their infantilism, but who later became in all respects satisfactory wives and admirable mothers. For them, marriage provided itself a sovereign remedy, for the genital congestion and increased blood supply of the organs, owing to sexual intercourse, the absorption of stimulating seminal substances and pregnancies (of which the first were abortive, but the later ones carried to term), finally contributed to perfect local development.

But all doctors know of women whose marriage was literally their doom, as a pronounced degree of genital infantilism rendered them totally incapable of meeting its requirements. Such arrested development causes a woman so much suffering (physical often, even more emotional and mental) that it were better she had never married, both for herself and her husband.

And even the husbands of women whose comparatively light infantilism is curable and cured by marital intercourse, require in the first difficult years, a fund of patience, magnanimity and tender self-restraint, which is not available for all! For only highly evolved and spiritualized or abnormally cold-blooded men are capable of a love so altruistic and which can never attain complete sexual gratification.

We may assume, without hesitation, that infantilism is the chief physical source of danger and discomfort to women, in marriage—apart from certain specific diseases of heart, lungs and kidneys. For this reason I must emphatically support the attempts now being made to standardize medical inspection and certificates before marriage. I would even suggest that it be extended and made exact and exhaustive, for all girls at adolescence, as a matter of principle. In this connection, exhaustive would mean a *general examination* by a hospital doctor (as is customary for life insurance) and a genital by a gynæcologist; and the latter can be quite thorough and yet not offensive or injudicious in any way. If it is preferred to entrust the latter to medical women—there is no valid objection. But such an inspection *should* take place.

It is possible to spare the young girls' modesty and avoid possible psychic and emotional harm by having the inspection betimes, while there is no marriage or engagement in prospect.[1] And if some serious defect appears, it is infinitely better to know of its existence in time. In cases of slight infantilism it is often possible to cure them by suitable treatment, before there is any question of marriage.

I have quite often had success in treating relatively severe cases of genital infantilism, which would have made marriage extremely difficult and painful, but by appropriate measures, were modified so far as to be equal to normal sexual requirements, and finally completely cured in marriage.[2]

Moreover, it is well to inform the future husband, early in the course of his engagement, of the existence of certain infantile traits and to impress on him the need of care and gentleness in sexual intercourse, at first, and also the probability of an initial anæsthesia (specific sexual coolness or indifference) on the part of his bride, which he must treat with appropriate skill and sympathy. The best person to tell him this, with authority and understanding, is the family doctor. It is obviously fairer to the man to let him know the factors which must inevitably be prominent in his married life—there will always be more than enough of the mysterious and incalculable! Moreover, it seems to me self-evident that he has just as much right as his bride or her parents, to be spared unpleasant sexual or general surprises, after marriage. The *general health* of both partners offers about the same possibilities and difficulties. *Genitally* for the bride, the most frequent and important matter is the *man's freedom from venereal disease.* For the bridegroom, if he marries a virgin, the adequate and adult development

---

[1] Prudent parents who lay special stress on preserving their daughters from shock or suggestiveness, can arrange for adequate medical examination after some slight illness; they can ask the doctor to pay special heed to sexual development, but make the examination as though for an insurance policy.

[2] See Van de Velde, *Zentralblatt für Gynäkologie,* 1926, No. 13, p. 799.

of her womanly organs, is equally important, though till now, it has not been recognized.[1]

Is there no risk of similar arrested development of the genital organs in the man? This question will at once occur to my readers.

The answer is: *in practice, No:* at least not to anything like the extent in which it exists in the woman.

Thus we have traversed the disputed territory of the medical certificate before marriage, and return to the subject of variations in individual genital proportions.

Inadequate development here is much rarer in men than in women; it is occasionally met with, however. It can manifest in defective seminal fluid, as well as in smallness of the erect phallos. If a small phallos is mated to a large vagina, the normal coital friction will hardly suffice to produce orgasm, and the sufferer here will be the woman, rather than the active partner. Moreover, the low potency or sexual efficiency of men of this type, and their slight inclination for coitus are inadequate to satisfy normal sexual desires on the woman's part. An unusually large male organ is more frequent than a very small one, even though extreme cases are rare. It is conspicuously hereditary and seems to run in families. And it is also *racial.* Negroes, for example, are generally longer and more massive, than white men; and they also number among them, proportionally to their own large average, more extreme "phallic giants" than the whites. On the whole, a phallos of unusual size must be more agreeable to women, on account of increased pressure and friction in coitus. It can only be considered a disadvantage when the vagina is infantile, or at the beginning of sexual relations. But physical disturbances of married life on this ground are rare, though men who know themselves to be unusually well endowed by

---

[1] The production and exchange of medical certificates before marriage, which could save so much misery and disease, has still to meet many quite comprehensible obstacles. It occurs to me that these would largely disappear, if either party would and could nominate an absolutely reliable and acceptable confidential representative; these could then meet, and discuss the circumstances in question, finally exchanging reports. Further, in certain cases a prenuptial instruction of the man in the special idiosyncrasies of the girl and in fact of woman generally, would be most desirable.

Nature, should exercise particular care till they are quite sure that they cause no harm to their wives.

An unusually wide vagina is also not an irreparable hindrance to marriage, although it implies less acute pleasure, especially for the husband. And we must admit frankly that the normal distension of the vagina and its introitus, after several births, is generally far from negligible in its effect on the husband. But these disadvantages may be largely met and compensated by careful surgical treatment after confinements and by exercise of the pelvic and vaginal muscles (cf. Chapters IV. and V.). And the special technique of variations in actual communion offers very efficient amends (cf. Chapter XI.).

If there is a diminution of stimulus and attraction, in spite of surgery, muscular gymnastics, and mastery of technique in attitude and position—well, that must be accepted as inevitable, just as so many other things must be, in life: Old Age and Death, for instance. And redoubled tenderness, devoted attention, psychic and mental companionship may make up for what Life has taken away.

CHAPTER XI

DURING the act of union, attitude and motion of both partners assume enormous significance.

Both from the scientific and from the practical point of view there is not the slightest necessity to enumerate here the famous one hundred—and so many—positions known to Oriental encyclopædias of the art of love.   But it would be an equal error to avoid the discussion of this topic, for it has great practical importance as regards:

(*a*) The increase of sexual pleasure;
(*b*) The prevention of hygienic dangers or injuries;
(*c*) The control (promotion or prevention) of conception.

As regards the last of these considerations, it may be said that every position in coitus which tends to promote the intensest possible orgasm in both partners simultaneously, or almost simultaneously, increases the probability of conception.   A position which facilitates ejaculation in the *interior* of the vagina helps the spermatozoa to penetrate into the uterus forthwith.   A position of the female genitals which involves depositing the semen in the immediate neighborhood of the cervix—even after the cessation of the orgasm—increases the likelihood of impregnation; as does also the retention of the erect male member inside the vagina, where it acts as a stopper or seal.   On the other hand, the chances of conception are diminished by an attitude which causes the semen to ebb back out of the vagina.[1]

---

[1] What is said here does not in any way conflict with the factors emphasized above.   The direct and immediate absorption of the spermatozoa by uterine activity during coitus, the mobility and tenacity of the sperm cells, which enable them—even in the minimum amount of seminal fluid!—to enter the vagina and the uterus, and traverse long distances after protracted intervals of time, to reach their destination, the egg cell in the ovary; these must always be the most important elements in the drama of impregnation.

The factors we now consider can only exert a favorable or unfavorable influence, but such influence may, in some cases, turn the scale.

Certain hindrances to coitus arising from physical peculiarities of one or both partners (*e.g.,* the enlargement of the abdomen in pregnancy or obesity) can be overcome by the appropriate positions and methods. Similarly, dangers incidental to union, especially for the woman, under such circumstances as disproportion of the genitals (liability to lacerations, and during pregnancy, etc.), can be avoided or minimized. In inappropriate positions, risks of injury may be increased.

Finally, the intensity of pleasurable feeling is dependent to a conspicuous degree on the attitude and movements during that supreme union.

And more: as the grade and locality of stimulation are different, according to the relative position of the two partners to one another, so therefore the sensations arising from such stimulation vary also, and not only in degree but in kind—and this in a wide range of variation. Thus diversity becomes possible in the act of coitus; and, as the Ancient World has testified in many oft-quoted aphorisms,[1] no pleasure is possible in sustained and repeated use unless adequate variety and shades of difference are introduced into it; so the subject of our present study has considerable importance for the weal or woe of married life.

POSITIONS

There are two possible main positions in coitus: the first, namely, that in which the man and woman meet face to face[2] or converse position (or anterior, from the woman's position), and the second in which the man faces forwards but the woman turns her back, the averse position,[3] posterior or *coitus a tergo.*

And in each of these two main *positions* various *attitudes*

---

[1] *Cf.* the saying of Publius Syrus: "Nihil est jucundum, quod non reficit variatum."

[2] A third position in which the face and abdomen of the man are brought into contact with the woman's side and flank is so little in harmony with both male and female physiology that it is only used as an occasional variation, with no charm but that of "difference" and various definite disadvantages. The Mohammedan recommendation of this position with intent to secure impregnation in cases of uterine displacement is based upon wholly erroneous anatomical views.

[3] Or position of flight and pursuit.

are possible, and many are practicable and successful from our point of view.

Many authorities consider this second position in coitus —the averse—as the essentially natural one, on biological grounds.

I am of the opinion, in accord with the majority, that the first or converse must be considered the more natural for human beings in their present anatomical structure, for this reason: that in this position the slight curvatures (declinations) peculiar to the copulatory organs—the vagina inclining forwards and the erect penis[1] backwards— correspond with one another. This does not mean, however, that the averse position is unnatural or physiologically inferior.

Let us now examine successively the various *attitudes,* according to their physiological significance, analyze them and ascertain by means of this analysis, when they are indicated: that is, let us decide in what circumstances and for what purposes each of them is advisable, or the reverse.

A.—First Position: Converse, Face to Face

There are six attitudes in the converse position, which we have to consider in detail, on account of their wide dissimilarities.

I.   Habitual or Medial Attitude

The normal or habitual coital attitude, which is not only *habitual* but also *medial,* as between extreme extension and extreme flexion, is as follows. The woman lies on her back; her thighs are separated and her knees slightly bent. The man lies upon his partner's abdomen, supporting his knees and elbows as far as possible on the bed or couch, in order to relieve her of his weight; his legs and thighs are between hers.

On the whole this attitude is both physiologically and psychologically appropriate.

---

1 From now on, the term "phallos," is used to denote the erect penis, in action, as the Greeks used it.

Psychologically, because it expresses the man's intense unconscious urge to *feel that he both protects and possesses* his partner, and equally the *corresponding psychic needs* of the woman.

This attitude, like some of its variations, also permits the couple to increase the joy of union by mutual kisses and caresses, and gives a greater range of emotion and sensation through the contact of the two bodies from thorax to thighs.

As against these advantages of the medial attitude in coitus there is an overwhelming drawback in certain cases, namely, the weight of the man's body—*overwhelming* in a literal sense, only too often! It is unnecessary to describe these cases in detail; they are obvious. I will only emphasize one objection: the danger of heavy exterior pressure on the pregnant uterus at a period in gestation when the whole abdomen is not so much enlarged that this attitude is obviously contra-indicated.

The stimulation which results in normal or medial coitus, in normally excitable couples, is itself "normal," *i.e.,* of medium degree, and sufficient to bring about complete detumescence and relaxation of tension in both partners. The intensity of its characteristic pleasurable sensations is also medial.

But if there is any disharmony, however slight, between the proportions of the male and female organs due to *the relative or absolute insufficiency of the phallos,* the necessary degree of stimulation cannot generally be attained in this "normal" attitude.

The prospects of impregnation are generally good.

II.   ATTITUDES OF EXTENSION   (Variation (a))

In the case of phallic insufficiency, during the normal attitude, matters may be improved by slightly shifting and stretching. After emission has taken place, in the normal attitude, the woman closes her thighs and stretches her legs out to their whole length, so that the man's thighs now enclose and clasp hers. For the man, this has the double advantage of increased stimulation of the penile shaft, in a somewhat crude but effective way, and of security that the phallos does not slip out of the vagina.   The attitude of extension is especially successful when the male organ is not in itself too small, but has had difficulty in attaining full erection, whether this disability be chronic or momentary, *e.g.,* owing to too quickly repeated acts of intercourse.

In the first place, the friction of the base of the penis against the *symphysis pubis* of the more favorably inclined female pelvis, against the folded *labia majora,* and even against the inner portions of the woman's thighs, contributes to the happy result.   And the pressure of these structures reciprocally causes an increased erection and congestion throughout the length of the intromittent organ.

In the extension attitude, the woman has the advantage of increased stimulation of the vulva and exterior vaginal orifice.   And, an even more important consideration for her, the clitoris in this attitude is offered more fully to the friction or stroking of the penile shaft.   The man's increased erectile capacity, of course, has great value for *her.*

But in this attitude the phallos cannot penetrate so deeply into the vagina.

The extended attitude with legs pressed together can be adopted by the woman—whether from the beginning of the act of intercourse or immediately after emission—in order to retain the semen in the vagina, by holding the phallos firmly clasped in the vagina between her thighs (until erection subsides).

The extended attitude of the woman is made more complete by keeping the upper part of her body quite flat and placing a cushion under her loins; it must not be *below* the loins, this would have the contrary effect, nor be too soft and flat; a rather firm, hard pillow or bolster is preferable. The thicker the pillow the better the angle of the female body in the extended attitude.   The result of such extreme extension of the lumbar region is an increased inclination of the pelvis, and accessibility of the *symphysis pubis,* and with it, the clitoris.

Symphysis and clitoris are thus pressed more closely and continuously against the anterior wall of the phallos than in the first-mentioned *prone* attitude and receive stronger stimulation. It is obvious that in order to receive the full effects of extension, the legs of the woman should be horizontal—whether closed or opened is immaterial, for any flexion of the thighs would decrease pelvic inclination and destroy the effect of the pillow beneath the loins. The greatest pelvic inclination is attained by stretching not only the spine but the thighs from the hip joints to their fullest extension, namely, by letting the legs hang down.

We obstetricians frequently make use of a similar attitude in our work (we call it Walcher's Suspension) in appropriate cases.

Second Extension Attitude

Suspensory (Variation (b))

Such extreme extension would have no purpose in coition and would hardly be possible. But certain Oriental treatises on erotics recommend an attitude based on the same principles, though less strained, specially to facilitate the rite of removing the hymen. This is very interesting from the scientific point of view and can serve as a helpful indication in medical practice. In this attitude the woman is placed near the edge of the bed or couch. The upper part of her body is prone, and stretched as far as possible backwards, the sacrum is across or even a little over the edge of the bed; her slightly parted legs hang down but her feet must rest against a firm support. The edge of the bed must also offer firm support and be high enough for the man to operate. He places himself between the knees of his partner, and, according to the Oriental prescriptions aforesaid, standing upright on his feet. A really supine attitude is, of course, impossible for him, with the female body at such an angle. But in practice, his vertical attitude becomes diagonal. He bends forward as far as possible, resting his hands on the bed, on either side of his partner.

Now what is the purpose of this attitude? Why is it recommended particularly for first intercourse?

The Oriental authorities do not give reasons, but the

method is logical and certainly arose as the result both of intuition and the empiric experiments of centuries.

When we consider the anatomical conditions, the explanation of this tradition seems to me to consist rather in the fact that in this attitude, the phallos during the process of immission is pressed downwards from its steep angle into an almost horizontal direction—even rather than in the increased stimulation offered to the clitoris. The intromittent organ and its base are pressed strongly against the woman's pubic arch, and they respond elastically. So the glans penis slips smoothly along the vestibule and into the vaginal orifice, gently stretching the free edge of the hymenal membrane, instead of immediately rending it. It is only torn by the pressure of the main portion of the phallos, while in other circumstances, *i.e.,* in the normal position it is destroyed by a sharp, sudden thrust of the glans penis from outside, in an unavoidably rougher, more painful manner.

But we need hardly point out that the suspensory attitude, in spite of its advantages, cannot be recommended to our newly wedded pair. We can only urgently recommend the man (basing our advice on the grounds given above) to introduce the glans and tip of the phallos, in first intercourse, as smoothly and gently and as much in front as possible and to stretch the hymen rather than split it forcibly. In the medial (normal) attitude, the simplest way is for the man to lie at an angle facilitating approach and intromission from in front and from above downwards, so that the phallos is pressed downwards in its passage through the pubic arch of the woman.

But I have myself recommended the Oriental suspensory attitude occasionally, and with success, if necessary after a short interval of abstinence and repose, when, in spite of successful rupture of the hymen, there were still obstacles to complete intercourse owing to painful soreness and even acute inflammation of the fossa navicularis.[1]

---

[1] The fossa navicularis is that portion of the vestibule lying immediately in front of the posterior junction of the inner lips (frenulum labiorum, No. 17, in Plate I.). It is often proportionately larger than in the Plate, and can form an appreciable depression behind the attachment of the hymenal membrane; and if the phallos continually presses and rubs this area, a lesion can ensue, as mentioned in the text. If our advice to perform the act of intercourse in the extension attitude—in order to spare the hymenal

Otherwise this attitude is only in question as a form of occasional variation which concentrates stimulation in the region of the clitoris and posterior vaginal wall for the woman, and in the frenulum præputii (præputial region) and the anterior penis shaft for the man. As the same effects may be obtained in attitudes less arduous and inconvenient for both partners, the exhaustion which follows coitus in the suspensory position is not compensated by any special advantages.

This attitude does not promote the reception of semen in the uterus, as the phallos can only penetrate a comparatively little way, and the fluid ebbs back and out of the vagina, for the vaginal orifice lies below and downwards from the *portio* or cervix.

III. ATTITUDES OF FLEXION

The direct contrast to this attitude of extreme extension which came to us from the Near East, is the extreme flexion of the woman's body in coition, which is extraordinarily popular among the Chinese, as is proved by the pictures in their "Bridal Books." The extreme practicable form of this method is as follows:

The woman lies on her back, lifts her legs at right angles to her body from the hips, and rests them on the man's shoulders; thus she is, so to speak, doubly cleft by the man who lies upon her and inserts his phallos; she enfolds both his genital member and his neck and head. At the same time the woman's spine in the lumbar region, is flexed at a sharp angle and the pelvic opening directed as far as possible upwards, so that the vulva lies sloping and almost flat, instead of vertically as in the normal medial attitude, and the vagina is directed almost vertically downwards. At the same time the tissues of the perineal region are drawn tensely "tight" by the position of the pelvic fissure.

Therefore the forms of stimulation during intercourse in

---

area—is to be successfully followed *the man must exactly realize what he is doing and why.* Otherwise there is risk of an exactly opposite effect, as the phallos, especially in incomplete erection, instead of gliding from in front into the vagina, misses the way and touches the fossa.

this attitude differ much from those experienced in the extension attitudes described above.

The phallos does not enter the vagina from the front, but presses forward across the perineum. The clitoridal region situated in the anterior part of the vulva, is not touched at all. Only on *entering* the vagina does the glans meet the anterior vaginal wall. As the phallos penetrates further it has to adapt itself to the direction of the vagina which clasps and contains it, and is strongly pressed backwards; thus the elastic base of the male organ responds with an equally strong counterpressure, against the anterior vaginal wall. This strong double pressure provides an appreciably heightened stimulation in comparison with the normal attitude where phallos and vagina have the same direction, and there is hardly any direct mutual pressure. In the normal or medial attitude, stimulation is as it were distributed more thinly and evenly over the whole genital apparatus. In the attitude we are describing, it is concentrated on the anterior interior wall of the vagina and the posterior rim of its orifice, on the upper edge of the glans penis and the lower surface of the base of the phallos.

Which of these two methods is to be preferred? That depends not only on the momentary moods and desires of the partners, but especially on the conditions of the feminine parts. If they have been expanded and distended and if the muscles of the vaginal wall have lost their tenseness and contractile power (which generally occurs simultaneously, for example, often after several births), then the clasping of the whole shaft of the penis as described in Chapter IX., which implies a certain parallelism of phallos and vagina, as in the normal attitude, is no longer possible. Thus one of the chief advantages of the normal attitude is canceled.

Moreover, the relaxed voluntary muscles (constrictor cunni and levator vaginæ) are often also incapacitated from efficient action. In these circumstances the perineal tension together with the backward pressure of the base of the phallos, attained by the flexed attitude, supply other compensatory stimuli.

Moreover, in this position which exposes and opens the pelvic fissure as widely as possible, the phallos can penetrate

the vagina right up to the hilt, where it joins the body at
the symphysis pubis, which is not otherwise possible.
Where the vagina has been much distended, this is of course
a great advantage.

In other cases, a certain caution is advisable, till the man
knows *precisely how far* he can penetrate.

But a vagina of average length and dilatability is able to
receive and contain a phallos of normal size, at maximal
penetration throughout its length.

To complete description of this attitude, we must mention
that here the profound penetration of the phallos and the
direction of the vaginal canal are both favorable to conception.

On the whole, extreme flexion is suitable as a variation,
and also in the case of women with too wide and slack
vaginæ.

But the extreme form of flexion in coitus has difficulties
and disadvantages for both partners. Not every couple is
capable of its gymnastic efforts. And the method which
entails placing the woman's legs on the man's shoulders
separates faces and breasts and the whole upper portion of
both bodies.

The extreme attitude is not, however, necessary, in order
to attain the advantages of flexion. The well-known
"lithotomy" attitude suffices fully, if the couple are careful to see that the direction of the intromittent phallos
keeps across the perineum and straight towards the anterior
vaginal wall.

The "lithotomy" attitude on the woman's part is as
follows: she lies on her back bending her legs at the hips
and opening her thighs as widely as possible, and also
bending her knees. This attitude exposes both vulva and
perineum even more advantageously than the extreme
flexion, because there the knees are not bent; its effect is
indicated by the name (a relic of mediæval surgery, and
the cutting for bladder-stones!) and by its widespread
utilization in operative gynæcology.

Intercourse in this attitude is much more convenient for
both partners than in extreme flexion, so on principle it is to
be recommended in preference to the preceding one.

There are a number of intergrades and modifications between the normal and flexed attitudes. The flexion can be lessened or increased *during* intercourse. Thus occasion offers of varying and heightening stimulation and compensating for any possible anatomical disadvantages.

In the attitudes previously described, the man's body was placed over the woman's. It is also possible to have intercourse with the bodies reversed; the woman above the man. An attitude which simply reverses the normal is not often found in practice; but may often have been attempted as an experiment. It has no special physiological[1] significance. But another attitude in which the man lies beneath the woman is of the utmost importance and interest.

IV. ATTITUDE OF EQUITATION (ASTRIDE)

This is the method of coitus which the Roman poet Martial considered so normal and obvious that he could not conceive of that paragon of married couples, Hector and Andromache, in any other attitude.

The technique here is as follows:—The man lies on his back, if necessary with a pillow under the sacral region, and with his legs slightly bent and supporting the woman's thighs. When immission of the phallos into the vagina has taken place, the woman lets herself down, sitting astride right across her partner's body, as far backwards as possible and facing him. The man keeps still; but she begins deliberate, slow, frictional movements; she remains sitting upright but alternately raises and lowers her body: she *lunges,* rhythmically with her whole trunk. During the downward motion, she increases the pelvic declination so far as possible, *i.e.,* she moves the symphysis downwards and backwards, and stretches the vertebræ especially in the lumbar region. As she moves upwards, the pelvic angle decreases so far as possible and the symphysis is raised and

---

[1] In the reversed medial attitude, as in the normal, vagina and phallos are parallel. The main difference is that the mutual friction is performed in a much more awkward and generally also uneven way and that the semen at once escapes from the vagina. Psychologically this attitude seems to me to have considerable defects compared to the normal, and to be quite inferior.

protruded forwards. The posterior rim of the vaginal orifice and the anterior portion of the perineum move in the same swing. The movements of the feminine genitalia, during intercourse astride, can be best visualized by remembering the approximate outline of the lower rim of the pubic arch, with the clitoris and introitus vaginæ. That is to say, an oval, whose axis throughout its maximum diameter is approximately upright, and whose axis through its minimum diameter runs from back to front; while the direction of the movements executed is as follows: from above, backwards and downwards, and from below, forwards and up again.

As regards the kind of stimulation and excitation which the male and female organs exchange with one another, here, during the downward motion of the woman's body, the same localization of sensation occurs as in the attitude of extension (II.). As she lifts, sensation approaches that peculiar to the flexed attitude. But at the moment of profoundest penetration, there is the exact congruence, the "fitting" which we have met in the normal, medial method. And if this moment is protracted by a slight pause in the rhythm of her movement, there is an enormous range of muscular vibration and contraction, as we have already indicated. In addition there are new possibilities of sensation here, which we have not met before. These arise because this attitude, like flexion, permits full penetration of the male organ into the vagina. Thus the tip of the phallos comes into close contact with the portio vaginalis or mouth of the womb. If this contact is prolonged and becomes a strong pressure, the *glans* and the *portio* or *cervix* can push each other rhythmically to and fro, as the neck of the womb droops freely and loosely into the vaginal canal, and the woman in this attitude (unlike Attitude III.) is able to move her pelvis and abdomen sideways in all directions. These swaying movements extend to the *portio* or mouth of the womb, rubbing it against the *glans* or tip of the phallos, which in the case of such maximal penetration, is itself almost motionless. This friction acquires a certain intensity on account of the steady and concentrated mutual pressure, culminating in stimulation whose special acuteness is not attained in any of the attitudes previously described. This is largely owing to the fact that the two surfaces engaged in friction, are of almost the same consistency and of approximate shape; thus they "fit" into each other.   This cervical friction can be performed in two ways.   In a straight line (sideways or backwards and forwards), through rhythmic swaying of the woman's body; or with a circular "corkscrew" motion of the pelvis.   Both these methods give as it were a different color-tint and *timbre* of erotic pleasure; in the *circular* movement the pleasurable sensations, at least on the man's side, are the stronger.   But the successful execution of this circular friction in the astride attitude, demands the highest degree of muscular control and co-ordination on the woman's part, and a considerable amount of practice.   In fact the whole astride method of coitus makes these two demands on the woman's physiology and erotic technique, so much so that we can unhesitatingly state that many are unable to learn or practice it. Moreover, there may also be anatomical peculiarities of individual structure which deny to certain women, or certain couples, this particular form of connection.   In the case of a comparatively short, inelastic or easily vulnerable vagina, the astride attitude involves too many drawbacks and even dangers.

The psychic factors require special mention here.   In the astride attitude, there is no possibility of mutual embrace or kisses.   On the other hand, the full unimpeded view of each other's bodies, especially of a finely formed feminine body seated upright and leaning backward, has a strongly stimulant effect.   And the opportunity, often missing in other attitudes, of gazing face to face, into one another's eyes, of beholding, in the reciprocal play of expression, the rising tide of excitement to its ecstatic culmination, greatly enhances all the other stimuli of this attitude.

The main disadvantage in complete and frequent practice of the astride attitude lies in the complete passivity of the man and the exclusive activity of his partner.   This is directly contrary to the natural relationship of the sexes, and must bring unfavorable consequences if it becomes habitual. Therefore, on these (profoundly psychological) grounds alone, we cannot recommend the choice of this attitude in connection. Also, physiologically, it cannot be beneficial during any natural function to insist on the maximum of possible tension, mobility, stimulation and culmination of stimulation in response, at every occasion. For there can be no doubt that coitus astride really can afford the summit in both excitement and response, the acme of specific physical sexual pleasure, to both man and woman. As in this attitude it is possible to combine all the various possible local stimuli, which can only be partially and separately experienced in other attitudes: and to blend and vary them in every shade of diversity and intensity, in one supreme act. Thus the main decisive factor in the choice of this attitude must be the wish to experience the keenest possible excitement and gratification. I repeat, however, with serious emphasis, that this attitude astride should be an exceptional variation, and not a normal habit in sexual intercourse.

It is, however, highly suitable when the partners are in an unequal state of bodily vigor and fitness, the man being tired and "slack," while the woman is full of energy and zest. This attitude spares the man as much exertion as possible,[1] without depriving her of her natural sexual relief. When the woman is languid and the man in full vigor, the astride attitude is quite inappropriate and should not be attempted. Nor should it be attempted when the woman is pregnant. A noticeably short vaginal canal (and of course *infantilism*, to an even stronger degree) are also contraindications, as we have remarked above. Great care and consideration are necessary during the first experimental ventures astride.

Finally, we must not forget the greater opportunity for the spermatozoa to invade the uterus in the very act of ejaculation, whereas this opportunity is much diminished, shortly after the act, by the ebbing of the seminal fluid out of the vagina.

---

[1] Note, however, and compare what is said on this point, under heading VIII.: lateral attitude, posterior (a tergo) position.

V. SEDENTARY ATTITUDE (*Vis-à-vis*)

After our detailed discussion of the attitude previously considered, we do not need to repeat ourselves on the subject of the whole scale and type of excitations afforded by intercourse in the *seated or sedentary* attitude: we consider in the first instance the converse position, where the partners are face to face.

The man is seated and the woman is *suspended* across his thighs, with her thighs apart; I used the term *suspended* intentionally, for the woman is *not strictly speaking seated* at all; her buttocks are not supported, for the man's knees are held apart, thus allowing him to open the woman's thighs, expose her sexual organs, and lift or lower her pelvis at will. He inserts his phallos with a rather strong *downward* pressure, which meets the elastic resistance of the clitoris. In this and the following stages of the act there is the same type of stimulation as in the extension attitude (II.) The woman can increase or modify the intensity of friction in the pubic and clitoridal region, by rhythmic movement of her pelvis to and fro. Then she decreases the pelvic angle as much as possible, and protrudes her vulva forwards and towards the man, who responds with a similar movement of his pelvis so that the phallos presses forward deeply into the vagina. The whole mutual rhythm is assisted and accentuated, as the man can clasp his partner's hips and thighs with his hands and press them against his own. And when maximum penetration is effected, we have again—as in Attitude IV.—perfect congruence, or "fitting," and the opportunity for all the voluntary and spontaneous muscular vibrations of and around the vaginal walls. And when the respective organs of both partners are harmoniously proportionate, we have here, too, the possibility of mutual friction between the mouth of the womb and the tip of the phallos, which is the special feature of the attitude astride. The sedentary attitude has this advantage over the preceding (astride), that *both* partners can move freely, though this freedom involves the possibility of uneven movement, of failing to "keep pace" with one another, and thus impairing the full possibility of sensation.

The scale of excitations in the two attitudes is similar, except that in the second (sedentary) it is not possible to enjoy the sensations of flexion. This, however, is not a conclusive contraindication, though *in practice,* the sedentary attitude does not permit of the delicate shades and semitones of delight, nor of the extreme intensity of the orgasm which may be experienced when the man is supine and the woman seated astride.

What then is the special significance of this attitude? It combines the main advantages enjoyed in Attitude IV. without its special disadvantages. Also, in this attitude, the act of immission can take place, with special gentleness and consideration of the hymenal area, as in Attitude II. Moreover, in Attitude V., it is possible to complete the act *superficially* and without profound penetration, thus avoiding close contact with the vaginal *portio*. The resultant excitation is, of course, strictly limited, but generally suffices to bring about mutual orgasm and relief in normally passionate people.

When the man is languid, fatigued, and below par in vigor, the sedentary attitude does not facilitate the act for him as does the preceding, and is thus not specially indicated under such conditions.

The occasional and even frequent employment of the sedentary method is reasonable in the case of slight frigidity, inexperience or recent initiation of the woman, for this attitude stimulates the clitoris more powerfully perhaps than any other, and enables the man, if necessary, to entirely play the active part allotted to him.[1]

The sedentary attitude is further indicated whenever the female organs need special care, and therefore specially appropriate during pregnancy. If intercourse takes place during gestation, in the sedentary attitude and as gently and deliberately as possible, the possibility of unfortunate effects, even in very delicate women, is reduced to the minimum inseparable from any stimulation of the sexual apparatus by reflex action on the uterus.

---

[1] In complete contrast to VI.

The influence of the sedentary attitudes in the case of profound insertion of the phallos, on conception, exactly resembles that of Attitude IV. In cases of slight or superficial penetration, the prospects of conception are decreased.

VI. Anterior-lateral Attitude (Sideways)

Ovid describes the lateral attitude in the face to face position with these simple but adequate words: "Of love's thousand ways, a simple way and with least labor, this is: to lie on the right side, and half supine withal."

The left side is equally feasible, but in practice the right side is generally preferred, for the woman, which, of course, implies the left for the man.

This attitude is hardly possible unless the woman draws up the leg on which she is lying. The lateral attitude thus becomes, for her, half-lateral, half-supine, with a corresponding half-lateral, half-superposed attitude of the man, which is possible by appropriate arrangement of pillows. The leg of the woman which lies uppermost can either be stretched or flexed at will.

Advantages, drawbacks, and type of sensations in the lateral attitude are about midway, between the medial and the flexed (I. and III.). Increase or decrease of the feminine—or masculine—pelvic angles permits of great variations here.

The principal advantages, laterally, are convenience (ease), and avoidance of the pressure of too great masculine weight on the woman's body. The special drawbacks arise from the localized pressure on the woman's leg—and this can only be avoided by approaching the normal horizontal attitude or through extreme flexion and lifting of the captive limb.

To some degree, also, the man is immobilized and has less freedom to operate in this attitude.

B.—Averse Position

We now come to the second possible position in human coitus—from behind, or in the *averse* position. (Position of flight and pursuit.)

VII.—Prone or Ventral Attitude

In the parallel, abdominal attitudes of both partners, the *directions* of phallos and vagina do not coincide, as in the first or normal attitude. For in the abdominal attitude of the woman, the vagina slopes obliquely upwards from outside to the portio vaginalis internally, while in the similar male attitude the phallos slopes obliquely from above at the base, downwards to the tip. This difference of direction is so great that coitus is impossible if it is not artificially rectified, otherwise effective penetration is out of the question, and the male organ misses its aim and slips out during the backward motion of the pelvis under the pelvic arch. It is generally possible to avoid this in practice, if the woman increases her pelvic angle as much as possible, by drawing in the loins—lumbar contraction—thus decreasing the upward direction of the vaginal passage and elevating the vulva and exterior orifice or *introitus*. As a rule this, with the altered position of the pubic arch, suffices to prevent the phallos from slipping out, and to facilitate deep penetration. The same accident is made less likely if the woman keeps her thighs closed, or presses them together, thus affording additional stimulus by friction.

The woman's attitude can be assisted if a small pillow is placed under her pelvis—*not* beneath the abdomen, which would alter the angle and spoil the desired result.

The ventral attitude in successful coitus is only possible for slim, lean people; ample adipose development of the female *nates,* and any appreciable abdominal corpulence in the man are equally obstacles here.

Also, the prospects of successful conception by the entrance of spermatozoa into the uterus are less here than in other attitudes, owing to a combination of unfavorable circumstances. For (*a*) the *glans*, or phallic tip, does not reach far enough into the vagina to shoot its contents into the mouth of the womb or against the vaginal vault, and (*b*) the seminal fluid poured forth on the anterior vaginal wall trickles out and away at once, owing to the slope of the passage, towards the external orifice.

It is obvious that (*a*) is not likely to help the woman to her climax of sensation and relief: on the contrary, it is unfavorable to the female orgasm.   Only an experienced, rapidly responsive woman can attain full gratification in the ventral attitude.   Others (erotically slower or recently initiated) have a bad chance of satisfaction—the more so as the clitoridal region is hardly or not at all affected—disadvantages peculiar to *intercourse backwards* in all its varying attitudes.   And there are further drawbacks from the woman's point of view: in the general discomfort and the weight of the man's body, which is generally more severely felt here than in the normal method.

For the man too, there are comparatively few allurements, though the drawbacks are less pronounced for him than for her.   We could, therefore, have omitted the ventral attitude from discussion, but for the interest of comparison between this second parallelism of the bodies with the first (horizontal, normal).   And in practice, ventral coitus does occur more often than we might expect, because of its comparative *prophylaxis against conception*.   This is intuitively perceived and utilized by couples who would shrink from more active interference with natural processes, from an almost unconscious or subconscious train of thought.

VIII.—POSTERIOR-LATERAL ATTITUDE

The posterior-lateral method has much greater practical importance in marriage than either the ventral or anterior-lateral attitudes.

During the course of married life, longer or shorter periods of time in which one of the partners—whether in general or in particular reference to sexual matters—requires special care and treatment must inevitably occur.

The other partner suffers often more acutely under such constraint than the one stricken.   If intercourse is quite prevented by circumstances, we must face and accept this necessity.   But it should only be prohibited on the most cogent grounds, for if this prohibition lasts for any length of time, it can have serious and far-reaching—even incalculable—effects. Therefore let me recommend the greatest reserve in denial and prohibition to married couples. And every medical man should think carefully before issuing an edict against coitus, especially for any duration of time. It is not infrequently observed that a marriage has been undermined and ruined by such an edict—which perhaps was itself unnecessarily strict and absolute. It happens much more often—and does not exactly promote the dignity or efficacy of the medical profession—that such a prohibition is simply disregarded with touching unanimity by both partners, and without any deleterious effects.

So we must exercise great discretion in forbidding intercourse. In the overwhelmingly greater number of cases it is wiser and better to advise *care*—of course not in a vague negative formula, which is quite useless and vain, but in precise technical physiological detail, appropriate to the circumstances of the individuals concerned. Such precise instructions will often be found to imply recommendation of the *posterior-lateral attitude,* with the particulars indicated forthwith.

Intercourse in this attitude can certainly be, for both partners, the least exhausting of any; it implies the fewest external obstacles, and the least exertion. The stimulation can be modified to the precise degree necessary for relaxation and relief; the male organ can be inserted just as far and no further than any special vaginal or vulvar irritation or inflammation make necessary or desirable. Moreover, there is no weight or pressure of bodies on each other, here.

The lateral position from behind may be dextral or sinistral. In practice both partners generally lie on their left sides, the man has his right hand and arm free, to embrace and clasp his partner, and stroke and caress her. It will be obvious, after what has been said about the respective angles of phallos and vagina when discussing the ventral attitude, that convenient coitus can only take place laterally and backwards, *if the two bodies are not parallel.* The difference in the angles and slopes of the genitals can only be modified to admit of insertion when *the trunks diverge.* Increase of the female pelvic inclination, and decrease of the male facilitate approach, and permit adequate penetration. So the woman should lie with legs somewhat flexed at the hips, and bending forward, the man at full-length. By modifying this attitude and the inclination of the two pelves, it will be possible to determine and vary the degree of penetration in a precise manner.

The type of stimulation is as in flexion. As in Attitude III., feminine excitation is localized in the posterior rim of the vaginal orifice, and the anterior vaginal wall. But this second stimulus, which is always the stronger, is more developed in flexion (Attitude III.) because of the elastic tension of the phallos against the vaginal wall; laterally, however, the operation is reversed, so that the friction is less against the anterior vaginal wall, and more against the posterior rim of the introitus, where it is less effective. We may almost say that the woman receives the greatest friction and stimulus where it has least response. As the clitoris has no contact with the male organ, in the lateral-posterior attitude, the stimulation afforded the woman is at its minimum, unless the phallos penetrates deeply. The excitations are just adequate for a slight degree of orgastic climax in a passionate woman who has attained to harmonious conjugal adaptation; but this relief owes more to psychic and adventitious factors than to specific local stimulus.

Under these conditions, a mild detumescent spasm or orgasm suffices for relief of tension, and is to be regarded as harmless in the majority of convalescent cases or such as require special treatment, and in any case as less deleterious than the prolonged genital congestion and psychic strain of ungratified sexual desire. A convalescent woman of cool and placid sexual temperament has hardly any benefit from posterior-lateral coitus, which affords her too slight gratification to secure any response.

The moderately excitable cases are here the most difficult of all. The stimulus afforded excites the woman too strongly to avoid local congestion and *erection* of the vulvar and vaginal tissues, and not strongly enough for the full

climax and relief of orgasm. In such cases it is best either
to abstain from all stimulation, *i.e.*, from coitus even in the
lateral attitude; or, if preliminary congestion and dilation
have been attained, to complete and intensify the stimulation.
This can be done in three ways; either by moving both
bodies and pelves, thus permitting deeper penetration of the
vagina, which increases the area stimulated and brings the
clitoris into touch with the under surface of the male organ;
secondly by more vigorous friction of the phallos; and
thirdly by simultaneous friction of the clitoris with hand and
finger (which is especially indicated when the two first more
acute grades of excitation are prohibited).

When coitus is performed laterally, and with the precautions described above, the gratification it supplies is
enough to achieve ejaculation and relief in a man of normal
sexual temperament. For him, too, this attitude is the most
convenient and least exhausting method of intercourse.
One might think that coitus astride would be less exhausting
for the male partner, as he has not to exert himself or move
at all, in this attitude, but he cannot decide or control the
intensity of the stimulation he receives, and this intensity
is much greater than in the comparatively tranquil lateral
method. The attitude of equitation (man supine, woman
astride) *can* be the easiest of all for him; but in the overwhelming majority of cases where it is performed, it will be
more exhausting—owing to the peculiar acuteness of the
sensations it provokes, than the active movements he must
make in the lateral attitude.

Indications for the posterior-lateral attitude, as aforesaid,
are (1) general conditions of weakness, or (2) local conditions of weakness or inflammation in either partner, or (3)
pregnancy. In the case of pregnancy, the gentleness of movement depends on the slight and superficial penetration of the
phallos. In these circumstances—very slight and gentle
immission—this method is the most harmless and safest,
even in cases of chronic inflammation of the internal female
genitals, as it neither wounds nor congests. (See detailed
instructions above.)

For conception the posterior-lateral method is about as
favorable as the normal (horizontal) attitude.

IX.—ATTITUDE OF FLEXION

As above I designate the attitude in which the woman kneels, while her body from trunk to thighs is inclined at a more or less acute angle. Her body can be stretched horizontally, supporting itself on hands and arms[1] or on a couch or chair of appropriate height.[2] A third variation is also possible; the woman's body can slope downwards from pelvis to head, with shoulders and elbows resting on a low couch or chair (*the famous knee-elbow posture used in gynæcology*), and form an angle to the upright thighs and legs. The man can kneel behind a kneeling woman or stand behind her as she kneels against bed or divan.[3] He can hold his body almost vertically, or bend over so far that he rests upon the almost horizontal back and shoulders of the woman. In this second male attitude, phallos and vagina lie more or less parallel to one another; but we must bear in mind in considering intercourse from behind, that in this position the slight curves of both male and female genitals do not correspond or "fit" in any of its variations or attitudes.

When the man holds himself upright, and the woman's back and trunk lie almost horizontally, the directions of phallos and vagina do not correspond, so that on insertion the *glans* or tip touches the *posterior* wall of the vagina. Deeper penetration is only possible here if there is mutual pressure by the vagina on the phallos, downwards and reciprocally upwards by the phallos against the wall of the vagina and backwards. This pressure and friction is somewhat intense and elastic, and increases the excitement of both partners.

The difference in direction of slope between male organ and vagina is increased if the woman lowers the upper part

---

[1] Example: The nymph in the bronze group, "Faun and Nymph" in the Museo Nazionale at Naples.

[2] As in the wonderfully tender and absolutely decent drawing by Gustav Klimt (Fig. 97 in Edward Fuchs' "History of the Erotic Motive in Art," published by Albert Langen, Munich).

[3] There is no substantial difference between the variations mentioned above, and an attitude in which the woman stands on her feet and bends her body as far forward as possible from the hips.

of her body and similarly by increasing the inclination of
the woman's pelvis.   So it is at the maximum of divergence
in the feminine *knee-elbow* (or knee-shoulder) *attitudes*
with tense lumbar muscles (and protruded nates) ; in this attitude the vagina even slopes slightly downwards.   As the
lower part of the pubic region here is pressed backwards, the
clitoris approaches the male organ and touches its lower
surface.   In this manner a stimulation of the clitoris by
phallic friction is achieved in the flexed attitude—an
exception to the usual rule applying to the backwards
position.

When the woman kneels (and even more decidedly in the
knee-elbow attitude), a factor emerges which we have not
had cause to mention in any previous attitude.   The contents of the abdominal cavity, especially the intestines, sink
down, under the force of gravitation, into the lowest-lying
portion of the belly in the immediate neighborhood of the
liver.   The abdominal wall curves and protrudes, and there
is a vacuum in the pelvic portion of the abdominal cavity.
The uterus droops, so far as its muscular ligaments permit,
forwards and with the main portion (*fundus*) lowermost.
The vagina is stretched, the cervix or mouth of the womb
is at its greatest distance from the *introitus* (vaginal orifice).   But the most practically important result is the in-
rush of air into the genital passage by suction as the passage
is dilated, and the posterior wall of the passage pressed backwards.   The air fills the whole cylindrical tube of the vagina, the walls distend, and the whole organ becomes—*what
it never is otherwise*—a really hollow space surrounded by
fairly smooth walls, for the characteristic folds and irregularities are smoothed out by the pressure of air, or at least,
partially obliterated.   We gynæcologists make use of
these phenomena in the knee-elbow (or quadrupedal)
position when we examine the surface of the vaginal
walls distended by pressure of air.   The same attitude
is used for the same reasons in certain gynæcological
operations.

In coitus, the rush of air into the vagina has an unfortunate effect, for the distension of the walls and obblitera-
tion of folds much diminish the chance of stimulation by

mutual friction for both partners.   And the piston-like
backwards and forwards motion of the phallos may occasionally force some of the air out of the vaginal cavity again,
to the accompaniment of unpleasantly suggestive and quite
audible whistling sounds.   Even when the air leaves the
vagina again on the resumption of a more normal position
after intercourse—or as much as some hours later—the
process is only too audible and extraordinarily repulsive in
its effect.

In the case of a comparatively small and "tight"
introitus, the danger of this unpleasant phenomenon is
much less, as the phallos is at once enclosed and clasped by
the woman's organ.   But in the case of a dilated orifice with
lax rim,[1] an *audible* result is practically certain after knee-
elbow coitus, and so this attitude is best avoided altogether
under such conditions.

The kneeling attitude is a very popular variation.   It is
perhaps the first variation to be tried by couples who seek
diversity from the normal method.

Why?   Are the stimuli it affords so potent, is the posture
so comfortable or so alluring, is the visual prospect so
æsthetically pleasing?   No, none of these suggestions meet
the case.   I think this attitude is preferred only because
people "want something different," but have not clearly
thought out *what* they want.   So they simply choose the
method which they observe to be usual in sub-human nature.
Nevertheless we may attribute the indisputable tendency
of human beings towards this attitude in coitus to subconscious atavistic instincts.

Attitude IX. favors the entrance of spermatozoa into
the uterus, especially when ejaculation takes place before
the woman's body is bent forward to its fullest extent, and
when she does so bend forward immediately she receives
the seminal fluid, and remains in this posture for some
time.

Moreover the kneeling method is appropriate in pregnancy, because the uterus, owing to the reasons described
above and to its own weight when gravid, is beyond the
reach of the full thrust of the male organ.   On the other

---

[1] As after several births.

hand, caution should be exercised in gestation, because of the *divergence of phallos and vagina,* and because the posterior (hind) wall of the vagina is extremely vulnerable in pregnant women, and should not be exposed to the full force of the almost vertical phallic thrust. Moreover, when birth will take place shortly, *all* contact of the upper and inner part of the vagina with the outer world is to be deprecated, because of possible invasion and infection by *bacteria.* Because of this, and because the uterus and the child in the womb should not alter their normal position at this period, the kneeling attitude should never be attempted in the last months of pregnancy.

X.—Posterior-Sedentary Attitude

The last attitude we have to consider is that in which the seated man takes his partner, who turns her back to him, on his lap, and performs coitus in this posture. The man separates his thighs slightly, but the woman spreads hers as widely as possible in order to open her vulva and facilitate approach. In the normal sedentary attitude, however, her body inclines more or less forwards, so that insertion becomes difficult, and there is risk of the phallos losing its direction, during the rhythmic movement of coitus, and slipping from under the pubic arch. This can only be avoided if the woman increases pelvic inclination, by arching her loins, and backward pressure of the vaginal entrance, and/or by simultaneously leaning forward, while the man leans back. Only by exercising or combining these measures is it possible to secure sufficiently deep penetration by the phallos. It goes without saying that the woman must be seated far enough back on the lower portion of the man's abdomen. Thus this last attitude has some resemblance to the attitude astride from behind, which particular variation has neither special advantages or special features compared with the posterior-sedentary attitude, and is therefore not discussed here in detail.

When the woman has attained a good degree of experience and adaptation, she is able, both in this attitude and the sedentary variation, face to face, to execute a sort of rotary "corkscrew" movement, which—enhanced by corresponding movements of the man—produces something the same type of sensation as the attitude astride affords. But it is much more difficult to perform these rotary movements in Attitude X. than in IV. And the result never equals what can be enjoyed "astride."

But on the other hand, if the phallos penetrates completely, even after slight modifications in the posture of both partners, there is "congruence" or "fitting," which when both organs are harmoniously proportionate, enables them to execute friction of the *glans* against the mouth of the womb. This friction produces the same acute stimulation as was possible when seated face to face, or (in fullest intensity) when astride. The stimulation in Attitude X. is less acute, because the penetration is less deep, and the pressure of tip and cervix less close. Thus, on the whole, this "seated from behind" attitude has fewer advantages and more defects in comparison with other variations and methods. It is generally adopted because in this attitude actual coitus may be most easily and conveniently combined with erotic play and manual caresses.[1] The indications suitable for modifying or employing the kinds of local stimulation possible in sedentary coitus, may be deduced from our description of its procedure.

A synopsis of the various attitudes in coitus and their special features, is here given in tabular form.

---

[1] *E.g.*, in the friction of the clitoris or pressure of the breasts by the man's hand.

SYSTEMATIZED TABLE OF ATTITUDES POSSIBLE IN SEXUAL INTERCOURSE WITH STIMULI PROPER TO EACH

		TYPE OF STIMULATION	
		TO WOMAN	TO MAN
First Position: Converse, Face to Face, or Forwards.	I. Normal Attitude.	Moderate throughout genitalia; slight in clitoridal area.	Moderate throughout the phallos.
	II. Extended Attitude.	Posterior wall of vagina. Region of the clitoris.	Frenulum præputii; dorsal surface of phallos.
	III. Flexed Attitude.	Front wall of vagina. Back rim of vaginal orifice. Clitoris not affected.	Dorsal surface of the tip. Ventral surface of base of phallos.
	IV. Astride Attitude.	The greatest possible stimulation of the mouth of the womb by the penile tip is here combined with all the stimulations peculiar to the first three methods.	As in the woman's case.
	V. Sedentary Attitude. Face to face.	Stimulation of clitoris. During profound penetration, stimulus as in IV. but less strong. During slight penetration only as in II.	See as in woman's case.
	VI. Lateral Attitude. Face to face.	As in Normal Attitude I. Modifications better, control easier.	The same.

Their Indications and Counter-indications and likelihood to produce Conception.

INDICATIONS	CONTRA-INDICATIONS	FOR CONCEPTION
For normal use.	Pregnancy after early months. Obesity.	Apt.
In cases of small phallos or imperfect erection. When inserting must avoid hurting hymenal region. With modifications in early pregnancy. With slight insertion when uterine adnexæ are inflamed or ovary prolapsed.	In case of superposition of man, for all the period of gestation. In all variations of this attitude, gestation after first months.	Less apt.
When the vagina is slack and widely distended.	In cases of infantilism, pregnancy, chronic internal inflammation and prolapsus ovarii.	Apt.
When the summit of voluptuous pleasure is desired by both. When the man is less vigorous.	Short vagina. Infantilism. Avoid this in the first acts of intercourse. Pregnancy, chronic inflammation, prolapse of the ovary. Not suitable for habitual use.	Less apt.
When inserting must avoid hurting hymenal region. With profound penetration if woman is not sufficiently relieved. With slight penetration in cases of sore vagina, etc., pregnancy, inflammation and prolapse of the ovary.	All indications favorable for "slight" penetration are unfavorable to "profound."	Profound penetration as in IV. Slight penetration less apt.
Convenience as in cases of convalescence or fatigue. Slight pressure on female abdomen.		Apt.

SYSTEMATIZED TABLE OF ATTITUDES

		TYPE OF STIMULATION AFFORDED	
		TO WOMAN	TO MAN
Second Position: Averse, Front to Back, or "From Behind."	VII. Ventral Attitude.	No clitoridal stimulation. Only the anterior vaginal wall and rim of the orifice are stimulated. Only excitable women are sufficiently stimulated.	Frenulum præputii and dorsal surface of phallos.
	VIII. Posterior-Lateral Attitude.	Minimum stimulation as in preceding attitude.	As in preceding attitude.
	IX. Flexed Attitude. From Behind.	Stimulation of the greater part of the posterior vaginal wall. If the woman is in knee-elbow position the clitoris is also excited.	Great stimulation of dorsal part of *glans;* and all dorsal surface of phallos. If woman in knee-elbow position, part of lower penile surface receives clitoridal and pubic contact.
	X. Sedentary Attitude. From Behind.	Front wall of vagina. Back rim of entrance. In deep insertion friction of tip against mouth of womb. Clitoris untouched. Attitude permits of caresses to thighs and breasts of wife.	Prepuce and dorsal surface of phallos. In deep insertion, tip is stimulated by friction of womb.

INDICATIONS	CONTRA-INDICATIONS	FOR CONCEPTION
	Pregnancy. Abdominal obesity. Heavy comparative weight of male body.	Less apt.
Most suitable for one or both partners if ill or weak. Superficial immission in pregnancy, inflamed adnexæ, prolapse of the ovary.		In itself not much less efficacious than the normal (I.) attitude.
Apt for conception. Care necessary in pregnancy. Also in prolapse of the ovary and in inflammation of uterine adnexæ.	If vaginal orifice is distended and slack, afflatus with noise results. Avoid during two last months of pregnancy.	Rather apt.
Advisable, combined with love play, when woman is not fully satisfied.	In cases of deep penetration inadvisable under infantilism, short vagina, pregnancy, prolapse of the ovary. (As IV.)	Not specially apt.

Final Remarks and Summary

We now conclude our study of the physiology of sexual intercourse and erotic technique. It has expanded into a systematic "Synousiology"[1] of respectable dimensions; and I do not regret it, for this hitherto fragmentary and incomplete chapter of physiology[2] had to be written out some day and by some one. It had to be written, both for the doctors and the laity. For the former, because it is not enough for them to know of the morbid and abnormal variations of the sexual act. If they are to guide those committed to their charge aright, in all matters concerning the marriage tie, they must have *precise and profound* knowledge of everything appertaining to coitus, within the limits of the normal and healthy variations: and they must not hesitate to impress this knowledge on the husband—if necessary with detailed information as to technique. Only precise detail can help here: platitudes and phrases are worse than silence. In cases of illness, in cases where it is desired either to ensure or to prevent conception, and in those—perhaps most of all—where *sexual disparities* threaten to destroy marital happiness, marital fidelity, and the bodily and psychic health (of one or both)—it is the doctor's duty to be able to come to the rescue, with precise technical instructions and suggestions based on physiological facts. But here too—power to help, depends on *knowledge*.

And the layman? In one of his effervescent aphorisms on marriage, Balzac has proclaimed that "In love—quite apart from the psychic element—woman is a harp who only yields her secrets of melody to the master who knows how to handle her." But who can play this delicate human harp aright, unless he knows all her chords, and all the tones and semitones of feeling? Only the genius—after long practice and many discords and mistakes!

But, in marriage, such discords are unspeakably painful. So the husband who wants to be more than a blunderer—

---

[1] From the Greek term for coitus.
[2] Physiologists, gynæcologists and specialists on sex have only treated separate portions of the subject-matter.

and if his marriage is to be happy he must be more!—must study the harp and the art of music. Till now, there was no accessible book of rules, for him. Here I have tried to put them before him; but let him remember that I have not written the preceding pages to be skimmed through—and still less, to be read as "spicy stuff"—honor and conscience forbid!—but for his earnest and reverent study.

Having once mastered their contents,[1] he may proceed from the main theme to the variations. And when he has mastered this science and this art—he may enter and enjoy the realm of free fancy according to his gifts. For behold! A miracle! Meanwhile the resonant harp has been itself transformed into an artist in melody, that seeks and sings, and so entrances the initiator, that he testifies, in grateful rapture: "Never was any woman so much a woman as thou, and none ever knew as thou knowest, how to kiss and how to give ever new ecstasies to the embrace of love." [2]

It is the supreme joy in intercourse, to complete and renew the pleasures of union *for each other;* and thus to prove that we desire to *give* joy, to *lavish* happiness, that we seek not only our own fulfillment, but another's, that *love the giver, love the comforter,* rules and decrees each detail of the sexual lives, and that which we seek to find and to give, in the ecstatic union of body with body, is essentially the merging of the souls into one.

"When ye unite one with another, do so with deep consciousness of the greatness, of the dignity of that which ye do! Give yourselves to this work of love; with your souls and with your minds, even as with your flesh!" [3]

---

[1] "No man should marry before he has studied anatomy and dissected the body of a woman." Catéchisme conjugal. Balzac XVIII. Careful study may well replace dissection.

[2] From a Georgian song, by A. Thalasso; reproduced in *Mercure de France,* 1907.

[3] Omar Haleby: "El Ktab."

CHAPTER XII

WE must now conclude our *Synousiology* by mention of the typical symptoms or manifestations of coitus, in the whole organism of both man and woman. Our previous, physiological and technical subject-matter has been neglected by authorities till now; but the general coital symptoms and phenomena have been treated at length in different medical works.

As we have seen, the actual genital processes during intercourse may be subdivided into glandular, venous and arterial, muscular and nervous. The same classification holds good *generally* throughout the body.

The activity of many glands is conspicuously affected and, on the whole, much accentuated. If sexual relief is too long delayed, the flow of saliva may be checked in a painfully perceptible way.[1] But the approach of orgasm increases salivation often to such an extent that convulsive swallowing becomes necessary. The secretion of urine is increased by sexual excitement, as well as by other psychic tensions. The sweat glands operate profusely, and not only at the supreme moments, as might be considered obvious, but for some time in advance. Individual differences are marked in this respect, but perspiration flows from the armpits and often from the hollows of the knees, in many women especially. And not only during coitus, but during the love-play and even the prelude. The glands of the skin, in collaboration with the quickening of secretory activity throughout the organism, serve the natural and unconscious purpose of attracting and exciting the love-partner, by the olfactory impressions which we have already realized as peculiarly potent in their sexual suggestions.

---

[1] *Cf.* the dry throat of extreme terror or suspense.

A further metabolic symptom affects the circulation of the blood. The tiny blood-vessels contract and dilate: a deep flush alternates with extreme pallor. The whites of the eyes are bloodshot. There is higher blood pressure, the heart beats harder and more rapidly.

And all these manifestations steadily increase, with the increase of bodily tension and emotional excitement. They reach their maximum immediately before the acme, continue at highest pitch throughout this experience and slowly ebb as sensation subsides. Their graph or curve is therefore approximately parallel to that of the normal coitus curve. The acute disturbances of circulation are enhanced by specific respiratory phenomena. As the supreme sensation approaches, the breathing of both partners becomes shallower, rapid and more and more irregular. Carbonization is hindered and there is a certain accumulation of carbon-dioxide in the blood, which excites those cerebral centers governing the blood supply and pressure. This reacts on the vascular tissues of the genitalia (phallos, clitoris, bulbi vestibulæ), and increases expansion which is at its height as the orgasm begins. Thus the disturbed and superficial breathing interacts favorably on the local mechanism of the act in both partners.

A less favorable—sometimes a most unfortunate—factor is the heightened pressure, which has caused a stroke or apoplectic seizure in many middle-aged men, with brittle arteries, during coitus.

The muscles also play their part. This is complex and includes the co-ordinated, wholly voluntary and also reflex or automatic specific movements of coitus, and the extraneous, more or less conscious muscular exertions which may become spasmodic just before or during orgasm; in fact which follow a certain tendency to sharp increase, followed by relaxation. The most conspicuous examples are the convulsive movements of the eyeballs and eyelids, which are so characteristic of the summit of sexual excitement that they form an unmistakable signal from the partners, to one another. In persons inclined to *cramps* of the thighs and calves, they may appear to a most unwelcome degree. And inarticulate sounds, groans, gasps and faint screams are also normally and almost universally uttered during the sexual act.

The involuntary muscles co-operate as well; both in the genitalia themselves, where they are basically important, and in the blood-vessels, where they cause the extra blood pressure and changes in circulation. And their frequently convulsive action also leads to occasional evacuation of wind from the bowels and to incontinence of urine, to spasmodic contractions of the bladder. Of course, in the male, there can be no urination during coitus, as the erection mechanically shuts off the anterior urethra. But if the relaxed penis is manually excited again after coitus, it *can* happen that urine is passed before full erection takes place again. In the woman, matters are different, as the congestion and expansion of her erectile tissues offer no obstacle to urination, and no occlusion of the bladder. Thus, in cases of extreme genital susceptibility or exceptionally acute stimulation, urine may be passed in quite small amounts.

These contractions of bowels and/or bladder are probably mainly due to the extension of excitement from the genital nerve centers to those of the adjacent organs. This extension of the affected nerve-areas, a gradual invasion of further and further citadels and territories in brain and spine, by the overwhelming urge, is a typical feature of the whole process of sexual desire. *Luciani* says: "It begins in the posterior lobes of the brain, with the centers governing hearing and sight, passes over the anterior lobes, governing tactile and motor centers, and from thence to the parietal centers of smell; and then, in the course of the sexual act, marches triumphantly along the whole spinal column." Sexual excitement affects the whole nervous system profoundly, producing manifold symptoms, local and general; indeed the circulatory, glandular and vaso-motor phenomena detailed above are *au fond*, of nervous origin.

There is greater affectability of all the sense organs. The retina is much more sensitive than normally to light rays; the expansion of the pupils which heralds the orgasm makes bright light quite painful. This peculiar sensitiveness, together with the muscular spasms mentioned above, cause the extraordinary action and expression of the eyes, characteristic of the orgasm.

The sense of smell becomes more acute. Moreover, there are certain intricate reflex connections, especially in women, between definite areas in the nasal mucous membrane and the sexual organs. During intercourse, there may be "sympathetic" phenomena such as sneezing and intense olfactory impressions.

Hearing is also more acute.

But the most significant *extension of sensory perception* is in *touch*. This is noticeable during the preliminaries of coitus, and increases progressively until the culmination of the act. Hence the phenomena of "ticklishness" with its implications and reactions, which favorably increase and promote sexual stimulation. It is specially localized in the genitalia themselves, and contributes its quota to the acme or orgasm.

Yet there is here a profound contradiction. In spite of this magnified receptiveness to sensory impressions during sexual excitement, an individual under its immediate impact, will pay no attention to extraneous things which would otherwise rouse most violent reactions. He is deaf and blind to the world. He may suffer the strongest shocks and pain—he ignores them, because he *will* not attend to them. Even if the temporary intensification of sensory impressions makes pain more acute—he deliberately closes his consciousness against it, as an obstacle to the supreme goal which focuses all his powers. For it is the signature of supreme sexual emotion, that the most complex cerebral and intellectual functions, the imagination and the will are dominated and absorbed, and "soul and flesh are one."

At this moment of highest vital intensity and activity and during its approach, each individual attains his highest possible degree of attractiveness and physical charm. The coloring becomes more vivid, the eyes larger and more luminous; the facial muscles tenser, so that even in world-worn middle-aged folk, wrinkles and lines are obliterated and youth returns for a few magic moments, and at the supreme acme the archetypal characteristics appear—power

in the man's aspect and expression, tenderness in the
woman's.[1]

Should we wonder if a function, which so intensely and
wholly dominates body and soul, implies an exertion which
is succeeded by a certain fatigue?

No, indeed! But if we aim at understanding and treating
this reaction correctly—as is *practically* important—we
must study it in some detail.

It must first of all be emphasized that normal sexual
intercourse is fatiguing, not because of its muscular exertions, but solely through its demands on the nerves. And
the sudden relaxation after such acute tension causes not
merely fatigue, but even a certain *exhaustion,* such as
we encounter in other (exclusively psychic and mental)
processes.

The higher the tension, the more abrupt its ebb, and the
more extreme the fatigue of exhaustion. The first factor
explains why a coitus carried out in a strictly matter-of-fact
spirit, with despatch, and without exciting accompaniments
(in short, so far as possible as a form of bodily "evacuation"!) is less exhausting (for a short while) than a communion between lovers, in which their whole souls, as well
as their bodies, participate with subtle art and intense
rapture. The second factor explains the ancient and universally recognized truth, that the woman, whose ecstasy dies
away gradually and gently (cf. Graph A) is much less
fatigued than the man. It was, indeed, a man who uttered
the famous phrase: "Post coitum omne animal triste"—
"After coitus, all creatures are sad."

Extreme and painful fatigue is, however, rare. As a rule
the sensation is drowsy, dreamy, and there is a need for
sleep. Only when *too much* is exacted of the organism,
either in the form of too rapid repetitions of the act, or of
one coitus in a state of previous fatigue—there is a sensation
of great tiredness and even comparative (though temporary) collapse. And, of course, the special exertion necessary in the *active* partner contributes to such collapse.

Equally, of course, this *can* do appreciable damage, but

[1] *Cf.* Havelock Ellis's description: "Studies in Psychology of Sex."

only very seldom, and then when several causes combine to deplete and overstrain.   For instance, when an already weakened or morbidly affected body is expected to perform exceptional feats.   *But, as a rule, moderate sexual activity does not harm even diseased people.*

Normally, sexual communion has a most beneficent effect on mind and body of both partners.   Especially when drowsy relaxation is followed by a short rest—it need not be by actual sleep—there develops a sensation of profound gratification, of mental and physical peace, balance, self-confidence, and power which is hardly attainable in such perfection through any other experience.

And the most profound and exquisite happiness which human beings can taste, is tasted by couples who truly *love* one another, during this pause of respite and realization, after completed communion.   Far, far more closely than even the rapture of mutual orgasm does this bliss and content of the *after-glow* unite true lovers, as they lie embraced, side by side, while nature recuperates, and their thoughts, in a waking dream, once more live through the joys they have experienced, and their souls meet and merge, even though their bodies are no longer linked.

This is the first stage of Epilogue—the After-play.

After-play is an essential and most significant act in the love drama, but unfortunately the most neglected of all. Many men are in the habit of going to sleep immediately after coitus; yes, even men who *love* their wives do this sometimes, from ignorance or negligence.   They turn round and presently lie torpid and snoring, while their wives feel the slow ebb of sexual longing, and thus they deprive themselves of the most exquisite psychic and emotional experiences, and they also destroy the illusions of the most loving wife, by showing that they have no idea of the woman's nature, of the æsthetic delicacy of her love, of the profound appreciation sexual pleasure arouses in her, of her need for caresses and sweet words, which lasts much longer than the orgasm.   This is a closed book to them.   In after-play the man proves whether he is (or is not) an *erotically civilized adult.*

He should be assiduous after his own desire is gratified to cultivate his wife's pleasure. And this can be so easily done! A word of love *will* do it, a kiss, a tender touch, an embrace! It will suffice for a loving wife to know that for him, too, all is not over at once, with the tempest of the orgasm, that his happiness endures and echoes through his whole nature, like hers. She herself desires nothing better than opportunity to prove the rapture he has inspired in her.

After-play is, as we have maintained, essential to ideal sexual union, and principally so, because it *seals* and confirms the intensification of love attained in communion. And it is a part of sexual intercourse because of its interchange of tender impressions and sentiments. It is no diminution of this interchange that it is of necessity predominantly psychic, so that bodily contacts are only *accessory.* On the contrary, this makes it the most delicate and ethereal and (in a sense) altruistic of all acts in our love drama.

For this reason we cannot treat it in detail here. Its intimate technique is not *physical* but *psychological,* and to do it justice would require a complete psychology of love— in its subtlest semitones, its slightest currents, cross-currents and under-currents; and this is not the place for such a study.

I confine myself, therefore, to *one* suggestion—cultivate this portion of your sexual relation with the greatest care and attention! But, at the same time, avoid excess! Extravagance and exaggeration are nowhere more out of place than here, where the imagination requires the utmost delicacy and grace.

Physiologically the technique of the after-play may be summed up in this formula; gradual diminuendo of excitement and return to normal balance and control: the ideal is peaceful relaxation and contemplation. As in the earlier stages, so here: methods must harmonize with physiological necessities. Therefore, until perfect equipoise and control return, *the golden rule enjoins no strong stimulation which*

might interrupt and deflect them. Even if married lovers in
the zest of youth, sometimes prefer to jest and laugh and
play after the tempestuous orgasm, until a new wave of emotion again bears them to the summit; even if more mature
men and women, of profound and rich vitality, often begin
erotic play anew before the last tidal wave has completely
ebbed;[1] all this means only that the *Epilogue is deferred, and
does not in any way cancel the golden rule, that the final ebb
and end of each erotic occasion should immediately follow
an orgasm, and should not be deflected by any further genital stimulation.*

The duration of after-play cannot be suggested, because
its end cannot be defined. In Ideal Marriage it passes im-
perceptibly into another prelude. For even after a lengthy
interval, the memories and echoes of the last occasion live
on, in a word of love, a look, a whispered reminder of shared
delight and a tender hope of its renewal.

And if such hope is in vain; if the husband and wife are
parted, even forever:—nevertheless memory and gratitude,
pride and delight remain, so long as the soul remembers
anything.

For the echoes of *this* peerless happiness are *never* si-
lenced.

We quote an extract from the fourth letter of the series
written by Heloïse to her husband, Abélard, long years after
their enforced separation: "Truly, those joys of love, which
we experienced together, were so dear to my soul that I can
never lose delight in them, nor can they vanish from the
mirror of my remembrance. Wheresoe'er I turn, they arise
before me and old desires awake." "Whilst I should
lament for what we did together—I rather sigh and sorrow
for what we can do no more! Not only the deeds that were
ours, thine and mine, but every place and every hour, that
saw them, have been printed with thine image, on my soul
so deeply, that I live them again with thee, moment by
moment. Nor brings sleep, respite nor oblivion. Often my

---

[1] In our next chapter we shall deal with repeated communions and
similar matters.

body stirs and betrays my soul's desire, and words escape me that I cannot unsay." . . .[1]

THIRD INTERMEZZO OF APHORISMS.

I.

The ignorance of woman's physiology which prevails among most men is boundless and incredible.

Camille Mauclair.

2.

Ye shall some day love beyond yourselves
So first learn loving !

Nietzsche.

3.

They who will learn Love, will always be its scholars.

Bernhardi. (Don Juan.)

4.

Si vis amari, ama ! If thou wilt be loved—love !

Seneca. Epistolae.

5.

Here is a perfect poem: to awaken a longing, to nourish it, to develop it, to increase it, to stimulate it and to gratify it.

Balzac.

6.

Amor nihil potest amori dene-gare.
Amans coamantis solatiis satiari non potest.

Love can deny naught to love.
The lover can never enjoy his beloved enough.
From the Codex Amoris of the Twelfth Century. (Provence.)

7.

He loves but little who
Can say and count in words, how much he loves.

Dante. Vita Nuova.

8.

In marriage alone, is the woman completed and fulfilled by the man, and he through her.
Man and woman together compose the fullness of humanity.

Hippel.

---

[1] Translated from Latin.
Cf. the concluding verse of Thomas Hardy's poem, "One Ralph Blossom Soliloquises."

9.

Laetitia perfectio est.   Joy is perfection.

Spinoza.

10.

I know not, whether I am entangled in error; but for me, the sexual problem is both root and flower, Alpha and Omega of all right living.   And though one works night and day for the weal of humanity and though one offers up goods and life itself on that altar, all this seems to me in vain, if one neglects and degrades *sexual functions, the eternal rejuvenators, and the elementary school of any true altruism.*[1]

S. H. Ribbing.[2]   (Sexuelle Hygiene.)

11.

The most precious joys of sense are received from the imagination and the heart.

De Vauvenargues.

12.

A husband's interest and honor alike, enjoin that he should never permit himself a sexual gratification which he has not made his wife desire as well.

13.

The chastest wife can also be the most voluptuous.

14.

If there are varieties (as of melody) between one erotic occasion and another, a man can always enjoy happiness with one and the same woman.

15.

To swiftly apprehend the shades and semitones of pleasure in love, to master and develop them, to give them a unique and individual style of expression—therein lies the genius of a husband.

Between couples where no love is, this genius is—vice.   But caresses inspired by love are never unchaste or vicious.

16.

To be a lover is easier than to be a husband.   For it is more difficult to show intelligence every day than to make pretty speeches from time to time.

(Last five Aphorisms by *Balzac.*)

17.

Cast we from us our garments!   Naked the body, Beloved
Shall meet its naked companion, in the embraces of Love.

Paulos Silentiarios.
(Greek Love Epigrams adapted
by Karl Preisendanz.)

---

[1] I have italicized these memorable words.
[2] Ribbing was a distinguished Swedish writer on sex.

18.

Know ye, each one, yourselves. The wise shall choose as it suits him
One and the same delight, does not enrapture us all.

Ovid.
Ars Amatoria. Book III.

19.

Press not, although the tempest urge, thy pace!
Lest she thou lovest linger far behind.
Soar side by side! And mingle flesh and mind
In one joint moment of supreme embrace.

Ovid.
Ars Amatoria. Book II.

20.

Lovers in their play, when they have been liberated from the traditions which bound them to the trivial or the gross conception of
play in love—are thus moving among the highest human activities
alike of the body and of the soul. They are passing to each other
the sacramental chalice of that wine which imparts the deepest joy
that men and women can know.

Havelock Ellis.
"The Play Functions of Sex."

PART IV

HYGIENE OF IDEAL MARRIAGE

Ethics and Hygiene of the cohabitation of man and woman are
alike determined by their mutual love.

Féré.

INTRODUCTION

DEFINITION, LIMITATION AND ARRANGEMENT OF MATERIAL

THE Hygiene of Marriage treats of everything tending to
place conjugal cohabitation on a wholesome basis, to promote the health and thence the happiness of their life together, and so far as possible to avert all that could endanger
this health and happiness.

In a general sense, therefore, it would comprise the whole
bodily hygiene of sex, and a large part of its psychology.
Readers will understand that to treat this whole range,
would be beyond our present purpose, and that we must confine ourselves to the hygiene of sex life in marriage, in its
exact and limited sense.

This may be conveniently subdivided into physical and
psychic hygiene. But we must never forget that bodily and
psychic factors continually interact and influence one another, and especially that the bodily functions of sex in a mutually loving couple, *i.e.,* in Ideal Marriage—have always a
strong psychic element.

CHAPTER XIII

BODILY HYGIENE

I. *First Intercourse or Defloration.—Honeymoon*

LET us begin at the beginning, namely with the bodily consummation of marriage. It is not by any means necessarily identical with *defloration* or the rupture of the hymen or maidenhead, for many women do not enter married life as virgins. For cases in which the newly married wife is already used to sexual relations, the subject matter of our next pages has, of course, no relevance, or only very limited application. But it is of the utmost urgency that the man who marries a *Virgo intacta* (untouched virgin) shall not imagine that the genital initiation of his young bride is in any way an easy matter, or one that may be lightly or inadvisedly undertaken.

For in her, he will meet resistance on two planes; spiritual and bodily.

The spiritual or psychic resistance *exists in every case;* however intense her love, complete her *theoretic* knowledge, and implicit her trust in him. It exists even when the bride succeeds in concealing it from him and her own conscious mind!

This can best be exemplified by a comparison which I have hitherto intentionally abstained from drawing, in these pages; namely by comparing the human maiden with the young sub-human female, who has not yet known the male of her species. Here, too, reluctance and resistance are fundamental! The sub-human female desires coitus, but if she has not before experienced it, her behavior differs strongly from that of those who already "know." Certainly the experienced ones often make tentative efforts to escape their wooers, but it is obvious that these efforts are only love-play intended to further excite the males, and probably also to prolong their own gratification. But the novices show very different symptoms. With them the attempted flight is far more than a playful allurement, and their movements and expressions betray a profound struggle between the elemental urge to yield and unite and a sort of shyness, and instinctive dread; and the victory of desire over dread is often very slow and difficult. The man who observes his canine friends, with the deep comprehension and mutual trust that can exist between man and dog, needs only to watch the expressive eyes of the bitches during the approaches of the males. The dread of the beginners is unmistakable, in spite of the visible and ardent instinct to mate; but the already initiated are all eagerness for the male.

And this profound and elemental dread which the human maiden shares with the animal, is assuredly something much greater than the virginal woman's fear of the impending pain from her torn hymen. It exists in animals that have no hymen and in whom even first intercourse gives no pain. It exists in the highest degree in the absolutely ignorant girl, who knows nought of coitus or the hymenal membrane.

We may not doubt that this instinctive dread, which masks unconscious resistance, has deeper origins and significance than the fear of short physical pain. The man who troubles to realize and understand this reluctance, need only remember that defloration means the beginning of the most important changes and events in a woman's life; the inception of active sexual functions, with all their results, duties—and dangers.

In any case, whether this reluctant dread be unconscious, subconscious, or—to the least extent—conscious, it has every claim to due recognition and respect. This does not mean that the bridegroom should meet it with weak submission, sentimentality, or least of all, misplaced pity. But it emphatically means that he has the first—but not the last nor certainly the easiest!—opportunity to show that delicate consideration and that technical proficiency on which both her happiness and his largely depend. For "the course of a marriage is determined by the wedding night."

The bodily obstacle to be encountered is the hymen alone; for there *must not be* any question of defensive struggles, gestures of repulsion, or closed thighs. If these distressing signs appear they prove conclusively that the psychic preparation of the bride is incomplete: and that she must be wooed into compliance. *Till then, all attempts at rupture of the membrane must be deferred.* "Thou shalt not begin thy marriage with a rape," wrote Balzac. And I would add: "For this offence avenges itself, for many years."

The main requisites in this part of erotic technique have been discussed in Chapter XI. We need only add here that the phallos should advance from above and in front—in the case of a recumbent woman, in the "normal" position— so that the *glans* slides along the vestibule and into the slight aperture that exists even in maidens. As the invading organ continues its pressure, the membrane stretches tensely, and then splits generally in two places, on left and right, backwards. Of course this is to some extent painful, for the woman. But the pain is quiet brief and bearable by a woman with a normally thin hymen and average nervous sensibility. And the duration of this pain is reduced to the minimum if the husband, at the moment of entry, meets the immediate resistance of the hymen by a quick, not rough but decided forward pressure. If the woman, instead of shrinking or starting back, can be induced to respond by a *slight rapid counter-pressure,* the hymen will be ruptured in a moment, and defloration effected with the entry of the penis. The woman's loss of blood from the small tears in the membrane is usually slight and soon ceases. But in exceptional cases it lasts longer and is profuse; the bride should then lie quite still on her back, with closed legs, and avoid all contact with the wounds. Do not dab or wipe them! The bleeding will presently stop of itself. Medical treatment is only very rarely necessary.

If the maiden membrane cannot be so easily ruptured as is desirable, and as has just been described, attempts at *perforation and penetration should not be continued,* but rather postponed to the next day, or even the day after the morrow. Too prolonged, or too soon repeated, or too vigorous efforts on the man's part generally cause only an increased sensitiveness to pain and nervous fear, and thus make success more difficult. In the same way, even the "decided forward pressure" recommended above, must be executed with care, so that it may be checked at once, if the hymen proves too tough, the pain too acute or the fear of the bride too great.[1]

"Advance then with mercy and with circumspection! Nor seek with a forcible thrust to break the shuddering resistance of her virginal chalice. Know how to bridle the powerful steed of thy desire. And if Allah hath made thee too mighty and great of girth, hesitate not to defer thy right of entry unto the next night, or even unto the third." It is the famous Muslim Sage, Omar Haleby, who speaks thus, in his great book, *El Ktab*.

How much wiser, more intelligent and more sympathetic are the Orientals (in this as well as other matters of love!) than most of our Western men, who feel themselves entitled to ignore all real consideration and regard on their wedding nights, in the fear of seeming "impotent" and "no good"! In many races, religious or social rituals prescribe postponement of first intercourse for two or three days after the ceremony.[2]

Nevertheless, here, too, the old rule "Ne quid nimis"— "Nothing in excess!"—holds good. Prolonged postponement of defloration can do harm in various ways. If precise suggestions are asked for, here, I would say: if after four nights, and thrice-repeated attempts, perforation and first coitus have not been successfully performed, the couple should consult an efficient gynæcologist who is at the same time a psychologist in sexual matters. Such a special-

---

[1] "No woman has been given her full share of the beauty and the joy of life who has not been very gradually and skilfully initiated into the sexual relation. . . . A really satisfactory lover must have insight and intuition as well as virility and passion; he must respect his mate's individuality and be able to exercise an iron self-control; his own enjoyment will be all the keener in the end." Quotation from Pamphlet 3, British Society for Study of Sex Psychology, "Sexual Variety and Variability Among Women," by F. W. Stella Browne.

[2] In the Banda Archipelago, for instance, the bridal pair may only have connection after three nights have passed. Till then, an ancient woman or young child sleeps between them. Ref. Ploss Bartel's "Woman," Vol. I., p. 549.

ist will almost always be able to put this difficulty right, whether through two small incisions in the membrane, or through psychic suggestion and persuasion, or by a combination of both methods.

If necessary, by treatment of or advice to the man, also. But if further delay occurs, the psychic lesions and impressions of pain and fear, together with local soreness, will make their own cure increasingly difficult.

When insertion has been successfully accomplished, only a few movements will, as a rule, suffice to produce ejaculation in the bridegroom, whose psychosexual excitement must inevitably be acute. The friction of these movements will *probably* be inadequate to give the bride her orgasm, on this occasion. And as, even if she be appreciably excited sexually, the psychic and bodily shock largely counteracts this desire, there is not much likelihood of specific gratification for her in the first sexual act, which makes her a woman. And I would not advise attempts to produce her orgasm by prolonged friction. It is much better for the small fresh wounds of the perforation, that they should not be touched more than is quite unavoidable. Their quick healing seems to me *on this occasion only* more urgent than *her full response and sexual enjoyment in coitus, to which, in all other circumstances I attach the greatest importance, as has been repeatedly made clear.*

But—can this full enjoyment, response and relaxation, not be achieved, after perforation, through genital stimulation, *i.e.,* the genital kiss or friction with the finger? I think the reply must be as follows:—if after the husband's ejaculation, the bride has actually reached such a degree of stimulation as to desire orgasm, and if the relationship of the young couple is already so spiritually intimate that no instinctive reserve opposes this desire—then genital stimulation should be applied until she reaches the summit of pleasure, but applied only to the clitoris; hymen and introitus should not be touched.

Should first intercourse be preceded by genital stimulation? This depends wholly on the psychic attitude of the bride. I should be inclined, on the whole, to discourage it.

The *sensory* result would be entirely canceled by the pain of defloration. And there are advantages in restricting her first coital experience to the removal of the hymenal barrier, and the opening of the sexual passage.

Moreover, a more detailed activity of the bridegroom on this momentous occasion, an initiative that went beyond what was strictly necessary, might easily deeply offend the modesty of a more or less timid and quite inexperienced virgin bride. This should be avoided, for the psychic stresses and conflicts of the situation are in themselves great! And womanly modesty is in itself something so beautiful and precious—and so often disregarded by modern customs and costumes—that the husband should show it all possible reverence.

Therefore, he should hold himself well under control during the less precise and localized love-play before the first sexual union. The Prelude, with all its tender affection and admiration, kisses, embraces, gentle caresses, should be given the main *rôle*. The more intensively erotic and definite stimulation should be sparingly applied. Especially is this the case with the intimacy of nakedness. The lines of Paulos Silentiarios cited in the XVII Aphorism of the Third Intermezzo apply in a more evolved stage of conjugal life. To demand that the timid bride should yield her body suddenly and completely to the gaze of even the most beloved man, would be unreasonable and inconsiderate. And to display the male member which would seem gigantic to her unaccustomed eyes, would only terrify her and accentuate her unconscious psychic dread.

But, of course, not every bride is a shy chaste child! And it is obvious that the forethought, control and consideration which are absolutely imperative in the initiation of such a child, would be inappropriate with a girl whose virginity consisted in an intact hymen, and nothing more.

In conclusion, a purely technical detail needs mention. As a bride does not generally attain full local congestion and "erection," the natural lubricant secretion (distillation) may not suffice to make the passage of the phallos easy. This prolongs perforation and can make it quite painful.

Therefore an artificial lubricant should be used and applied directly to the vulva. If the bridegroom gently explains that it is meant to avoid hurting her, she will readily permit this, and the suggestion of consideration and care will appeal to her. The substance should be both chemically aseptic and clean; and strict cleanliness is necessary in both partners of course. Not only for æsthetic reasons, but also because any wound or cut, however tiny, and wherever situated, must be kept free from "matter in the wrong place."

After the bridal night comes the honeymoon. Quite erroneous beliefs are current about this stage of married life, especially among young bachelors. Just as they depict or describe the bridal night (in their private thoughts or intimate talk) as a riot of supreme pleasure, so they anticipate a ceaseless succession of unrestrained sexual enjoyment, from the first weeks of conjugal life.

They are gravely mistaken. The honeymoon is—an apprenticeship. There is a striking consensus of opinion among serious specialists (both men and women) that the average woman of our time and clime, must *learn* to develop specific sexual enjoyment, and only gradually attains to the orgasm in coitus. As I am in the act of writing the last sentence, the post brings to hand the current "Zentralblatt für Gynäkologie" with a critique of a thesis by Edelberg and Galant treating of this and kindred subjects.[1] These specialists consider that inadequate sensibility in coitus at the beginning of active sexual life, must be accounted physiologically normal in women: they have to *learn how* to feel both voluptuous pleasure and actual orgasm. The frequency of temporary anæsthesia, these specialists estimate as absolute, 100 per cent.

Even if this estimate is too sweeping and should be somewhat reduced, the general tendency is undeniable. The wife must be *taught,* not only how to behave in coitus, but, above all, how and what to feel in this unique act!

So the beginning of married life is a school and an ap-

---

[1] *Monatschrift für Geburtshülfe u. Gynäkologie* (Monthly review of obstetrics and gynæcology), Vol. XVII., No. 6. Article in *Zentralblatt für Gynäkologie,* Jan. 24th, 1925.

prenticeship for her. There can be no doubt of this. And the teacher is her husband. As teacher he needs, first of all, a fund of patience and self-mastery. And those are two qualities which are peculiarly difficult for a man in any acute phase of sexual emotion. So for him, too, these longed-for honeymoon weeks mostly prove a time of education and testing, an apprenticeship in sexual altruism and abnegation, a true Purgatory (Hill of Purification). And this time of his married life will most forcibly recall the Russian proverb: "Even a good marriage is a time of trial." The woman's sexual awakening must be gradual; in some individuals it is, of course, much more rapid than in others. "Practice without strain," exercise and adaptation, are the wise prescriptions, in this, as in the development of all latent mental and bodily powers. She should receive full rest and consideration in the days just after defloration, while the hymenal area is still sore and tender. And very gentle exercise for some while longer, while the vulva shows any tendency to redness and inflammation from the unaccustomed friction and congestion.

The exercise must be adapted to her capacity of endurance and appreciation; step by step it must advance and must avoid all sudden or severe demands, on the refinements and complexities of erotic technique, in early days. Thus the variations of attitude and position are advanced instruction, and belong to later stages. That is, they are best deferred till after the honeymoon. That will leave adequate time for the "elementary education." The difficult and nervously exciting and exhausting initial stages should not be additionally complicated, with advanced erotic technique. The return to the new joint home and daily life together, is often psychically critical and precarious for the wife, whose husband's time and attention are again largely occupied by his work, and who tends to feel "lonely" and even "neglected," in consequence. But this crucial phase can be made infinitely interesting, beautiful and soundly helpful for the future for both partners, by beginning their education in the principles and practice of Ideal Marriage.

CHAPTER XIV

BODILY HYGIENE

11. *Influence of the Sexual Function on Physique and Psyche. Sexual Vigor or Potency*

WE are now about to consider the hygiene of Ideal Marriage. The dangers which would have arisen from unreasonable behavior in the earliest stages—dangers consisting in a consolidation of the bride's initial anæsthesia and/or in general or local irritability—have been surmounted through enlightenment and self-control. And the "vigorous and harmonious sexual activity of the pair," which we postulated in beginning our study, has been established.

What are its laws of health?

To understand them, we must study the sexual efficiency, vigor and potency of both partners, and clearly recognize in what manner and degree the external influences of life affect this quantitative vigor as well as sexual intercourse in general. From these considerations, a rational and wholesome rule for sexual activity may be clearly deduced:

First we will consider the general influence of this functional activity, physical and psychic. Most of what is important here has been fully discussed already in this book, and need not be reiterated here. We will therefore confine ourselves to a brief summary.

Sexual activity *in itself* has *an extremely favorable influence on a woman's mind and body.*

I say *"in itself."* Note, however, that one of its physiological results—and from the racial point of view the most important, naturally obvious result—*pregnancy,* has complex and contradictory effects, on body and mind. It has very favorable and beneficent consequences, and also others of an opposite character. It is pregnancy which alone makes

the womanly organs "full blown" and completely functional; and at the same time begins to "deface" them. It
heralds the utmost bodily maturity and efficiency, and at the
same time changes many bodily processes (*e.g.,* metabolism)
so greatly, that even in thoroughly normal cases these processes approach morbidity or become morbidly deranged.
Finally, pregnancy, to a woman of normal instincts is
enormously desirable, for it means *Motherhood;* it is the
most overwhelming and wonderful experience possible to
her; yet it provokes, simultaneously and almost normally,
the unequivocal signs of anxiety neuroses.[1]

We can only touch on all this in passing. It offers ample
material for a monograph. And, in many respects, we are
only just beginning to understand the whole subject of pregnancy.

But we must emphasize one point especially. It is certain
that the thought of pregnancy plays an enormous part in
the sexual relations of most couples. Only when the circumstances and conditions *of communion are such that they can
liberate their minds from this fear, can sexual intercourse
realize all its possibilities.*

Fear of pregnancy often impairs sexual processes and
reactions on the psychic side to such a degree that bodily
reactions are sympathetically affected and even *inhibited* or
checked. Many marriages are totally ruined by this fear
and its consequences.[2]

In our introduction, we envisaged these facts, and equally,
the fact that sterility may also ruin married happiness, and
therefore we immediately added to our demand for vigorous
and harmonious sexual activity, a solution of the problem of
parentage in accordance with the wishes of both partners.
For the first is impossible without the second.

To return to the influence of sexual activity *per se* on the
woman, we recognize that a regular (*i.e.,* not an occasional,

---

[1] See the dream analyses of *Heberer* in his Essay, "On the Psychology
of Pregnancy" in the *Zentralblatt für Gynäkologie,* 1925.

[2] *Cf.* "Physicians who make a life study of human sexuality know that
the fear of impregnation is a heavy burden on the mind of every intelligent
and responsible woman in the world. . . . Many cases of 'frigidity' are
really due to fear of pregnancy." Wm. J. Robinson, M.D., "A Doctor's
Views on Life." (George Allen and Unwin. London, 1927, p. 56.)

possibly very infrequent) functional activity of the genitalia, has very happy anatomical and biological effects, *e.g.,* it can often cure previous irregularity or pain in menstruation. It also invigorates and develops the physique generally, and replaces infantile outlines and proportions by those typical of maturity. This is especially the case with the bosoms, and has often been confirmed in everyday life, when we meet a lady of our acquaintance, whom we have known as a maiden, after a year or two, without having heard in the interval that she has been married.

Which of the complex factors in action during coitus causes this development is hard to decide.

It is *not exclusively* the numerous orgasms, even though we may attribute something to the increased blood supply and congestion they entail whenever they occur. Girls who habitually practice self-relief (masturbation, auto-erotism), acquire enlargement of the labia and clitoris, but not increased all-round development.

Nor is it due entirely to the absorption of seminal products; for women who have regular intercourse wherein full absorption is prevented (coitus condomatus) also show improved general and mammary (bust) development, though perhaps somewhat less than when communion is biologically normal and complete.

We may perhaps attribute the beneficial results of regular coitus to a *combination* of all the factors in play. Hence, it follows that failure of any single factor involves some damage, or at least some decrease of benefit.

And the *psychic* factor is not the least among them. Sexual harmony in activity is a real psychic panacea. It develops all the latent strength and sweetness of a woman's character, ripens her judgment, gives her serenity and poise. This is not only the case in the long run, as a result of the sum of sexual acts and impressions; it is also true of each single successful occasion. Each such satisfactory erotic experience revives and refreshes the healthy woman throughout her soul and body.[1] Only when the excitement is too prolonged

---

[1] "The sexual relation when happy and harmonious, vivifies a woman's brain, develops her character, and trebles her vitality." F. W. Stella Browne in "Sexual Variety and Variability." (1916)

and involves paroxysms repeated at too close intervals there ensues, instead of unspeakable *bien-être,* a certain fatigue and lassitude, a physical and mental languor. If this only lasts a short time and is not repeated, and accentuated, it may be disregarded as unimportant. If it survives some hours of natural repose, or appears more than once, it is a danger signal that the limits of wholesome activity are being exceeded. If these symptoms last for more than a day, moderation is imperatively indicated.

Where the border-line between exertion and excess is to be drawn *varies infinitely in each individual woman.* The amount of stimulation a woman is able to receive and of relief she is able to experience, depends on her constitution, her temperament, her state of health, her psychic attitude especially, on other causes of fatigue and, finally, on general extraneous conditions, to which we shall refer again.

So this Rubicon is different with each different woman. Nor is it always in the same place in the same woman. On the contrary, at one time excess is easily reached; at another, the woman's vitality matches much higher demands. But, on the whole, it is elastic and not too easily or closely drawn, for the sexual vigor, efficiency (and technically *tolerance*) of the healthy, erotically awakened woman is very great; decidedly greater, indeed, than the potency of the average man.

And this is not surprising. For the man supplies the seminal *ejaculate* containing millions of the most complex cellular structures (spermatozoa), though otherwise, the psychic tension and physical exertion are about equal as between the partners.

Of course, it means no undue demand on the male organism to supply the spermatozoa, if they have accumulated in a sufficient amount during a certain (variable) space of time, and have collected (together with the by-products of the prostate) in a supply, as it were, on store, and ready.

But the position is very different if further ejaculations are expected after the available supply has been spent. For the excitations which summon further emissions mean an

enormous strain on the sensitive local nerves and tissues of
the organs which secrete the vital fluid. Also, great effort is
needed from the whole brain and body, to produce the state
of tension necessary for the effective collaboration of the
whole organism in the genital act.

So any and every man cannot meet such demands always
and at any moment. Even within normal limits, *male sexual potency* varies considerably; it depends on age, constitution, temperament, race, habit, practice, erotic influences,
psychic influences and interests other than erotic in character, and many other circumstances. And, it is above all, an
idiosyncrasy, an individual peculiarity, whose determining
factor is quite unknown to us. There are both sexually
weak men and sexual athletes. And this special aptitude or
deficiency has nothing at all, or only very little, to do with
general bodily robustness or debility. It may possibly be determined by a special productivity (or apathy) of the glands
secreting the sperm; or it may depend to some degree on
the amount of fluid expelled on each occasion. It is notable
that some men declare they can voluntarily *retain or hold
back a portion of their ejaculate,* if they wish to follow the
first coitus by a second, soon after. But we have no *exact*
knowledge of these causes. We only know, and indisputably,
that there are perfectly healthy and normal men in their
most vigorous years who can only execute coitus twice a
week—and at the very utmost and in exceptional circumstances, once a day—and that there are others who can
repeat the act three or four (or more) times in succession,
or at very brief intervals during several days, without any
injury to their health and zest.

If *more* is demanded sexually from any man (potent or
weak) than he can perform, his body simply refuses. In
spite of the most acute excitations, his discharge does not
occur. This temporary and occasional apathy is, so to
speak, quite normal; in contrast to the genuine *impotence,*
which fails before quite moderate incitements and is distinctly morbid. The *occasional* sexual incapacity of the
healthy man is not only normal but *beneficial;* it is, so to
speak, a natural self-defense of the organism against exac-

tions and excesses.   When it occurs, *all further stimulation should cease* till the body is rested and once more potent. This generally happens fairly soon.   But repeated sexual physical fatigue and temporary impotence due to over-exertion must not become too frequent!   Moderation, as in all things—so here.

Of course, we need not explain that it damages a man's general health if more is habitually expected of him, sexually, than he is able to give.   It also harms the woman by depriving her of full reactions and relief.   But an occasional failure of this kind, after extreme pleasure, need cause no alarm.

The woman can not only *tolerate* the performance of coitus better than the man; she can also *admit* him to coitus even when her own excitement fails.   She can at least partially protect herself against excessive fatigue, by keeping *passive* through deliberate mind-control; but this does not make the act itself impossible.   She is not subject to temporary absolute incapacity, as he may be—unless through morbid symptoms definitely associated with various diseases.

Excessive sexual activity is more often expected of a man in a *relative* than an *absolute* degree: and most often in the form of too rapid repetition of coitus.

The *criteria* of "excess" are about the same in both sexes.   We have enumerated them already.   In the man the most conspicuous are slight pains across the loins, and more important—diminished clarity and concentration in brain work.   This particular deleterious effect should be avoided, as it may quickly become obstinate, and possibly chronic.

On the other hand, it should be recognized that two or—in strong potency—even three successive acts of communion, *can* be—in certain circumstances—of great advantage. After a few days or a longer period of abstinence, the man often has ejaculation so soon that the preceding stimulation is not enough—or only just enough—to gratify the woman. In these cases, coitus will give both partners *relief,* but a minimum degree of specific *pleasure,* and is therefore

inadequate as an *expression of their love. But nothing is
more fatal to love than disappointment in sexual intercourse!*
So the first relative failure may be redeemed by a prompt
repetition of communion.   Whether this should occur
immediately, or after an hour or so of repose, or on the next
morning, depends so much on masculine potency, on mutual
inclination and on so many other factors besides, that a
system cannot well be propounded or definite advice given.
Nevertheless, if some suggestions are asked, I would say:
if the man's potency is adequate, *then the after-glow or
epilogue of the first act should be interwoven with the prelude and love-play of the next.*   This gives excellent opportunities for prolonged and delicately varied love-play.   During its slow summation the male organism will have had
time for recuperation and fresh accumulation, and the stimulation will be mutual and harmonious.   There will be ample
opportunity to taste all the delight of mutual love, and give
expression to all fancies and desires; and the woman may
appropriately take a more active *rôle* than usual.   If after
this experience, the man is able to rest thoroughly and
especially to sleep, there is little likelihood that he will be
unduly fatigued.   It is advisable, for this reason, that
repeated sexual acts should take place early in the evening.
But if he should feel the mental lassitude and lumbar pains
mentioned as signs of sexual strain, the next day, instead of
the increased vigor, psychic refreshment and mental and
physical efficiency which should normally follow coitus,
then he should "put on the brakes," and postpone the next
occasion, for a few days.   And this experience can also
teach both partners the desirability of greater sexual activity
and initiative on the woman's part, in multiple coitus, *e.g.,*
Positions I., V., and X., in Chapter XI.

Some of my readers may perhaps feel that the greater
feminine *aptitude* or *tolerance of excess in coitus* compared
to the man's *potency* as just described, is hardly compatible
with what has been stressed in earlier chapters, *i.e.,* her less
rapid and facile excitability and the frequency of feminine
sexual anæsthesia, "coldness" or frigidity.   But any one
who is acquainted with the sexual histories of a large number of women, and has been able to observe them throughout

changing phases and periods of their lives, will know that
this contradiction is only superficial and apparent. And the
attentive reader of these pages will not feel any contradiction
or confusion. But for the sake of clearness, we may summarize as follows: the newly married woman *is as a rule,*
more or less completely "cold" or indifferent to and in
sexual intercourse. She must be *taught to love,* in the complete sense in which we here use the term. The husband
may perhaps not succeed in imparting this erotic education;
generally that is because he takes no trouble about it.
She then *remains* permanently *frigid,* which explains the
heavy percentage of anæsthesia which all authorities confirm; or else the husband's grave omissions are made good
by another man. But even if the husband proves a good
teacher, the young wife does not generally at first attain
to an equal sexual ardor, a delay which should be allowed
for and made good in the ways we have suggested. Only
gradually does she develop erotic maturity and experience,
and when she does reach her zenith, the comparatively
slight provocation which will cause ejaculation in the husband after some days of abstinence, may well be insufficient
for her. We have also shown how to meet her requirements
in such cases. Her *desire* for sexual intercourse, in happy
married life, will have become *at least* equal to his. And her
quantitative sexual efficiency and endurance surpass his.

Education and habit have obviously great influence here.
A certain practical maxim (which I have fairly often
observed to be sound in the course of professional work)
may be deduced, and is best expressed in the form of a
caution. I would warn husbands not to recklessly *habituate*
their wives to a degree of sexual frequency and intensity,
which they (the husbands) may be quite unable to keep up
for any length of time. There are many women, of moderate sexual temperament, who keenly enjoy occasional long
festivals of erotic expansion and activity, in which their
husbands both give and demand their utmost, but who do
not suffer nor resent when the tempest subsides, and a calm
follows. But there are also others, though they are perhaps
less numerous among Northern races, who, when once

introduced to the maximum of sexual pleasure, cannot modify their desires when this maximum is no longer available. Then, indeed, the husband cannot exorcise the spirits he has invoked! He has the painful choice between chronic "nerves" [1] on his wife's part, which destroys marital peace and happiness, and equally chronic sexual overstrain and fatigue on his own. This overstrain and fatigue reduces him to a mental and physical weakling—a "neurotic." Often no choice between these two evils is possible, and nerves, health, love and happiness are wrecked all round. The analysis of such painful cases is instructive and not difficult. Most readers will be able to fill in the outlines of our sketch for themselves. In any case, the husband who has married a woman of ardent temperament will do wisely, even in his most passionate moods, not to pitch her expectations *too* high—or his recklessness may cost him dear, indeed.

A further point of great practical importance may be considered in the light of the possible incompatibilities and disharmonies we have just mentioned, especially as they are generally ignored or not adequately recognized. What should be the relative ages of the partners from the rational and scientific point of view? Some idealists maintain that men and women should all marry quite young, which, of course, eliminates appreciable differences in age. Another view champions the desirability of definitely greater age and experience on the man's part, and if about ten years older he can, of course, no longer be "quite young." I am of the opinion, expressed in these pages, that *at least* in sexual matters, the husband has the duty of *teaching* and *guiding* his wife. Therefore, however sympathetic the *ideal* of boy and girl marriages is in theory, I cannot approve entrusting so difficult and delicate an office to a youth ignorant of life and the world. In the beginning of married life the union of a man of thirty with a girl of twenty has every advantage; but for *prolonged* sexual harmony as regards the *quantitative* aspect (potency and frequency) it

---

[1] It is now universally recognized and accepted by neurologists that the feminine psyche reacts to every repression (conscious or unconscious) of sexual wishes, with neurotic symptoms.

would seem better to have less difference in ages. The man of fifty begins slowly to grow—if not old—"older." If he continues moderate and regular sexual activity (as recommended at the end of Chapter VII.), he may long preserve his vigor and be able till advanced old age, to have coitus with full satisfaction to both his partner and himself. But his ability to repeat the act at *brief* intervals, and his specific sexual desire, slowly and gradually grow less.

In our modern days the woman of forty is still young. As the psychologist James Douglas correctly observes: she is no older than the woman of thirty was a hundred years ago. "Middle age" generally begins in the middle forties (forty-five), and quite often later—of course, I deal in "round numbers" here. But between forty and the definite establishment of the menopause her sexual frequency is not diminished and her desire is, if anything, more intense than in her earlier years.[1] This late efflorescence has been exaggerated in modern literature, and represented as "the dangerous age" of woman. Persons of balanced judgment and insight protested against this distorted view without delay. But there are, of course, individual cases of this kind. Every gynæcologist of psychological perception and experience knows poignant examples.

Moreover, even if her specific desire is only slightly quickened or unchanged—if a mature woman who has been accustomed to active and satisfactory sexual intercourse for years, feels that she receives less attention and gratification than formerly, just at a period when the thought of impending changes and past youth must certainly obtrude itself on her conscious mind—the deprivation is quite enough to unleash mental conflicts. Such mental and psychic conflicts may take incalculable forms and produce incalculable results. It is fortunate if their manifestations are confined to the individual soul and to slight "nervous disturbances."[2] They may be exacerbated into severe psychoneuroses or domestic tragedies—all the more tragic as their "pity and

---

[1] Dr. R. Latou Dickinson in his detailed study of Average Sex Life of Women found that in Northern Europeans and Anglo-Americans, forty-nine was a more usual age for menopause than forty-five.

[2] *Cf.* the portions of Chapter VI. which deal with climacteric and pre-climacteric.

terror" supervene after years of mutual happiness and without "guilt" on either side.

I am therefore of opinion that a difference of ten or fifteen years between husband and wife at the inception of marriage is excessive and inadvisable if the bride is only twenty. I would suggest that about half this difference is preferable, *i.e.,* that the man should be not *less than five, or more than seven, the senior.*[1]

In short, I would retain thirty as the desirable age for marriage in men, and raise that of the girl from twenty to twenty-three or twenty-five. There are many advantages here. The risks of "comparatively late maternity" I am quite prepared to accept, having fullest confidence in our modern obstetric technique.

---

[1] When the difference is great, *e.g.,* exceeds fifteen or twenty years, the results may be happier. The marriage of an *elderly* (senescent)—not, of course, an *old* (senile)—man to a quite young girl, is often very successful and harmonious. The bride is immediately introduced and accustomed to moderate sexual intercourse; the husband is able to continue this for many years, and the wife neither expects nor desires more.

CHAPTER XV

III.   *Personal and External Factors Affecting Sexual Intercourse*

PERSONAL and external circumstances may affect sexual functions in many different ways.   We have already discussed some of them in the previous chapter, also in Chapter II., dealing with sexual emotions and endocrine and psychic stimuli, and in Chapter III., which treats of sensory impressions in relation to sex.

In these portions of our survey, we learned that innumerable factors, from within and from without the organism, may promote or inhibit sexual desire.   And it is obvious that in married life, where normally there is opportunity to gratify this desire, *intercourse itself* is promoted or inhibited, as well as the emotion of which it is the fulfillment.   But, of course, we must never forget that *two* persons are affected here, and their interests and wishes must coincide or be brought into harmony.

In the last portion of Chapter VI. we dealt with fundamental characteristics of the woman, and in Chapter VII. with attributes of the man, which must be taken into account here.

Finally, in the Third Section of this treatise we discussed the sexual act and its accessories, and enumerated many factors which influence the manner in which it is performed, its frequency and its modifications and, as it were, modulations.   So we need not repeat all this, but will only supplement it and emphasize certain points which have not previously been stressed.   These can be grouped under certain main headings of principle and practice.

Till now we have not treated of the effects of *food and drink on desire and potency*.   These we shall now briefly survey. This subject can be and has been exhaustively discussed. Certain books, written in the sixteenth and seventeenth centuries, describe in minute detail all solid and liquid varieties of nourishment calculated to incite sexual desire (libido), to intensify sexual pleasure or enjoyment (voluptas), and to favor potency or efficiency in the sexual act. Both the European, and especially French literature of this description, and the Oriental, describe not only the various dishes which promote sexual stimulation, but their preparation and ingredients. But many of these recipes are obviously fantastic, and recognizable as such at a glance. Thus symbolism and sympathetic magic are unmistakable when a preparation of orchids is recommended! *(Orchis* is the Greek term for testes.) Nevertheless, it is undeniable that in this department, as in so many others, the art of love among us has suffered retrogression and decline, and fails to make use of all the resources which might be employed without ill-effects. It is quite the exception for housewives to possess inherited manuscript recipes and prescriptions, which they find specially efficacious here. I have, however, heard from a reliable source of a cookery book in manuscript, compiled with a view to erotic effects, and bequeathed from mother to daughter, in a private family. I have not, to my regret, been able to examine it myself. But the dependable man who told me of it, and who himself had considerable erotic experience and genital potency, categorically declared that he had not only looked at the recipes but often himself enjoyed their efficacy.

It is universally known that abundant food excites to sexual activity, and a spare diet, especially *underfeeding,* inhibits these functions. Meat is stimulating, and venison especially so. Eggs have a traditional reputation for tonic efficacy, both as a stimulant and a restorative after special exertions in coitus. And it is said that an egg diet favors the production of spermatozoa. Apart from this latter merit, milk-rice dishes are said to resemble eggs, as do also beetroots, carrots and turnips (root vegetables), stewed in milk sauce. The most effective dish in the *haute cuisine* is supposed to be crayfish soup, which resembles the Oriental bird's-nest soup in both flavor and stimulant quality.

Of the essentially appetising and/or aphrodisiac substances, the chief is *celery,* famed in popular stories and saws; more expensive delicacies are *artichokes* and *asparagus,* which owe their repute to the specific effect of their substance on the kidneys—for it is filtered and eliminated separately, and somewhat excites the urinary passages. Truffles, which form a transitional stage or link between foods and spices or condiments, are also not to be ignored. Then there are the condiments themselves, and principally saffron,[1] cinnamon, vanilla, pepper, peppermint, ginger.

Alcohol is the chief sexual stimulant among drinks. In small amounts its invigorating influence is universally admitted; in large quantities, it paralyzes the genital function on the physical side, while at the same time it breaks down psychic inhibitions and controls. Habitual drunkenness (apart from occasional excess) is extremely deleterious to the sexual organs and functions. An unfavorable result may also be recognized after excessive use of tea, coffee and tobacco. Possibly, small amounts of all three may stimulate slightly (as does alcohol), but only a very few, specially sensitive persons, are in a position to confirm this personal experience.

It is particularly useful to know that acid drinks (such as lemonade), in large quantities, seem generally to diminish sexual desire.

Besides the foods habitually or occasionally consumed for purposes of nourishment or enjoyment, there are special substances taken on special occasions which may affect the organism sexually as well as generally. This effect may be intentional or indirect. Thus, medicinal preparations of bromide and valerian, and various sedatives and narcotics, not only relax general tension and excitability but also lull the sexual impulse into quiescence. Thus, they may be helpful in mastering and quelling an unfortunate sexual preoccupation.

---

[1] Saffron was known and extensively used by the ancient Phœnicians as a love-spice. It flavored the moon-shaped cakes baked and eaten in honor of Ashtoreth. Some traditions of Phœnician cookery are said to survive in South-western England, Cornwall and Devon.

Other medicaments of a tonic and restorative character favor sexual as well as general vigor and health. Among tonics are some, such as the various combinations of *phosphorus,* which have a decidedly strong *positive* influence, *sexually.* Others, again, diminish general tension and inhibit, *e.g.,* the functions of bladder and bowels, but stimulate desire; the chief of these is *opium,* with its derivatives.

It is, of course, evident that doctors in prescribing should bear in mind these accessory aphrodisiac or anaphrodisiac effects of various medicines.

The term aphrodisiacs (negative anaphrodisiac, cf., anæsthesia) derives from the Greek goddess of Love, Aphrodite; it is applied to means of exciting or increasing sexual desire and reproductive capacity. In Classical Antiquity the love-potion (philtre, philtron), played a great part, as also in the Assyrian, Egyptian, Persian and Chinese civilizations. The women of Thessaly were supposed to be the greatest adepts in philtres. The recorded ingredients are incredibly disgusting: the caul of a foal, other portions of the equine placenta, the vaginal discharge of mares in heat, the tongues of certain birds, pigeons' blood, fishes' roes and fins, insects, lizards, and other equally loathsome substances.[1]

In Rome the wholesale compounding and marketing of philtres became such a public scandal that the Senate forbade it under heavy penalties.[2]

The aforesaid nauseating animal ingredients were simply symbols of sympathetic magic. But there may have been some measure of primitive science in the employment of calves' brain—a frequent favorite which might well have a strong effect, owing to the amount of *lecithin* it contains—or of the glands (testes and uterus) of animals. It is questionable whether there was any *rational deduction* here, but even though unconsciously, these Thessalians were the fore-

---

[1] *R. Paasch* in an interesting Essay in the *Archiv für Frauenkunde und Konstitutionsforschung* (Vol. XII., Nos. 1 and 2, 1926) gives further relevant details and bibliography.

[2] Needless to say, in vain.

runners of modern organic therapy for sexual deficiency; as such they are medically of interest.

The vegetable *materia medica* of the love philtres was also selected on a symbolic and magical basis, in most cases. For the philtres were almost always administered with the intention of rousing irresistible desire for one special person who administered them.[1]

Throughout the Middle Ages folk brewed and believed in love potions. Alongside the magic draught that inspired love, full-grown and irresistible, at one lightning flash (as in the tale of Tristram and Yseult)—we find the increasing systematic attempt to help physical potency by means of drugs. Even though such ingredients were originally purely symbolic—since the Renaissance especially, substances of the most dangerous kind were lavishly employed.[2] They acted first on the urinary organs, especially the urethra, which were violently stimulated: the stimulation then extended to the adjacent genitals. This was the case with the preparations of cantharidine ("Italian elixirs," and "pastilles galantes"). The stimulation and congestion, however, easily reached to the bladder and kidneys, and caused most painful and serious complications.

Only of the most recent years has pharmaceutical science acquired compounds which really influence the genital functions. Or, to be strictly accurate, and apart from organo-therapy by means of endocrine extracts and trans-plantations—it has been reserved for the medicine of the last two decades to compose *one* such effective drug: Yohimbin. This substance is an alkaloid, derived mainly from the bark of the Yohimbe tree, and really does stimulate and intensify sexual processes in both men and women.

---

[1] Substance and potions of an opposite nature are far less popular in legend and literature. As a traditional antidote to love excited by magic means, I may cite the extract of the stem and roots of the white water-lily. Genuinely effective herbal sedatives, known from time immemorial, are such popular remedies as valerian, roots, and hops. As a main ingredient valerian has the advantages of a repulsive smell and strong persistent taste.

[2] *Cf.* the famous household cookery book of Caterina Sforza of Pesaro (1500). *Cf.* also Montague Summers' "The Marquis de Sade," in the Fourth Pamphlet of the British Society for the Study of Sexual Psychology. Also the description of the trick played on Cesare Borgia by French courtiers, recorded by Brantôme.

This proves two important circumstances. Firstly, such medicinal stimulation is possible; and secondly, that traditional and popular recipes may have genuine scientific value. For among the Negro tribes of tropical West Africa, the rind of the Yohimbe, has been valued as an aphrodisiac, for untold generations. It is highly probable that among the sovereign remedies recorded in ancient or modern popular belief, there are some others which have sustained or will sustain rigid scientific tests. But substances with so acute and definite an influence must leave *some* traces on the whole organism. And this, Yohimbin most assuredly does. The medical expert makes use of it in definitely indicated and limited cases—not only of male impotence, but *e.g.*, of serious menstrual disturbances in women—in the justified expectation of benefiting his patients. But laymen should not touch this powerful toxic substance (either in its concentrated form, or masked among the much-advertised secret remedies to "restore virility")—without professional consultation and advice. Impotence is so serious and complex a condition—it may arise from so many different causes—that its treatment is a matter for the medical specialist. And attempts to force up sexual desire and the normal degree of sexual vigor, by powerful artificial means, must, sooner or later, cause damage. If, on exceptional occasions, *e.g.*, to meet the wishes and needs of a beloved partner—it is advisable to "level up" temporary sexual inadequacy, the *culinary* resources mentioned above may be used, with good results.

Further aids which can at least have no harmful reactions, are hot cushions or pillows applied to the lumbar region. And also medicated (carbonic acid) baths. In certain cases the hot pillow is surprisingly helpful.

I have successfully prescribed baths to both men and women; they can be taken either as sitz-baths, or with total immersion. Natural and artificial carbonic acid solutions are both helpful. In various watering-places, long series of total immersions are prescribed as cures for sexual anæsthesia in women. Occasionally successful results can be verified, especially when the husband helps, *i.e.*, is in residence together with his wife, and when the frigidity was only partial and relative. And other factors besides "the waters" may play their part. But, as a rule, a frigidity which the husband could not overcome in his own home, is too serious for a watering-place to cure.

For men, total immersion in carbonized water is particularly appropriate when normal desires are impaired by slight languor and fatigue. It removes the lassitude—if this was not too strong and caused by real overstrain and also exercises a slight stimulation on the genitalia and lumbar region. If pelvic and genital stimulation alone is sought, both sexes may be helped by sitz-baths or hip-baths; a simple and easy procedure, concentrating the effect on the pelvic zone. In slight cases of local insensitiveness and delayed sensation, it can be of help as a *preparation* just before sexual intercourse. But the physician who prescribes this, will do well to remember *that measures which are too obviously part of a timed and planned coitus may offend a woman's taste, and inhibit her erotic feeling.* This difficulty is avoided by taking the warm hip-bath regularly for a time every evening before retiring. If sexual intercourse follows closely, it does not lose the *spontaneity* essential to its full beauty and normality.

And though there are no objections to the occasional use of such deliberate aids, both partners should never forget that they cannot possibly replace proper preparation, bodily and psychic, for the sexual act. Almost every sexual tepidity and inexperience of one partner—so long as it is not positively morbid—may be compensated and conquered by an adequate prelude and especially by an artistic love-play, both in general and genital stimulation. Nothing can really replace technical skill and resource here. And the wife, too, should not hesitate to employ them, especially to help her husband through temporary anæsthesia or fatigue.

Further factors which we have not yet considered, are the bodily stimuli caused by movements in *locomotion.* I refer to the more or less rhythmic percussion or vibration, received for more or less long periods of time. Men may experience an erection while on horseback, or driving in a carriage or traveling by rail; more rarely, perhaps, when motoring or bicycling. It might be deduced that the short, rapid, vigorous vibrations are the more stimulating and the more elastic swing-like and prolonged, the less so. It must be remembered that these erections do not proceed from erotic thoughts or fantasies. They may begin while the mind is absorbed in quite different directions, and only reach the consciousness when they are unmistakably evident. Of course then they may arouse erotic mental associations, which, if opportunity offers, may lead to acts. This is an explanation of the relatively high frequency of sexual intercourse during or immediately after a journey, even between couples who have full opportunities for it, otherwise.

I have only quite inadequate information of the effect of locomotion on women, in this respect. I have known ipsatresses[1] who lamented to me that journeys *drove* them to indulge in a habit their minds resisted and disapproved. I know also some normal women who have never felt such special excitement due to locomotion. For a man, even if he be a doctor, has very seldom opportunity of asking women about intimate sexual things of this kind.

Opinions still differ widely, both as to whether the urge to sexual activity varies periodically in human beings and as to what, if such is the case, are the types of periodicity. These differences of opinion will probably persist, because human beings tend innately to generalize on the basis of their own observations and experiences, and because a certain periodicity of sexual desire has often been recorded, but at very different intervals and durations.

The question itself has not any fundamental value for the hygiene of Ideal Marriage, unless *personal observations are assumed to be universally true.*

For if there be a normal maximum of desire in spring, as most authorities believe—a maximum analogous to the breeding season of animals and birds, and manifested in the spring festivals of primitive races with their overwhelmingly

---

[1] *Ipsation* is the more modern and accurate term for what was known as *masturbation*. Other accurate terms are *autoerotism* and *self-relief.*

sexual coloring—this vernal efflorescence[1] affects both partners alike. The same would be true of a second maximum in the autumn, or of a winter ebb of desire, neither of which, however, I can personally verify from observation; and so such seasonal sex fluctuations would not cause disharmony between man and woman.

More importance would attach to a fortnightly or monthly crescendo of desire which some men insist on having verified in themselves. If this type of periodicity were to *alternate with a fourteen days' feminine cycle,* it would, of course, be more than usually difficult for the partners to achieve complete unanimity and harmony.

The periodic fluctuation of sexual desire is reputed to be much more marked and common in women than in men. But paradoxically, the many authorities who have expressed themselves on this subject (and generally with such conviction that they have attempted to enthrone their own view or experience as Natural Law), are as little in agreement on details as are the individual women whom one can consult about it! The most emphatic support is given to the theory of a cycle which has maxima at fortnightly intervals, and these are generally allotted respectively to the days just before menstruation and to the days midway between one menstruation and the next (the intermenstruum or intermenstrual period). According to the books, both these maxima last for three or four days. The one which precedes menstruation is the more acute and constant, while the intermenstrual is not infrequently described as fainter and indeed hardly or not at all perceptible in relatively cool or insensitive women, so that their fortnightly cycle of desire is practically a four-weekly or monthly cycle. And in cases of certain diseases, of physical exhaustion and mental fatigue, of chronic overstrain, nervous depletion, or prolonged worry, the intermenstrual increase is the first to be suppressed, while the premenstrual increase only disappears if these disturbances and damages become worse.

Of late years this theory has been most exhaustively

---

[1] Statistics indicate a maximum number of conceptions in May.

defended by *Marie Stopes,* who in the book[1] quoted in our footnotes on pp. 202-3, has visualized her relevant observations and experiences in a striking graph.

If we compare this graph with the diagrammatic curves showing the rhythm of vital processes in the feminine organism, as represented in Plate V. of this book, we find that the premenstrual "crest" of Dr. Stopes' observations coincides with the maximum intensity of the various functions indicated by variously colored lines in my plate. Its correspondence with the temperature curve is very remarkable, and I have already explained that this temperature curve could be regarded as typical and representative of the tendency of all vital processes.

It is obvious, therefore, that this premenstrual accession of aptitude for sexual intercourse in women may be regarded as one manifestation of the intensification of all vital processes in their organism, and that both general process and special symptom may be attributed to the stimulating secretions of the *Corpus luteum,* which at that time in the twenty-eight days' cycle, is just in full efflorescence.[2]

Incidentally, we may also conclude, that inadequate sexual aptitudes and inclinations in women are curable by absorption of ovarian substance in appropriate form. We have reports of such practical experimental results, but not yet unequivocally. And there may be another, purely local (and secondary) cause of premenstrual sexual desire; the extra congestion and blood supply in the genitals. The second "Crest" in Dr. Stopes' curve begins immediately after the day on which I have marked *Ovulation* or rupture of the Graafian follicle, in my diagrams. Thus it corresponds to the upward movement of all vital processes heralded by the formation of a new Corpus luteum, as described

---

[1] "Married Love." By Marie Carmichael Stopes, Ph.D., D.Sc.

[2] Of course the activities of the Corpus luteum and ovaries generally are not autonomous. If we seek for more profound origins we must probably assume (with *Aschner, L. R. Müller, Mathes & Ewald,* etc.) a determination and regulation of these processes from the vegetative centers in the medullary section of the brain. (*Cf. Zentralblatt für Gynäkologie,* 1925, No. 10.)

But I do not feel that this deduction brings one any nearer to genuine understanding here.

in Chapter VI. But here we have the remarkable circumstance that the intermenstrual desire, according to Dr. Stopes, subsides again after three or four days. But the curves of temperature, uterine membranous proliferation, glycogen formation, ovarian tension—all continue to rise, in correspondence with the evolution of the Corpus luteum. Teleologically, a quickening of the urge to sexual activity immediately after ovulation must be very appropriate to Nature's aim of reproduction.

Moreover, the accentuation of desire postulated on the twelfth to thirteenth day after the beginning of the menstrual flow, is very far indeed from being constant. It is not even frequent. Even though I must confirm Marie Stopes' view that many women feel an accession of desire just before menstruation—though I make some reservations on the frequency of this experience—I must maintain as regards the intermenstrual period, that I have often been told desire was rather less than usual on those days selected by Dr. Stopes, instead of more.[1]

I should rather be inclined to concur in *Marshall's* view that the time of the strongest sexual feelings is generally that immediately following the conclusion of the menses.[2]

This intensification of desire for intercourse at the end of each menstruation, and sometimes before the flow has ceased, has been mentioned fairly often, even in Classical Antiquity. Furbringer is of opinion that it is due only to the temporary abstinence during the menses, and I am inclined to agree with him.[3]

Other authorities, again, especially those who assume the rupture of the Graafian follicle at an earlier date than I feel justified in maintaining, emphasize the increase of desire after menstruation, with reference to the normal phenomena

---

[1] I mean, of course, less in comparison to the days just before them. In order to avoid misunderstanding I repeat once more that I, too, have observed cases of increased desire from the twelfth to fourteenth day. But these were exceptions.

[2] "Physiology of Reproduction." Cited by Dr. Stopes.

[3] "Zur Frage der Sexualperiodizität beim Weiblichen Geschlecht" ("On the Problem of Female Sexual Periodicity"), *Monatsschrift für Gynäkologie u. Geburtshülfe* (*Obstetrics and Gynæcology*), Vol. 47, No. 1.

in sub-human mammalia, as peculiarly likely to help reproduction.[1]

Similarly, and with equal justification, I would refer to the intensified sexual feelings, which I have quite often observed from the eighth to the tenth day after menstruation, combined with a distinct congestion of the genitals. These are the cases which I had in mind, in my brief dissertation on the increase of tension owing to the maturing of the Graafian follicles.

And the maximal points already mentioned are not the only acute periods of feminine desire. Women occasionally are quite emphatic in recording other days, *e.g.,* those of the menstrual flow itself, as their special erotic season. Then there are yet others, who state that they have no regularly recurrent accentuation of desire. And these may perhaps be in the majority, apart from the premenstrual accentuation, which I consider fairly common.

Taking data all in all, my attitude on this certainly complex subject is, to *deny the existence of a law of periodicity in sexual desire for "the woman" of our age and geographical region; just as I also deny it in the case of the man.* But—in contrast to the man—*I admit there are regular recurrent temporary accentuations of desire in not a few women.* The most frequent maximum is found just before menstruation. But besides this or instead of it there are other maxima, which *are individually characteristic but not typical of the race.*

It is self-evident that in Ideal Marriage the husband must study and consider the acute periods of his wife's desire. It seems to me equally right and obvious that he should not be asked to *restrict* intercourse to her maximal periods. Mrs. Stopes considers it "normal" for the wife, whose fortnightly rhythm of desire she assumes, to expect several acts of union during the three or four days of each maximum period, and to dispense entirely with sexual intercourse in the ten days between, except under the influence of some extraneous factor which excites both partners.

---

[1] *Cf. Greils'* Essay, "The Etiology of Sterility" ("Zur Ätiologie der Sterilität"), in the *Zentralblatt für Gynäkologie*, 1925, No. 5, p. 233.

Here are her exact words:

"The mutually best regulation of intercourse in marriage is to have three or four days of repeated unions, followed by about ten days without any unions at all, unless some strong external stimulus has stirred a mutual desire."

"He will then endeavor to adapt his demands on her, so that they are in harmony with her nature" (p. 73).

The error of this view is, in my opinion, not only the generalization from her own personal observations but, and principally, the assumption that the sexual indifference of the woman during the (two ten days) intervals is truly "normal."

Fortunately, this assumption does not coincide with actual facts. The woman who is neither anæsthetic nor inexperienced, and who *loves* her husband, has—even outside and apart from her idiosyncratic maximal periods—a sexual desire and capacity not in any way inferior to the man's average.

And therefore Mrs. Stopes' suggestion that the wife should demand recurrent ten days' abstentions will not do the harm it might. For the wife will not wish such deprivation any more than the husband!

But in the case of a woman who is somewhat tepid and deficient in sexual vitality, Mrs. Stopes' view might influence her to such an extent, that her husband's attempts at a cure by skilled erotic education, would be counteracted, and *both* partners harmed thereby.

For this reason I consider the theory of the famous biologist as somewhat risky—which is why I have devoted so much time to it.

The demand that the woman's wishes shall be paramount and alone decide, is also both unjust and, what is practically more important, incorrect. It offends against the *fundamental principle of sexual altruism,* just as much as does the traditional view of male "rights" and female "duties," [1] which Mrs. Stopes condemns.

I fully sympathize with the repudiation and condemna-

[1] "The result has been that the supposed need of one of the partners has tended to become paramount, and we have established the social tradition of a husband's 'rights' and wifely 'duty.'" ("Married Love," by Marie Stopes.)

tion, as will have been clear from everything I have written. But it is wrong and unhelpful to replace the old mistake by another, equally fatal. We possess ampler and more efficacious means than those recommended in "Married Love," for bringing about harmony and equipoise of masculine and feminine desires in marriage—or at least, in Ideal Marriage.

Of course, man and woman have in Ideal Marriage *equal* "rights" and identical "duties." The right to be gratified, the duty to gratify—or far better—the right to give gratification.

The "rights" of the man must not encroach and predominate—and equally, the woman's must not do so either!

"Let the husband render unto the wife due benevolence; and likewise also the wife unto the husband. The wife hath not power of her own body, but the husband: and likewise also the husband hath not power of his own body, but the wife.

"Defraud ye not the one the other. . . ." (I. Cor. vii. 3, 5.)

CHAPTER XVI

BODILY HYGIENE

IV. Sexual Intercourse in Special Bodily (or Physical) Circumstances. Sexual Intercourse during Menstruation

FOR large categories of the human race, for whole peoples, for the faithful of many creeds, there is nothing problematical on this occasion. The menstrual woman is "unclean"; to touch her is forbidden defilement. And that ends the matter! Even though there are no such *ritual* prohibitions among Occidental peoples, and the ancient rule only formally binds individual Hebrews among us, yet the immemorial dogma has such force of suggestion, that sexual abstinence during menstruation may be almost regarded as customary. "But it is certainly an open question, whether this abstinence be indeed hygienically necessary, or whether we have to do with a primeval but baseless superstition." If so serious and eminent an authority as the late *Kossmann* (whose early death is a great loss to medicine) expressed himself, thus,[1] there is ample warrant for examining the subject thoroughly and without prejudice.

Here, too, we shall have to distinguish between bodily and psychic considerations.

In women the wish for intercourse *may* be increased during menstruation, or during certain days of the flow. And the man's impulse of sexual approach may be instinctively aroused by the menstrual condition of the woman. There are certainly profound and complex influences in play here. I refer to what we have already said about *olfactory stimuli*. There are men—and perfectly "normal" men—on whom this stimulus casts a spell that is almost irresistible. And

---

[1] In Senator Kaminer's "Krankheiten und Ehe" ("Marriage and Disease"). First edition, p. 172.

even without its special appeal, the knowledge that menstruation has begun drives many a man into the embrace of the wife he loves. His fervid preference may be partly caused by memories of previous experiences, for, with some couples, communion at the beginning or the close of the monthly period achieves the supreme sexual pleasure,[1] but in the main, it probably expresses primeval stimulus and primeval instinct.

It was with intention that I used the phrase, "drives many a man into the embrace of the wife he loves": both substantive and qualifying clause are important. For a woman must be truly *loved* by a man if he feels so attracted to her at the monthly period, and she must be his *wife, i.e.,* his mate, sharer of and in a permanent sexual partnership which implies mutual habituation and adaptation.

If these conditions do not prevail, the disadvantages of menstruation prevail easily against its special appeal. And such disadvantages are considerable and exist on both sides. Apart from concern for the woman's welfare, they include æsthetic factors, modesty and fear of exciting repugnance, involuntary associations with *ritual* "uncleanness" which suggest *actual* "uncleanliness." They are much strengthened by Biblical traditions of the customs of ancient pioneer peoples, who were also—it must be remembered—polygamous peoples!

But this inhibitive suggestion vanishes for those who face and reason out its origins, as the Christian Moral Theologians rightly recognize.[2]

Of course, the inhibitions are in themselves quite intelligible and justified, as the loss of blood may be considerable and accessory symptoms more or less conspicuous. Thus, while the loss of blood is greatest, there is more ground for abstinence than when it commences or ceases.

And what of the purely physical "pros and cons"?

We will consider the man's case first. It has been stated

---

[1] Probably because of the tumescence and congestion of the woman's organs, and at the end of menstruation also because of preceding abstinence.

[2] Dr. Alphonso de Liguori expressly sanctions coitus during menstruation.

that the menses contains substances which may cause inflammations of the mucus lining of the male urethra (Urethritis). I do not believe this. Whatever may be the case regarding special toxic properties of the perspirations and secretions of menstruating women, there is absolutely no proof of the corrosive and irritating nature of the feminine genital secretions *in themselves*. In my opinion the explanation of these cases of urethritis is bacteriological. I, too, have met cases—and not so very seldom—in which "clap," like urethritis, which was not caused by *Gonococci* in the man, followed coitus during menstruation. And I succeeded in every case in fixing the micro-organisms which caused the inflammation, by means of bacteriological test cultures.[1] Of course, such inflammations may be slight and generally quite curable, but they are not invariably so (see footnote), and the symptoms are highly unpleasant both in themselves and their sinister suggestions. When there has been no previous infection of the woman, I am convinced that they arise from simple neglect of proper cleanliness, especially of the vulva and vagina. Apart from such dirty neglect, there is practically no risk.

Of course, risk may menace from real gonorrheal germs. Gonococci may lurk in the genital passages of both men and women from a previous (perhaps forgotten or unconscious) infection, and may have lost their active virulence for a while. *But they may renew this virulence in the menstrual secretions,* and pass with such secretions into the male *urethra,* and *there renew acute symptoms of gonorrhea.* Thus, an old infection which has been latent and imperceptible for years may suddenly "flare up" after a sexual act during menstruation.

For the woman there are not only the *psychic* disadvantages common to her partner as well, and those, equally significant, and considered in detail in Chapter VI., such as unstable balance of judgment and emotions during menstruation. There are also the following physical factors :—

---

[1] Most of these urethric cases healed quickly and completely, after simple antiseptic douching without further treatment. But in one case general infectivity developed, with resultant heart disease. The germs were traceable in large numbers in the blood.

(1) The particular discomforts (headaches, disturbed digestion, etc.) felt by many women during a time, which for them really, is "being unwell."

(2) The initial and inevitable congestion of the genital organs, which, while it promotes sexual tension and enjoyment alike, may also make them sore and tender.

(3) The special flow of blood to and from the genitals in response to stimulation. In association with (2) there may be a positive hemorrhage, or an excessive loss which has ceased may begin again during coitus. And these congestions may cause pains, more or less acute, which after repeated infliction and natural sensitiveness may become chronic.

(4) A certain special vulnerability of the local tissues, so that vulva and vagina may, more easily than at other times, sustain slight lacerations. This is due to the combined congestion of the tissues and the effect of the mucus secretions during some successive days. Its significance in normal cases, and apart from such factors as arrested development, disproportion of the organs, and masculine violence (cf. Chapter X.) lies almost wholly in the danger of infection through tiny lacerations. And menstruation gives special liability to infections! Moreover, more serious lacerations may occur more easily under adverse conditions.

(5) This special liability to infection and contagion, which is both general and genital, or local. And most such micro-organisms and germs find a particularly favorable medium in the menstrual secretions and proliferate with enormous rapidity and virulence. This is the case both with germs already latent in the feminine organs and those introduced during coitus, from outside.

(6) The tendency of latent, chronic or sub-acute illnesses to "flare" during menstruation. Where there are any morbid or inflammatory affections of the genitals, this tendency is greatly increased by menstrual coitus.

Such are the results gleaned from practical experience, observation and scientific investigation. The conclusion as to the advisability of sexual intercourse during menstruation in the light of such practice, observation and research, can, I think, only be as follows:

Apart from the ritual customs of Oriental races, and assuming as an indispensable condition, the utmost personal cleanliness, then *moderate* and *mutually desired* sexual intercourse between *healthy* partners during menstruation is quite unobjectionable. But for æsthetic reasons, it is better to abstain during those days when the discharge is greatest. And in case of even slight disturbances, inclination to hemorrhage, hypersensitiveness and similar symptoms of the feminine parts, and especially in even latent inflammations of the ovaries and tubes—every and any erotic approach, even on psychic lines alone, is best avoided. And if there is any ground for supposing that morbid germs may be lurking, in either the man's or the woman's organs— even in so latent a state that they cause no perceptible effects —then complete sexual abstinence during menstruation is indicated.[1]

The problem of sexual intercourse during *pregnancy* is much more involved and many-sided than during menstruation. It is extraordinarily difficult for a doctor who possesses not only clinical and scientific knowledge, but also experience of life and human nature, to decide on which principle to take his stand, and what advice to give. For on him there may often depend, not only the physical destiny, health and even life, of expectant mother and unborn child, but also the happiness of a marriage. At a time when I could at the outside lay claim to knowledge of medicine, but not of life, I was solely preoccupied with the *physical* welfare of the women under my care, and issued many a decree forbidding marital embraces—only to regret

---

[1] In a more precise sense we may say that when such germs are located in the female genitalia the woman should have no intercourse during menstruation. For the man it would suffice to take especial precautions against the risk of contagion, which is very great at that time. If, on the other hand, the man is the germ carrier and the woman still free from them, it is always needful to avoid contagion, but above all during menstruation. In such a case, only *Coitus condomatus* would be permissible. Practically in married life, the first case does occur, but the second is somewhat rare. It is extremely difficult to judge which partner, if either, is contagious or if they both are. Correct diagnosis demands repeated and minute investigations and knowledge and experience on clinical, bacteriological and biological lines. Where it is impossible to consult a competent doctor, married couples would do well to follow the old saw: "In dubiis abstine"; in this case, if they feel all is not well, do not have intercourse during menstruation.

it later, when life had taught me what more precious and basic things there may be than the avoidance of bodily dangers. I console myself with the reflection that my urgent prohibitions were probably met with secret smiles and prompt infringement! Especially if and when the damage I prophesied, showed no signs of occurring!

And yet, anyone who would deny that coitus during gestation *can* have dangerous results and not infrequently *does* have such results—would make a mistake quite as serious as the error of *considering this aspect of the matter exclusively.*

We must realize the pros and cons, as clearly and accurately as possible. And in doing so, bear in mind, that our knowledge of many relevant factors is full of gaps, and of others, equally relevant, still almost a minus quantity.

On the basis of what we do know, we shall try to balance arguments for and against and to discern when and how it is possible to find a middle way between the two extreme positions.

Let us therefore begin with the *acte d'accusation,* and review the reasons which may be validly urged against sexual intercourse during gestation. They may be mainly summarized as follows. Immediately during coitus the uterus may be convulsively agitated, and expel its contents. In other words, and according to the precise stage of gestation, coitus can bring on an abortion, a premature delivery (alive or still-born) or the labor pains of a birth more or less normally due. In the two first cases, there is direct injury to or even destruction of the unborn life. And in the third case (premature parturition) we often find untimely ruptures of the amnoid membranes, which prolong birth and thus may harm both mother and child.

Moreover, in all these cases there is the risk of puerperal infection, if the male organ introduces germs of disease or decomposition into the recesses of the vagina, where they proliferate, under the favorable conditions of the ensuing birth or miscarriage, and find the best opportunity of ascending further into uterus, tubes and abdominal cavity, where they may permanently injure or kill the woman.

A further argument against intercourse when pregnant is

furnished by the state of the tender and congested genital tissues; they are even more *vascular* (full of blood) and more *vulnerable* than in menstruation. Thus, during coitus, small lacerations may occur, which are more dangerous than in the menstrual period, both because of weakening loss of blood and infection; and any considerable laceration in the genitals of the gravid woman, which are absolutely saturated and distended with blood—represents imminent risk of very serious bleeding. In practice, these substantial lacerations happen *quite seldom*—unless, indeed, the man is extraordinarily and inexcusably rough and clumsy—which is probably due to the simultaneous expansion of the vagina and its greater flexibility. And the small and extremely minute tears which mostly occur in the rim of the introitus can be completely avoided, if proper care is taken, and adequate lubricants used, to facilitate entry.

So that, all in all, the local vascularity and sensitiveness during pregnancy are less of an absolute barrier than a very strong reason for the greatest care and consideration in intercourse.

A less cogent reason against sexual intercourse during pregnancy is the objection brought forward because of abdominal distension, and the typical high stomach of advanced pregnancy. Of course any marked pressure on the woman's abdomen is quite wrong in the later months—but it is equally certain that appropriate positions and attitudes will avoid such pressure. (Cf. Chapter XI.)

We do not know, as yet, whether the seminal *substances* absorbed by the woman's organs are harmful to her in pregnancy. It is certain that the vaginal membranes are peculiarly absorbent in that state. It is also quite likely that the organism reacts by defensive special secretions, against substances which might be injurious. There is *no* proof as yet of chemical injury to the pregnant woman in coitus. If such proof is established, the use of condoms is indicated.[1]

The same remedy as in the case of latent disease germs in pregnancy applies, as in menstruation, with reference to

---

[1] And why should the absorption of sperm substances not have as tonic an effect on the pregnant woman as on the non-pregnant?

"flaring" following coitus. *The risk is greater in pregnancy.* If there should *appear to be any infection or contagion (of any kind) of the female organs during pregnancy, they should not be excited through coitus under any considerations.*

The belief in the danger that the man may contract urethritis from vaginal secretions of a healthy pregnant woman has as little or as much foundation as the same belief about menstrual secretions. *The remedy is the same: careful cleanliness in both partners.*

We see, therefore, that apart from former or initial morbid infection or contagion, only the first group of objections are serious and fundamental, as the other negative arguments may be disposed of by suitable precautions and modifications.

But the serious problem of the danger of coitus in pregnancy crystallizes round these two points:

(*a*) Is the probability of premature labor, or premature birth or miscarriage, immediately after coitus, great?

(*b*) If birth follows coitus, is puerperal infection probable?

For it must be admitted that such puerperal infections occur far too often.

This is proved by the statistics published by Bübens, but his number of cases is far too small to be accepted as wholly representative or conclusive. Moreover, women from the poorer classes of a Hungarian city are probably no more shining examples of personal cleanliness and wholesomeness than are their husbands. I consider that likelihood of puerperal infection is very much reduced when both partners habitually wash and cleanse their sexual parts, as I have suggested throughout.

We have no "sources" on which to base an answer to Problem (*a*) : no means of knowing in what percentage of cases the womb expels its contents after and because of coitus. But those who have seen much behind the scenes of married life, can only say that this percentage must not be over-estimated: if coitus invariably or generally brought on parturition, the number of still-births and premature births would be much greater than it is.[1] Medical experience teaches us that the danger is greatest during the first three months, and that it is specially great among women of a particular type, which shows a constitutional tendency to miscarriage and/or premature parturition—often still-birth. Finally, we need hardly emphasize that towards the end of pregnancy, the probability of labor-pains after coitus, progressively increases.

There is some justification for the case against coitus in pregnancy. This we do not attempt to deny.

But: if the woman is healthy; if the uterus shows no tendency to premature function—(slight blood-stains, convulsive pains)—or has not shown such tendency in the previous pregnancy or pregnancies; if all necessary care and consideration are exercised during the act;[2] and excessive stimulation of vulva and vagina, avoided; if both partners are absolutely *clean*,[3] and if, for the last—say four—weeks, total abstention is observed, then in my opinion the risks to the woman are reduced to a very slight amount.

The arguments "pro" are wholly *physic*. We must primarily try to realize *whether the woman herself desires sexual intercourse during pregnancy*. In putting this question we at once meet the difficulty that it is impossible to make a valid generalization on changes of a typical character or universality in the intensity of feminine desire during pregnancy. Most writers who express a definite opinion on this subject, declare for a decided ebb or diminution of sexual desire in pregnant women, and almost invariably they stress the analogy of sub-human female creatures. Others, but fewer, authorities are of the opposite opinion, holding that the sexual desire of a woman often increases,

---

[1] The enormous number of miscarriages which admittedly do occur, must not be taken as evidence, here. Even if a considerable number are brought on by reckless intercourse, the overwhelming majority are artificial (illicit) abortions, which make remedial measures very difficult.

[2] Avoid deep penetration.

[3] The introduction of germs and dangerous matter may often be better prevented if the *anterior sedentary attitude* is favored, rather than the *posterior lateral*. (See Chapter XI). Another wise precaution is the use of a pure and *non-greasy* lubricant, compounded with a non-irritant antiseptic.

owing to the congestion and sensibility of the genitalia in the gravid state.

In my professional experience, I have observed a great many cases of undeniable quickening of desire, in the early part of pregnancy. It may be so pronounced and characteristic, as to form the most reliable sign that conception has again occurred.[1]

In any case there is no universal valid rule about the influence of "pregnancy" *per se* on "woman" in general, as concerns sexual emotions. Rather does the pregnant state influence desire in most diverse ways, according to individual temperament and constitution, and the stage of gestation. For several years, I have given special attention to this, whenever and so far as it was possible. The sum of my information and observations may be generalized thus:—

Where, previous to the pregnancy, the sexual relationship of the husband and wife was more or less lukewarm, and the specific gratification of the woman during intercourse, only moderate or quite inadequate, there, desire, if it still exists at all, vanishes quickly and wholly, as soon as the woman knows she is pregnant. Quite frequently, there is marked dislike to any erotic contacts or approaches.

But, if the sexual relationship, between husband and wife, before conception occurred, follows the lines indicated in the third section of our book: then, as a rule, the woman's desire, in the first half of pregnancy, does *not subside* in the least; on the contrary there can be, as mentioned above, a temporary accentuation of desire. In the second half of pregnancy this slowly diminishes, but remains to a certain degree, till the end.[2]

---

[1] I think the explanation must be sought in the evolutionary changes which take place in the ovaries, and their functions, immediately on impregnation, and which alter the processes of metabolism. (See Chapter VI.)

[2] It does not even vanish with the onset of labor pains. The fact that during the preliminary stages of birth, coitus takes place relatively often, has been emphasized in recent research into the causes of puerperal infection; is this to be ascribed to a sudden "flare" of sexual emotion in the wife? It may seem the essence of paradox, but I think it is by no means impossible. However, at present it is not possible to make more precise statements. I attribute *communion* between a *loving* pair under such conditions, largely to erotic altruism, whose psychic strands must be so rich and various: pain, fear, the need for protection and consolation, the

Before passing from the instinctive and primitive sexual urge to the discussion of more evolved and conscious feminine emotion, it should be made clear that it is fortunate for the expectant mother if and when she belongs to the category whose desires are not diminished or obliterated by gestation.

Has not modern psychology which probes and unveils the unconscious, revealed to us "that the soul of woman reacts to the suppression of erotic wishes by morbid symptoms, of which anxiety[1] is the most conspicuous (the so-called anxiety neuroses)"? And in my opinion there is but one obvious logical conclusion, from this recognition: the admission that it is wise and right to continue normal intercourse during pregnancy. The psychology of the unconscious can supply formidable ammunition to our affirmative case.

And her conscious and half-conscious mind must strongly counsel a woman who loves her husband, to continue her former intimacy with him, on all planes, psychic and physical. Her need of attachment and dependence is enhanced by her condition. More than ever before, does she long for her husband's attentions, his courtesy, his tender wooing. As pregnancy advances, the consciousness of her altered appearance depresses her and irks her. She fears to lose charm for her husband. And his intentional abstention from intercourse must then seem to her callous neglect, and inflict an emotional wound far more serious than any physical harm that could result from sexual activity—(postulating, of course, that both she and her husband are *healthy*).

And so, in Ideal Marriage, the wife desires to continue

---

need to protect and console, etc. (I would refer to what is said in Chapter III.) The conventional explanation which would reduce these acts to the coarse recklessness of brutal male egotism, and the credulous stupidity of women who believe that coitus will make birth easier (a prevalent popular superstition), is not the only one. It is probably true in some cases, but in others the motives are those I have suggested. Many and many times have I been convinced of this in my professional practice. But, of course, prolonged or vigorous sexual intercourse in such circumstances, however favorable and beneficial psychically, must be absolutely discouraged from a medical standpoint.

[1] Note, of course, indefinite, unconscious anxiety, *dread without an object*, unlike conscious *fear* which refers to something definite. On this significant subject I would refer to the interesting Essay by *Heberer* in the *Zentralblatt für Gynäkologie*, No. 7, 1925, "On the Psychology of Pregnancy." Our observations on the desire of pregnant women diverge, however.

sexual intercourse with her husband, during pregnancy, as before. She would desire this, even if her own instincts did not impel her. She desires it with her whole heart, and also with her brain and judgment. *And she is right.* For it is nothing less than impossible for a man accustomed to active sexual life, to stop complete functional satisfaction, more or less suddenly, for several months, and nevertheless to continue to play the wooer to his wife: to repeat the approaches of the prelude (which will mightily increase a sexual excitement that has become clamant through enforced abstinence), and then, again and again, to break off. No; and again no! Even those writers who enthusiastically proclaim the harmlessness of sexual abstinence, must admit that such repeated sexual repression and psychic *dislocation must* lead to neurotic symptoms or at least to very difficult moods and impaired efficiency in (specially brain) work; and that if the man is to abstain entirely from his wife's person, he can only do so by keeping at a definite distance, and practicing a systematic reserve.

But a loving wife desires to prevent this *distance* and *this reserve,* at all costs. Even the woman to whom "Marriage" means nothing greater or more intimate than a haven of refuge from the need of self-support, will share the real wife's anxiety. For who shall guarantee that "thus far and no further" does not drive the man into the arms of another? Who shall guarantee that he will return, when "changed circumstances" permit her to receive him once more?

Enough! For me there is no doubt at all. The reasons in *favor* of continued coitus during gestation are far more imperative and profound than those against it. Therefore "doctors must be extremely sparing in prescribing abstinence during pregnancy, and confine such prohibitions to the most urgent cases," as Kossmann says. Under such "most urgent cases" I would include, apart from special diseases, *only the menace of miscarriage, and the imminence of birth. And these urgent exceptions I must specially emphasize to my lay (non-medical) readers.* And further, I strongly urge them, in coitus during gestation, to use all the caution and gentleness which we have seen to be necessary for the welfare of the woman and the unborn.

Is it necessary, in conclusion, to point out that special regard is necessary to the complex physical and mental symptoms of pregnancy?

Surely not, for the husband who has stood the test (as guide and friend as well as true lover), of preparing his wife for the high festival of Ideal Marriage, will not fail her at a time when such enormous demands are made upon her, and such possible dangers face her.

How long should be the repose and abstinence after birth?

We will here disregard the elaborate rituals of Semitic cultures, the customs of many primitive peoples, and the tradition of the "uncleanness" of a mother after childbirth. To discuss them here would merely repeat what has been said, in relation to menstruation. Let us rather consider the matter from a purely physiological point of view.

The confinement in the everyday, non-medical sense, lasts from eight to fourteen days. A quite arbitrary duration, varying according to race, region, social position, financial means, and many other factors. I think it advisable to assume the longest time—a fortnight.

The confinement in our medical sense is the interval during which the genital organs return to their normal state, after the stresses and changes of pregnancy and birth. This process is known as *Involution*.[1] It lasts from five to eight weeks, and depends on climate, race, and personal idiosyncrasies. Involution generally lasts six weeks. In women who do not nurse at the breast, it closes with the reappearance of menstruation. The indiscriminate use of the term, "confinement," for involution, is inaccurate and causes confusion; we shall therefore not employ it in that sense.

Thus, *Confinement* lasts a fortnight, *Organic Involution*, including "Confinement," about six weeks in all. And *accoucheurs* generally omit to give any precise counsel about renewal of intercourse, either to their patients, or the ladies' husbands. And they are only asked for such advice, in exceptional cases. And so, with women of the poorer classes who, as happens in many cities, leave the hospitals after

---

[1] Otherwise the puerperium.

eight or ten days, and return home, coitus recommences much too soon.

On the other hand, the smaller number of writers who have expressed themselves on this subject, recommend an abstention of needless length; *i.e.,* throughout the whole involution. Only occasionally do they admit that this separation may be shortened without risk, by "a week or two."

I cannot see why the necessary abstention should be observed throughout six weeks, if health and recovery are normal.

There are three principal perils to be avoided, with reference to the feminine organs:

1. Infection or Contagion.
2. Hemorrhage.
3. Irritation of wounds which have just begun to heal.

Well, I have dismissed thousands of women, from hospitals or private treatment, between twelve and fourteen days after delivery. If the last examination showed normal recovery, I have seldom advised abstinence. I know that several—and I infer that most—of them renewed sexual intercourse as soon as they returned to their homes. I have re-examined the overwhelming majority of these women, six weeks after delivery, and, apart from certain fresh gonorrhœal infections (which would have happened, sooner or later, even after prolonged abstinence), I cannot remember one case, in which any disturbances of normal involution or any morbid symptoms, could be ascribed to coitus, though it had generally happened very frequently.

And why should it cause any such disturbance or disease? The gates stand wide to the bacteria of puerperal fever, in the days immediately following delivery. But after a fortnight that is no longer the case. Any lacerations (even larger perineal lacerations) have had time to heal, if the doctor does not dismiss his patient too soon. As for the peril of uterine hemorrhages, sexual excitement certainly causes local congestions, but it also promotes strong muscular contractions, which compensate and balance possible ill-effects of the increased blood supply.

And the general, bodily and emotional state of a healthy woman, a fortnight after delivery cannot justify a ban on coitus. *Consideration* she surely needs, for she has just performed a great and perilous office, and if nursing, is still performing it. She should have all possible opportunities of special rest, and demonstrations of special regard, but these are quite compatible with the renewal of sexual intercourse in its tenderest mood, with special accentuation on the prelude, on verbal endearments, and only gradually assuming more pronounced and vivid sexual coloring. If sexual intercourse is performed with the utmost consideration and caution (because of the vulnerability of the local tissues), without excessive genital stimulation, and in the normal attitude, I think it is favorable and beneficial rather than the reverse, to a healthy woman, who has not suffered exceptionally, in birth and confinement, after a fortnight has elapsed.

Of course a fresh impregnation would be most inadvisable in every way. But conception rarely occurs during the six weeks of involution. Especially if the woman nurses at the breast, the risk is less than under ordinary conditions.

Finally, a word in reference to the recurrence of menstruation, which is to be expected in women who do not suckle their infant, about six weeks after delivery. It sometimes occurs earlier. The loss of blood is apt to be quite profuse. It is therefore wise not to increase the congestion by genital exercise and stimulation, and to abstain entirely from the first symptoms till two days after it completely ceases.

My opinion of the advisability of sexual intercourse during the interval between conception and the end of involution may be summarized as follows; with special gentleness and care, sexual connection may be continued for the first half of pregnancy (four to five months) without excessive stimulation, and assuming healthy and normal conditions. From the middle of the fourth month it should become gradually less frequent, and cease entirely at least four weeks before delivery is expected. Fourteen days after (normal) delivery, intercourse may be resumed, very gently and carefully, and increased gradually till about six weeks after delivery, when it may return to habitual frequency and fervor. During the first menstrual period, there should be a complete abstention.

A few remarks are necessary, on *sexual conduct in cases of illness.* They cannot be exhaustive or detailed, as that would be impossible in this treatise, although the subject in general has great interest and importance.

We must clearly differentiate the direct influence of sexual activity *in itself from its biological results of gestation, birth, and involution. For most kinds of serious illness, these reproductive processes have far graver and more adverse results than has the sex act. We devote our attention to the last, alone.*

It is, of course, self-evident, and hardly needs stressing that coitus is to be forbidden (unless all appropriate sanitary precautions are taken) in cases where an illness of one partner might be caught by the other.

Equally self-evident is it that *acute* diseases of either male or female genitalia, absolutely bar coitus.

Chronic genital inflammations themselves prevent the sexual act as a rule, on account of the pain they cause. In other and milder cases, coitus is apt to bring about renewed inflammation and relapse.

Nevertheless, I am of the opinion that many gynæcologists are too severe in their prohibitions here. We should not forget that, in long illnesses, complete abstention between husband and wife has its own dangers. Therefore, if occasion offers, the doctor should confine himself to advising *temperance in indulgence, and at the same time emphasize the technical resources for avoiding possible harm: (e.g., Positions in coitus:* see Chapter XI.). Or else *operative measures* should be boldly suggested, if it is probable that they would make safe and painless sexual intercourse possible once more. A woman patient who was frankly and fully informed of the risks and disadvantages attendant on the surgical operation on the one hand, and on "doing without it" on the other, will surely not often refuse it, and prefer the almost certain destruction of marital happiness, to the perils and discomforts of an operation—which have been greatly reduced of late years. And we doctors should not hesitate too long, before suggesting surgical aid, as otherwise, when the marital relation has been destroyed, it will still be necessary to have recourse to the scalpel.

With only few (but all the more significant and helpful) exceptions, doctors still give far too little attention to the preservation or restoration of sexual efficiency and sexual activity: at least so far as women are concerned. Such demands are only made very seldom by women, in explicit terms, and generally not even adumbrated. Most doctors evade the whole subject, whether from perfectly comprehensible but mistaken reserve or inadequate understanding of its importance. But the importance of sexual activity, efficiency and experience is at least just as great as that of fertility and reproductive power, to which we—quite rightly!—attach so much value, in our professional judgments. It is not even inferior to effective economic power or earning capacity by either manual or mental work. It may even outweigh risk to life itself. For how often does all that makes life worth living or preserves the "will to live" depend on the power to experience the joy and inspiration of sex? And so, not only in the cases in reference to which I have felt compelled to make these suggestions, but in *all cases affecting sexual activity and experience,* whether directly or indirectly, we doctors should give this function the significant and fundamental place in our comparisons, our diagnoses, our advice and our therapeutic methods, which is its rightful due.

General morbid conditions have of course a very lowering influence on desire and potency (especially in men), through the exhaustion they cause. But *fevers* often accentuate sexual desires, and even, though only for a short while, and to a slight degree—genital potency. And then the general organic tension of the act is followed by collapse. We must remember the peculiar mixture of weakness (exhaustibility) and irritability in sexual matters which is the frequent result of the effect of illness on the nervous system; and this very difficult condition may be made worse by disappointments and refusals. Neither the marriage partner nor the medical adviser has an easy task in deciding, among so many complex and contradictory factors, whether to grant—or deny.

Finally we must refer to the fatal consequences of coitus in *many* cases of men with arterio-sclerosis, on account of the high blood pressure, which invariably attends it. And to the equally established fact that regular, normal sexual intercourse *can* exercise most favorable influence on all morbid conditions which are mainly of nervous origin.

SUPPLEMENT TO CHAPTER XVI

Care and Cleanliness of the Organs of Copulation

I would suggest the following details, regarding the care of the genital organs, and especially the proper method of cleansing and washing them. These hints may *appear* trivial: but they are important.

The technique of cleanliness here is often not only neglected but applied in a way that does positive harm. But we have repeatedly stressed its importance!

Cleanliness is particularly difficult in these organs; because the folds and interstices are somewhat inaccessible, and the *smegma* is rather adhesive. We have discussed this fully in Chapters V. and VII., and I would ask my non-medical readers to read through the relevant passages again, before turning to these paragraphs.

Very frequent and exact cleansing of the genitals removes both *smegma and decomposing organic particles,* which will otherwise certainly collect, on or near them. The *urinary orifice* is set in the exterior genitalia, and the *anus* is in their immediate neighborhood, especially in the woman's case. So there is great need for frequent ablutions and purifications.

Therefore the following directions are *absolutely necessary,* to deal with smegma, excretory particles and germs of disease!

For Men

(In addition to the usual baths and ablutions)

(i.) Cleanse the *glans* or *tip* carefully, both morning and evening; also the inner surface of the prepuce, and the *rim* or *corona,* especially, pulling back the prepuce to do this. Use clean water and a small piece of lint,[1] dipped in the water beforehand. Use a fresh piece each time!

(ii.) Avoid staining underclothing during urination. If stained, the underclothing should be changed. Change underclothing as often as possible. The same rule holds good for night-shirts and pajamas.

(iii.) It is advisable to use a piece of clean lint for dabbing and wiping after urination.

(iv.) After sexual communion or at the end of the afterplay, the penis should be washed and the *glans* cleansed, as directed above (i.).

(v.) If the organ shows irritation after too vigorous use —as may occur if lubrication is too slight and manifests itself by itching, burning, slight swelling, and redness especially on the rim of the prepuce—cleanse very carefully with lint, drawing back the prepuce, dab dry and powder thinly all over with talc powder; powder especially on the *glans* and the *corona.* This powder-stratum is designed to prevent friction of glans and prepuce.

For Women

(In addition to the usual baths and ablutions)

(i.) Every morning and evening, *thorough* cleansing of the vulva, with special attention to the folds and interstices around clitoris and Labia minora. Use a clean piece of lint on and over the *bidet,* and clean with warm-tepid water. Dab dry—do not rub!—with a clean towel.

---

[1] I am aware that surgical lint is rather expensive just now, but must persist in this requirement. Only very small pieces are necessary, the costs are small and bearable even by modest household budgets! And if regarded as an insurance against disease, they are really low enough!

(ii.) Whenever possible, cleanse after urination, to remove all traces of urine. Use bidet, lint, and lukewarm or *cold* clean water. Rub dry with clean towel.

(iii.) Cleanse the anus most carefully after going to stool. Use enough good toilet-paper to remove all solid detritus! Wipe only from the front to the back, *never* in the opposite direction! Then wash; from front to back! The perineum should be cleansed very carefully. A wrong method of removing excrement has really caused widespread harm! Finally, with fresh water and fresh lint, cleanse the vulva from drops of urine. Any soiling of the vulva with excrement should be avoided and prevented at all cost.

(iv.) Avoid soiling underlinen by excrement, urine, or discharges. Change linen if soiled. Change sheets in like case. Frequent change of bed-linen and body-linen, essential!

(v.) Cleanliness *during menstruation* should be carried to the utmost possible limit. Diapers or sanitary towels should be changed frequently, and only perfectly clean special sanitary towels used. Change underlinen once a day at least, if not twice.

(vi.) After sexual communion or at end of after-play, carefully wash the vulva, as directed above (i.).

(vii.) If the vulva shows symptoms of irritation after vigorous use, especially if lubrication is difficult, or if the menstrual (or other) secretions cause redness, burning, itching, slight swelling or any, even the tiniest lacerations: then the vulva is to be cleansed most thoroughly but very gently, *dabbed* dry, and then powdered with lint and talc powder. Powder the vulva, and Labia minora. If a second person can be entrusted with this, use a powder sprinkler, and repeat after every cleansing.

In any irritation, double cleanliness is essential. Till recovery (which should be prompt) avoid further irritation of the parts.

(viii.) *No* "cleansing" douches, so-called. They destroy the chemical process of the vagina, which are a natural antisepsis, and should only be employed on medical prescription. But the modern gynæcologist is sparing with such prescriptions.

For Men and Women

Use clean water! If no filtered water available, boil water before use.[1]

No sponges!

No powder-puffs!

Avoid woolen underclothing in the genital regions.

Only touch the genitals, whether your own or your partner's with perfectly clean hands! This is particularly necessary in women.

I beg my readers, in their own interests, not to dismiss these directions as exaggerated and "too much trouble." Such negligence can have serious results, even if the exact connection between cause and effect is not always demonstrable.

And—Ideal Marriage can only be achieved under the protection of physical cleanliness.

---

[1] *Not* an exaggerated demand! In 1907 I published an account of nine cases of an infectious disorder of the female genitalia, caused by washing in unfiltered spring water, and—communicated to their husbands. Further particulars in my Essay, "Blastomycætes and Inflammation of the Female Genitals" in *Zentralblatt für Gynäkologie*, 1907, No. 38.

CHAPTER XVII

PSYCHIC, EMOTIONAL AND MENTAL HYGIENE

HYGIENE means—care of health.

The health of any organism is preserved and promoted in two ways; firstly by striving to improve its normal functions; secondly to combat hostile factors which threaten it. And it must be borne in mind that the degree of functional vigor and efficiency attained helps the whole organism to overcome damage and disease. Thus the effort to attain the greatest possible functional efficiency has *double* hygienic value. But such effort must not be *overdone* in any direction, or harm will follow, instead of improvement.

Let us assume that the Ideal Marriage of two partners is an independent living organism, and study it in the light of our hygienic motto of *exercise without excess; efficiency without exaggeration.* We have endeavored, in the preceding chapters, to lay the foundations of physiological and technical proficiency, which will enable this organism to bring its most important function, namely sexual intercourse, to the degree of perfection which is due to it.

We have suggested how to avoid mistakes and mischief arising for those who share in this function, through errors in its execution and have, finally, taken every opportunity of warning that neither one nor both partners should be physically over-strained by exertions or exactions of a sexual character. *And we have explained that sexual activity only is an inspiration and benefit to the psyche (mood, mental capacity) of both partners, as and so long as it is in harmony with their general and specific (genital) powers.* But we will stress this point once more: excess in this direction is harmful, genitally and generally, and especially to the man. Vigorous sexual activity and concentrated intellectual effort are in many persons, men especially, antagonistic, and with difficulty compatible.

The partners in the Ideal Marriage of a constant brain worker, must make full allowance for this difficulty.

This necessary consideration leads us to the particular fundamental principle of hygiene which decrees that it is *never* good to make any *one* function of any organism, even the most important function, so predominant and absorbing that the others—and the whole entity—suffer thereby.

Applied to Ideal Marriage, this means that the highest development of mutual relationship on the sexual side, must not invade and impair their mental life in common, and their psychic sympathy and partnership; bodies, emotions and brains must be equally in harmony. As a rule, if and when Ideal Marriage is achieved, this universal harmony prevails of itself; for in Ideal Marriage, husband and wife, through the very range and intensity of their mutual erotic life, remain *lovers*. And lovers, as we all know, have souls attuned to one another.

Thus, there is not much risk of psychic starvation; on the contrary, danger threatens from an excess of emotional absorption and dependence, for these, in the long run, weary the recipient of such unremitting devotion.

It would take us too far from our main theme, to discuss the reasons and remedies of this satiety. To point out its peril should suffice and should enforce this practical lesson and rule of life: *Let there be love, let there be attachment, let there be mutual partnership in things of the mind; but, with all the utmost possible sympathy in word and deed— leave each other enough leisure, enough space, enough repose! Respect each other's personality and privacy! Learn when and how to leave each other alone!*

Another important life lesson; if every sexual desire is fully gratified, the danger of satiety arises, for satiety follows all excess. Its blighting shadow falls, sooner or later,

on all the sexual relationships of the average marriage.
Even Ideal Marriage is not wholly immune! Even although
its "vigorous harmonious sexual activities" having the
charm of variation and versatility, do not pall as do the
monotonous exercises of sexual ignorance—nevertheless,
just their very perfection and completion have the fatal possibility of "Too Much Loving."

This is a tragic possibility; all the more tragic because it
strikes lovers who are wholly unconscious of its danger, and
slide down the treacherous incline, from their Heaven of
Happiness, unawares. To avoid its havoc is one of the
greatest psychic tasks. Psychic hygiene must avert satiety
by a tactful delicacy, a wise reserve at appropriate intervals.
A husband can do nothing wiser than to bear in mind Balzac's aphorism: "The husband who leaves his wife nothing
more to long for—is indeed lost." And—the exquisite
charm with which occasional coyness and reserve on the
wife's part, can invest her, in his eyes, has been immortally
celebrated in the description of Imogen, in Shakespeare's
Cymbeline:

> "Me of my lawful pleasure, she restrain'd,
> And pray'd me oft, forbearance: did it with
> A pudency so rosy, the sweet view on't
> Might well have warm'd old Saturn."

But the wife should not forget that exaggerated coyness
and caprice are *most* hostile and dangerous to Ideal Marriage. It all depends on the manner and method in which denial is expressed. *Remy de Gourmont* wrote: "Women have
ways of—*not* giving themselves which are more delightful
than anything else." But such refusal can only arouse delight when it is itself full of tenderness and pleasure in some
aspects of the man's love and personality: and not when it is
an ungracious, egotistic fit of temper—or calculation! And
such elusiveness should be compensated on another occasion,
by a certain demonstrativeness and initiative. This whole
interplay of reserve and advance, hesitation and attraction,
gives fullest scope to womanly intuition and charm, and is
a valuable and legitimate exercise of coquetry and flirtation
as defined and described by us in Chapter VIII.

Personal reserve has another helpful office in avoiding incessant intimacy in the most commonplace aspects and details of life. Here, too, a swift *aperçu* says more than pages of explanation. The *aperçu* is by Balzac—(we have referred once more to his knowledge and vision, but he has said it best of all) :

"The man who enters his wife's dressing-room, is a sage of consummate wisdom—or a fool !" [1]

Sapienti sat.

We have touched on a subject which though at least equally important in Ideal Marriage, applies also to ordinary conjugal relations, and is not characteristic of their highest evolution. We now turn again to Ideal Marriage—in the light of psychic hygiene, to ask whether there are no inevitable drawbacks, which accompany its *extension, intensification* and *transcendent clarification* of the sexual relationships between the partners? Even the happiness Ideal Marriage can bestow would be bought too dear, at the cost of psychic equipoise, of full human efficiency and experience, and moral stature in all other departments of life.

And this would certainly be the case with persons who were *ascetic* in temperament or theory, or both; whether or not they belonged to a definite religious creed. They do not need the happiness of Ideal Marriage : or they do not wish to need it ! They condemn such highest human bliss, because it contradicts their concept of "Purity": of "that sanctification of life, which means deliverance from all earthly ties and their translation into a spiritual sphere." [2]

Certain groups of Christians go fairly far, in the effort to free themselves from earthly wishes, and in the view that such wishes must be combated; other (certainly less numerous) go almost all the way ! Thassilo von Scheffer in his book, quoted above, points out that "The concept of original sin, with special reference to sexual desires and

---

[1] "L'homme qui entre le cabinet de toilette de sa femme est un philosophe ou un imbécile."—*Physiologie du Mariage.*

[2] *Cf.* Thassilo von Scheffer : "Philosophie der Ehe," p. 152 ("Philosophy of Marriage").

experiences, affects the whole Christian attitude to 'the lusts of the flesh,' which are branded as 'sin' instead of glorified as both the core and summit of existence, as in many other cults." [1]

Of course, with those who sincerely hold this faith and try to make it their rule of life, there can be no conflict between religion and Ideal Marriage: for their conscience will exclude Ideal Marriage.

Others, again, have no traditional religious prejudices or beliefs. For them, too, there is no question of divided allegiance, here.

But what of those persons in whom ethical idealism, traditional religion, and sexual desires, all have power, and whose souls they all affect profoundly, so that, in many cases, they are operative turn and turn about or simultaneously? In other words and from the *practical* standpoint: *How do the dogmas and precepts of the chief religions of the Western World affect the principles of Ideal Marriage, as we have formulated them in the preceding sections of this study?*

We may not ignore or evade this subject. It affects the psychic side of Ideal Marriage most profoundly. For if this highest evolutionary form of human marriage really offends accepted religious dogmas and rules of conduct, it could obviously lead to psychic conflicts and disunion on the part of husband or wife, or both, which might disturb and endanger the psychic and mental side of their relationship.

The subject is unavoidable because of certain ascetic tendencies of traditional organized Christianity.[2] But the conflict is not, as a matter of actual experience, necessarily acute. For, where certain details which we consider wise and desirable, are opposed to religious doctrine and practice, we find that Ideal Marriage may adapt itself, while wholly retaining its essential character.

It is somewhat difficult to summarize the theories and

---

[1] "Philosophie de Ehe," p. 154.
[2] Especially derived from early Christian times, which were exclusively occupied with the Kingdom of God on earth, that was believed to be imminent.

precepts of the various creeds in question. There are contradictions and cross-currents.[1]

---

[1] I have corresponded with several theologians of the most diverse views, on this subject, and ransacked many libraries. In these pages, as well as privately, I wish to express my thanks to these gentlemen for the time and trouble they took on my behalf. I am especially indebted to the courteous help of the authorities of the *Bibliotheca Nazionale* in Palermo, where I found most of the sources for Catholic moral theology, and to those of the Zentralbibliothek, at Zürich, which enabled me to refer to some of the relevant Protestant literature.

To my keen regret I have been obliged, owing to considerations of space, to let fall my plan of discussing this absorbing series of problems in detail and illustrating them by quotations. I shall therefore confine myself to reproducing the general impression these studies made on me, and only here and there mention some detail of special significance.

For the technical scientific aspect, I would refer readers to the following list of sources used by me. The religions are arranged in chronological order :—

JEWISH

Julius Preuss. "Biblisch Talmudische Medizin," 23rd Edition (Medicine in Bible and Talmud). Berlin, 1921. S. Karger.
Original sources, being in Rabbinical Hebrew, were not available to my use.

CATHOLIC

Capellmann-Bergmann. "Pastoral Medizin," 19th Edition. (Paderborn, Bonifazius Press.) The relevant passages are printed in Latin. This book suffices as a practical manual for clerical and medical use.
For detailed study :
Th. Sanchez. "Disputationum de Sancto Matrimonii sacramento auctore Thoma Sanchez, Cordubensi e Societate Jesu." Antverpiæ apud Jac, Meursium. Anno MDCLII. (On title page of the copy in the Palermitan Bibliotheca Nazionale, formerly belonging to the Jesuits, is written in ink : "Editio non prohibita.") Tomus II., Lib. 9. *De debito conjugale.*
S. Alph. Mariæ de Ligorio. "Theologia moralis." Neapoli, 1827. Tom. VIII., Tract 6. *De Matrimonio..* (German translation by R. Grassmann, Extracts from the "Moral Theology of the Holy Doctor, Alph. Mar. de Lig." 34th Edition. Publisher, R. Grassmann, Stettin.)
Petr. Scavini. "Theologia moralis universa," 3rd Edition. Paris, 1859.
D. Craisson. "De Rebus Venereis ad usum Confessariorum." Paris, 1870.
J. P. Gury. "Compendium Theologiæ Moralis. Antonii Ballerius adnotationibus locupletatum, 6th Edition. Rome, 1882. German version, Regensburg, 1868.

PROTESTANT

Luther's words : "On the Babylonian Captivity" and "On the Monk's Vow."
Heidelberg Catechism.
Ames (Amesius). "Medulla Theologia de Conscientia, eius jure et casibus." (1633.)
Francis Wayland. "The Elements of Moral Science." (1835). Book II. "Practical Ethics."
Gottschalk, in Herzog. Realenzyklopädie für Protestantische Theologie und Kirche." Art., "Ehe" (Marriage) and "Ethik" in this encyclopædia. (Publisher, J. C. Hinrichs, Leipzig.)

The position is most simple as regards the oldest of the
three faiths represented among us. The Hebrews have a
precise and definite traditional rule, developed from the
Mosaic Code. The principal features are the prohibition of
all sexual intercourse—and even physical contact, with the
woman (who is considered "unclean") during menstruation
and involution, until and before she has had the ritual bath
or purification, ordained after a certain length of time.
There is no point in citing these regulations in detail: my
Hebrew readers know them well and for the Gentiles they
have no importance. We may say, however, that this special code *sets up several seasons of abstinence between husband and wife, but otherwise does not oppose the principles
of Ideal Marriage.* In fact, in one respect, they emphasize
my advice; they insist on a close season for the freshly-
perforated bride (which however from the medical point
of view, is needlessly long). They regard the slight loss of
blood from the ruptured hymen, as identical with the end
of the menstrual period, and prescribe a seven days' abstinence in that case as well.

In condemning coitus during menstruation, orthodox
Calvinists refer to the same Biblical texts as do the Jews:
Leviticus, XV, 19: XVIII, 19: and XX, 18. I do not
know whether these Calvinist Protestants go so far as to
include the seven days after menstruation in the season of
abstinence, but there is no doubt that certain circles *incline*
to this purely Mosaic view of sexual matters.

A fundamental principle of the Roman Catholic sexual
Code which corresponds with precepts in Protestant and
Jewish doctrine, based on the Old Testament, is the rejec-
tion of all actions tending to prevent conception.

It must, however, be clearly recognized that this ban is
quite independent of the basis of Ideal Marriage.

Steffen, in Schiele. "Religion in Geschichte u. Gegenwart" (Religion,
Historical and Contemporary). Art., "Ehe" (Marriage). (Publisher,
J. C. B. Mohr, Tübingen.)
"Encyclopædia of Religion and Ethics," Vol. 8, Art., "Casuistry" (Moral
Theology). Literature cited at conclusion of this article. Nothing of im-
portance in this way in article "Marriage."
Of course with regard to all these creeds the first source of investigation
is the Bible.
See further Bibliography to English version.

This basis implies that physical sexual relationships, through sound knowledge and appropriate technique, are directed and developed so as to give permanent and complete satisfaction to *both* partners, to intensify their mutual love, and contribute to a life of lasting happiness together. This basis, therefore, does not *necessarily* include the practical methods of contraception. For such methods *as are known and practiced to-day* often contravene the demands of Ideal Marriage, by diminishing stimulation, disturbing and dislocating normal reactions, offending taste, and effectually ruining spontaneous *abandon* to the act of communion.

Of course it is obvious that the pros and cons of pregnancy are of crucial importance for married happiness, and often ruin sexual relationships; experience shows this only too often. But this whole subject is, at once, so intricate and so important, that, as mentioned in the preface, only a separate monograph can hope to do it justice. For that reason, and also in order not to further complicate the numerous problems discussed in these pages, I have excluded contraception from my present study.

Briefly I maintain: (1) that Ideal Marriage is not necessarily in any way incompatible with the Catholic ban on contraception or the disapproval of contraception from religious motives. (2) That my advice to married people contains nothing—(with the exception of certain definite prescriptions in case of disease)—that could offend the conscience of devout Christians or Hebrews, in sexual matters.

What of other aspects of Ideal Marriage?

I gladly stress the fact that the views I express on bodily hygiene in Ideal Marriage must be in full consonance with religious doctrines and ethical principles, for they are *the practical application of the Golden Rule of doing NO harm or injury either to one's neighbor (in this case one's marriage partner) or to the unborn child!* I have to repeat that my advice on coitus during menstruation and involution (after childbirth) does *not* coincide with Hebrew ritual laws or with the views favored in certain Protestant circles. I do this, in order to avoid misconstructions and for the benefit of those whom it may concern. *But the principle of Ideal*

Marriage is totally unaffected thereby. Catholic Moral
Theology permits coitus during these special periods, without demur—in so far as no dangers arise, to the wife's life
or health.

The various religious standpoints referred to agree in
general with my medical views on coitus during pregnancy
and disease; there may be some individual differences here,
where also "doctors disagree"!

Hebrews and Protestants take no explicit objections to
any variations of position and attitude in coitus. There is,
therefore, no reason to suppose that they regard the "Normal attitude" as the only one decent or permissible. Catholic moral theology treats this subject in detail; it regards
other attitudes than the "normal" *as at the worst, venial*
sins.

Finally, concerning the initial processes which I have
termed *love-play* and *genital or local stimulation.* Here, too,
Hebrew and Protestant authorities preserve unbroken silence, so that *they certainly do not expressly forbid;* while
Catholic moral theology is much exercised over what
is here illicit, and what is allowed. On the whole, its
conclusions harmonize with mine. It allows local stimulation, if used as preparation for or completion of normal
coitus.

It is of especial interest to compare Catholic moral theology, which forms the basis of the precepts and prohibitions
of the Church, with the definition given by me at the beginning of Chapter VIII. (on purely physiological lines)—of
normal sexual intercourse. Such comparison is most illuminating if made point by point. I must regretfully omit
such a comparison here, and I leave it to any readers to
whom it may appeal: but of course profound and detailed
knowledge, of both moral theology and physiology, are
requisite here. But I would emphasize with all seriousness,
that such a study would prove complete correspondence
between Physiology and Theology, and that the sets of
equations; physiologically normal = divinely ordained =
morally good = ecclesiastically lawful (as well as their
exact opposites) are positively startling.

What is the attitude of Protestantism to this whole complex of ideas and problems?

It is extraordinarily difficult to form an opinion here, for Protestantism forms no organic unity, like the Hebrew and Catholic creeds. The numerous distinguished divines of many sects and lands, to whom I applied for information, replied without exception that they had neither experience nor convictions in this department of human conduct; that the question of what was lawful in marriage and what was not, had never been raised between them and members of their flocks; and that the technical literature—with one exception—was unknown to them. Only one professor of theology, to whom I owe a special debt of gratitude, helped me to access to this literature; but there, too, I could only obtain partial and fragmentary answers to the questions I sought to put.

The general impression I received is on the lines of the following historical quotation from the British "Encyclopædia of Religion and Ethics": "Lutheran casuistry tended to be mild if not lax; mediated by Pietism, it gave place to Christian Ethics in the sense now current. Meanwhile casuistry of a stricter type, and more penitential in reference, grew up in Calvinistic-Puritan circles."

If I judge correctly, the Lutherans of to-day still approach the Catholic system of ethics, which is both detailed and grandiose without being in the real sense of the word, lax. The Protestant Modernists[1] resemble the Lutherans, and the Reformed Churches, or Orthodox Protestants, especially the Calvinists, have examples of the whole gamut of ethical tendencies, from complete liberty of private judgment to the demands of Pietists which go very far in the direction of abstinence.

In the English Church, it appears to me that the "High" Anglicans resemble the Catholics in this respect as in others; and that the Low Church approach Calvinism. The Orthodox Protestants of the United States model themselves apparently on the old Puritan dogmas.

---

[1] *E.g.*, the English Broad Churchmen; and various neo-Anglicans, *e.g.*, Maude Royden, Conrad Noel.

In short, Protestants are not regulated or directed by creeds or rules in any way, as regards sexual conduct within the marriage bond; but are subject alone to the guidance of their individual consciences. This guidance varies according to early religious instructions and individual idiosyncrasy between complete freedom within the limits of normality, and the most rigid possible restriction.[1]

Taken all in all, we may answer our question as to the reconciliation of traditional religious views, and Ideal Marriage, as follows. For all those who hope to find peace of mind and soul, or the fulfillment of their desire for happiness in an exclusive spiritualization of life, and liberation from the earthly and physical, *Ideal Marriage is out of the question.* They may find peace elsewhere, and even happiness, for every sacrifice, offered up with serious purpose, brings its own psychic reward. But their ascetic philosophy is incompatible with ours.[2]

But for those who reject these extremes, I hope to have proved that religious faith and Ideal Marriage are not incompatible, and that they may seek happiness, inspiration and moral support from both these great sources, without hypocrisy or conflicts which imperil their psychic health.

But, of course, on this indispensable condition: that Ideal Marriage is understood in its *true* sense.

Its true sense and significance implies Love: as I have always emphasized. And Love in its spiritual sense; or, more comprehensively and accurately, in the *unity and*

---

[1] The work of "Copec," as shown in its conferences and publications, is significant here.

[2] It is unimportant whether this philosophy is supported by texts from the Old Testament, from the New Testament, or from other sources. But it is helpful to remember that this asceticism is far from being so entirely and essentially Christian, as many Christians seem to take for granted. We find tendencies to sexual asceticism and negation in all places and ages, in small groups, and among exceptional individuals, who gather bands of followers around them.

A pre-Christian example is the Neo-Pythagorean School, which viewed sexual activity as spiritual defilement, and enjoined complete abstinence. As this School of Philosophy arose in Alexandria, during the first half of the first century B.C. and flourished during the earliest Christian era, it is possible that the ascetic tendencies of the new faith were partly due to its influence.

As post-Christian examples, we may refer to certain ethical teachers who combined mysticism with ascetics.

transfusion of the psychic or spiritual and the bodily elements, in sexual love.

It is an enormous error to regard perfect technique in sexual intercourse as *an end in itself.* They who make this mistake will find the same disappointments and disillusionments, with this expert knowledge, as without it. For sexual intercourse is not an end itself, but the certainly indispensable means to an end.

Voluptuous pleasure *alone,* however refined and varied, cannot bring real happiness, without that solace to the soul which humanity desires, and *must* forever seek. Such pleasure is not only condemned by Moral Theologians and Heidelberger Confessors; Agnostic and Rationalist Ethics are equally severe in their judgment. No person of fine æsthetic insight or emotional nature can think for a moment of winning happiness from sensuality *without* any psychic element. No such person can or will consent to play the love-play *Ideal Marriage requires, to perform genital stimulation, if Love does not inspire them; Love that unifies flesh and soul. Otherwise they would be impossible, for they would inspire instinctive loathing and repulsion.*

What husband and wife who love one another seek to achieve in their most intimate bodily communion, and, whether consciously or unconsciously, recognize as the purpose of such communion is: a means of expression that makes them One.

And *this* means of expression is the only perfect one that nature puts at their command. And so, there must be mastery of this means of expression; of its range, of its diversities, of its delicacies.

May Ideal Marriage help them to this mastery! And may it help them also to preserve this means of expression, in all its fullness, throughout their allotted years!

BRIEF LIST OF THE PRINCIPAL PREVIOUS
WORKS OF Dr. Th. VAN DE VELDE (SOME
80 IN TOTAL NUMBER)

OBSTETRICS

Diagnosis and Anæsthetics.—Contributions to the Third International Congress of Gynæcology and Obstetrics and to the Proceedings of the Dutch Gynæcological Society.

Care of the Puerperium and the New-born Child.—Numerous Essays and Articles dealing with the protection and care of infants and mothers in their own homes; including Reports submitted to the International Congress of Infant Education at Brussels and the International Congress for the Protection of Infants at Berlin; also a monograph in the *Revue Philanthropique,* of Paris.

Pathology and Therapy.—Experimental and Clinical Research on eclampsia, placenta prævia, disturbances of labor owing to the contracted pelvis and arrested development of uterus, puerperal sepsis. Articles in Dutch, French and German, medical papers, monographs and contributions to the Proceedings of the Thirteenth German Gynæcological Congress and the Seventh Congress of Flemish Doctors and Biologists.

Obstetric Surgery.—Papers on vaginal operations (Fifth International Congress of Gynæcology and Obstetrics, at St. Petersburg). Cæsarean Section (Dutch Gynæcological Society), and especially on Pubiotomy (in Dutch, German, French, American and Italian periodicals), and the effects of this operation in permanently expanding the pelvis (Twelfth Congress of German Gynæcological Society, Dresden).

GYNÆCOLOGY

General.—Monograph on the Physiology of Menstruation and the Ovarian Function; Articles in Periodicals on Marital Fitness and Advice; Monograph on Women's Costume.

Etiology.—Contributions on Blastomycætes as Cause of Morbid Conditions of Genitalia and on the Relations of Tubercle Bacilli to the Female Genital Organs. (See under Bacteriology.)

Therapy.—Reports on Modern Methods, *e.g.,* on the Treatment of Gonorrhœa in Women by means of a Vaccine (Sixteenth German Gynæcological Congress).

Radiotherapy.—Several articles in Dutch and German Periodicals on Röntgenisation and Application of Radium in Inflammations of Uterine Adnexa and in Cancerous Diseases.

Gynæcological Surgery.—Contributions on various subjects in the Proceedings of Dutch Gynæcological Society; Report on the Comparative Efficacy of Operations for Retroflexion (Fifth International Congress of Gynæcology and Obstetrics, St. Petersburg); Prevention of Post-operative Peritonitis (Sixth Congress, Berlin); Evolution of Cæsarean Section (Eighty-second Assembly of German Physicians and Biologists, Königsberg), and Essays on Temporary Surgical Sterilisation.

BACTERIOLOGY AND SEROLOGY

A Monograph on Staphylococcal Sera, in Wolff-Eisner's "Manual of Serotherapy," and a series of Articles demonstrating the Detection of Micro-organisms in the Blood on the Biology of the Gonococcus, and on the Clinical Significance of Streptotrichætes and Blastomycætes.

PLATE I.

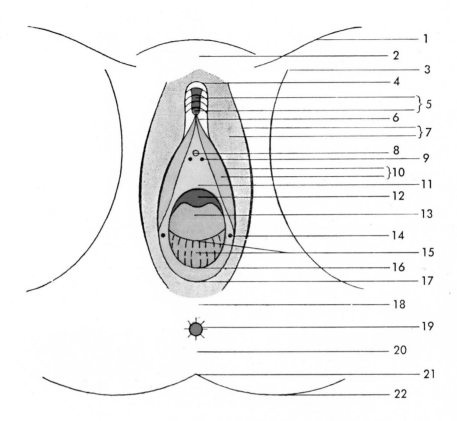

1
2
3
4
} 5
6
} 7
8
9
} 10
11
12
13
14
15
16
17
18
19
20
21
22

External Genital Organs of Woman; or Vulva.
(Schematic.)

1. Line of groin. 2. Pubis (*Mons veneris*). 3. Line of thigh. 4. Fore-skin of the clitoris (*Præputium clitoridis*). 5. Shaft and tip of the clitoris (*Corpus* and *glans clitoridis*). 6. The *Frenulum clitoridis* which connects the tip and the prepuce, enclosed in the preputial sack. 7. Rim and inner surface of the outer lips or *labia majora* (double). 8. Orifice of the female urethra (*Ostium urethræ*). 9. Orifice of the smaller or minor vestibular gland, otherwise Skene's gland (double). 10. Rim and inner surface of the inner lips or *labia minora* (double). 11. Vestibule or *vestibulum vaginæ*, that is the entire space between the two inner lips. 12. Anterior wall of the front passage or vagina, protruding into the orifice. 13. Entrance to the vagina (*Introitus vaginæ*). 14. Orifice of the larger or major vestibular gland, or Bartholin's gland (double). 15. Anterior rim and outer surface of the *hymen* or maidenhead, vertically lined. 16. Posterior wall of the front passage or vagina (only visible after the destruction of the hymen). 17. *Frenulum labiorum,* which connects the inner lips. 18. Perineum, between the outer lips and the anus. 19. Anus. 20. Posterior perineum. 21. Tip of spine (*Coccyx* or *Os coccygis*). 22. Buttocks or nates.

NOTES TO PLATE I.

1. The shaft of the clitoris is covered by the foreskin, and only the glans or tip is uncovered or can be uncovered if the foreskin or prepuce is drawn back.

2. The Frenulum of the Labia joins the inner lip, behind. Often it does not exist, as the lips do not extend far enough backwards. Or it can be obliterated, as the result of frequent sexual intercourse.

NOTES TO PLATE II.

1. 9. 10. and 11. Ovaries and Tubes with ligaments are bilateral organs, lying on either side of and slightly behind the womb. In the Diagram only the right ovary, tube and ligament are shown, and not in section like the rest of the organs.

2. The rectum is represented as broken off suddenly because it makes a curve to the left.

Plate II.

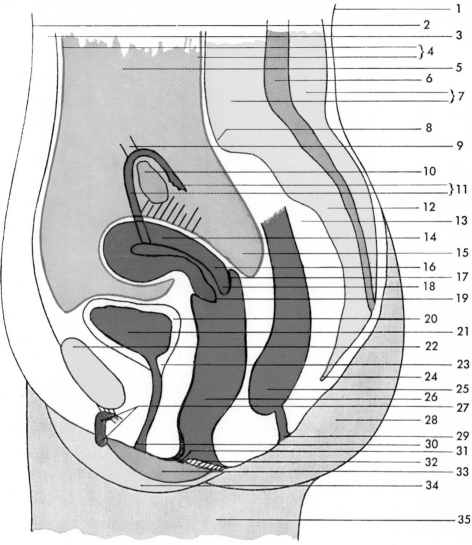

1
2
3
} 4
5
6
} 7
8
9
10
} 11
12
13
14
15
16
17
18
19
20
21
22
23
24
25
26
27
28
29
30
31
32
33
34
35

Vertical Section: Interior Female Genitalia.
(Diagrammatic.)

1. Skin of the back. 2. Skin of the abdomen. 3. Front, or anterior, inner abdominal wall. 4. Abdominal membrane, or *peritoneum*. 5. Abdominal or peritoneal cavity (*Cavum peritonei*). 6. Spinal canal or cavity (below the lumbar region called sacral canal). 7. Vertebral or spinal column. 8. Promontory of the sacrum. 9. Suspensory ligament of the ovary (*Ligamentum sus pensorium ovarii*). 10. Ovary. 11. Oviduct, salpinx, or Fallopian tube (*Tuba uterina Fallopii*). 12. Hip bone (*os sacrum*). 13. Pelvic cavity. 14. Womb or uterus (main portion or *Corpus uteri*). 15. Douglas' cavity (*Cavum Douglasii*), *i.e.*, portion of the abdomen between the rectal and uterine organs. 16. Neck of the womb (or *Cervix uteri*). 17. Posterior (hind) vault of the vagina (*Laquear posterius, fornix vaginæ*). 18. Portio (*Portio vaginalis uteri*). N.B.: 14, 16, and 18 together compose the uterus or womb. 19. External orifice of womb (*Ostium uteri externum*). 20. Posterior wall of bladder. 21. Bladder (*Vesica urinaria*). 22. Pubic bone or symphysis (*Symphysis ossium pubis*). 23. Neck of the bladder with muscle (sphincter) which holds it taut. 24. Extremity of the spine or coccyx (*Os coccygis*). 25. Rectum or lower gut: the enlargement towards the vagina is called the *Ampulla recti*. 26. Vagina. 27. Clitoris with protruding tip (*Glans clitoridis*). 28. Inner surface of the right buttock (*Nates*). 29. *Anus* (opening of rectum). 30. Opening or orifice of the urethra (*Ostium urethræ*). 31. Opening of vagina (*Introitus vaginæ*). 32. *Hymen* or maidenhead (diagonal lines). 33. Inner surface of right inner lip (*Labium minus dextrum*). 34. Inner surface of right outer lip (*Labium majus dextrum*). 35. Inner surface of upper portion of right thigh.

PLATE III.

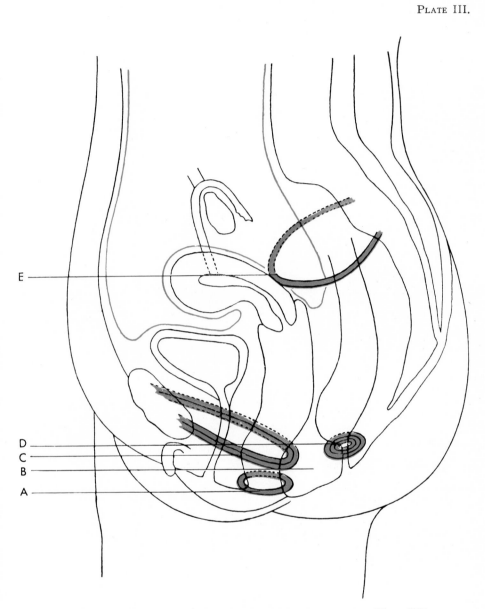

Important Muscles. (This plate shows the same contours as Plate III.)
(Schematic.)

   A. Circular group of muscles round the introitus (*M. Constrictor cunni*).
   B. Crossing network of fibres joining A to D.
   C. Muscles which grip and encircle the vagina (*M. Levator vaginæ*).
   D. Muscle which closes the anus (*M. Sphincter ani*).
   E. Group of muscles attached to the *cavity of Douglas,* drawing the lower part of the *Uterus* upwards and backwards (*M. retractores uteri*). The last group E are smooth or *involuntary* muscles; the others transversely striated or *voluntary.*

PLATE IV.

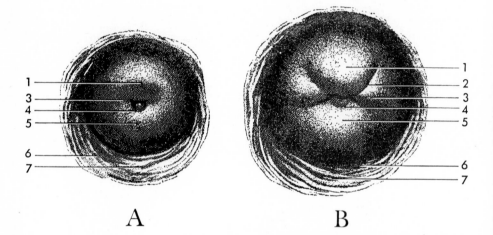

Vaginal Portion of Uterus or Womb.
(Natural size.)

'A. In a nullipara (woman who has not had children).
B. In a multipara (woman who has had several children).
1. Anterior lip of the womb. 2. Fissures in the mouth or *ostium,* following births. 3. Exterior of the *Ostium uteri,* round or oblate in the nullipara, horizontal fissure in the multipara. 4. Part of the mucus plug or Kristeller suspended from the *Ostium.* 5. Hind or posterior lip of the womb. 6. Posterior vaginal vault (*Laquear posterius*). 7. Posterior wall of vagina. (Taken from Hofmeier's "Manual of Gynæcology." Publisher, F. C. W. Vogel, Leipzig, 1921. Kristeller's plug and letterpress added by Dr. Van de Velde.)

Plate VII.

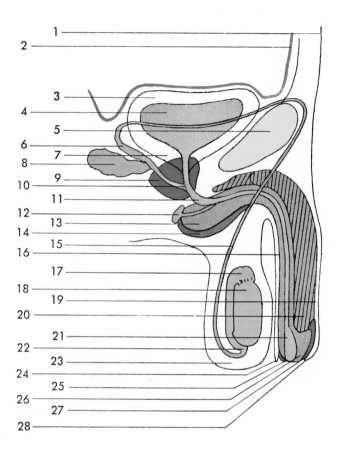

The Genital Organs of Man.
Vertical Section. (Schematic.)

1. Abdominal wall. 2. Peritoneum. 3. Wall of bladder. 4. **Cavity** of bladder. 5. Pubic bone or symphysis. 6. Seed reservoir (duplex or bilateral). 7. Neck of bladder with constrictor muscle. 8. *Vesicula seminalis* (seminal vesicle bilateral). 9. Prostate gland. 10. Urethral crest, junction of seminal ducts. 11. *Urethra;* here is the point of junction between anterior and posterior urethra. 12. Cowper's gland, with its duct (duplex or bilateral). 13. Bulb of the urethra *(Bulbus urethræ)*. 14. *Musculus bulbocavernosus*, which takes main part in ejaculation. 15. *Vas deferens* (duplex). 16. *Corpus cavernosum urethræ.* 17. Head of the epididymis (duplex). 18. *Testis* (duplex or bilateral). 19. Skin of the back of the penis. 20. *Corpus cavernosum penis.* 21. Enlargement of urethra just behind its orifice. 22. Appendage or tail of the epididymis where it joins seminal duct. 23. *Scrotum*, containing the testicles. 24. Rim of the foreskin, *Frenulum præputii;* only visible if the foreskin is drawn back. 25. Orifice of the urethra, or *Ostium urethræ.* 26. Tip or *Glans penis.* 27 Preputial sac; colored red in diagram. 28. Foreskin or prepuce.

Plate VIII.

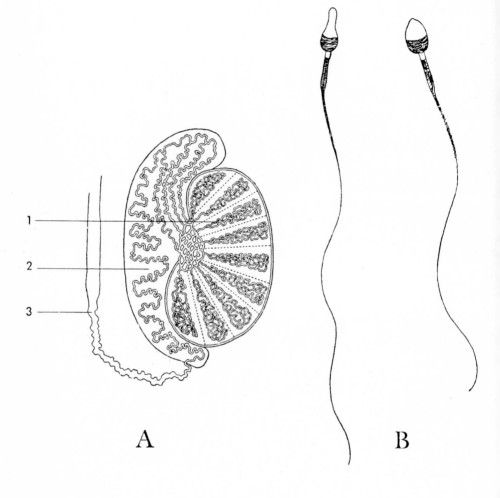

1
2
3

A

B

A. *Male Genital Gland.*

Showing plan of its structure. Vertical section in natural size; the epididymis is relatively too large, for the sake of clearness.

1. Testicle.   2. Epididymis.   3. Vas deferens.

B. *Sperm Cell of Man.* (*Very much magnified.*)

Left: Side view.   Right: Full view.